D1526736

Religion and Spirituality in Psychotherapy

An Individual Psychology Perspective

Thor Johansen, PsyD, is a Licensed Clinical Psychologist in the State of Illinois. He received his bachelor's degree in psychology from Arizona State University and his Master's Degree in Counseling Psychology and his Doctorate in Clinical Psychology from the Adler School of Professional Psychology in Chicago. He is a staff psychologist with the Samaritan Interfaith Counseling Center in Naperville and adjunct faculty at the Adler School of Professional Psychology. Dr. Johansen is a member of the American Psychological Association, the Society of Clinical Child and Adolescent Psychology, and the North American Society of Adlerian Psychology. Dr. Johansen has published numerous professional articles on topics such as misbehavior in children, psychotherapy, hypnosis, and religion.

Religion and Spirituality in Psychotherapy

An Individual Psychology Perspective

THOR JOHANSEN, PsyD

SPRINGER PUBLISHING COMPANY

New York

Educ.

Springer Publishing Company, LLC
11 West 42nd Street
New York, NY 10036
www.springerpub.com

BF
175.5
.A33
J64
2010

Acquisitions Editor: Philip Laughlin
Project Manager: Megan Washburn
Cover Design: Steve Pisano
Composition: Publication Services, Inc.

ISBN: 978-0-8261-0385-7
E-book ISBN: 978-0-8261-0386-4

09 10 11 12/ 5 4 3 2 1

The author and the publisher of this Work have made every effort to use sources believed to be reliable to provide information that is accurate and compatible with the standards generally accepted at the time of publication. Because medical science is continually advancing, our knowledge base continues to expand. Therefore, as new information becomes available, changes in procedures become necessary. We recommend that the reader always consult current research and specific institutional policies before performing any clinical procedure. The author and publisher shall not be liable for any special, consequential, or exemplary damages resulting, in whole or in part, from the readers' use of, or reliance on, the information contained in this book. The publisher has no responsibility for the persistence or accuracy of URLs for external or third-party Internet Web sites referred to in this publication and does not guarantee that any content on such Web sites is, or will remain, accurate or appropriate.

Library of Congress Cataloging-in-Publication Data
Johansen, Thor.
   Religion and spirituality in psychotherapy : an individual psychology perspective / Thor Johansen. — 5th ed.
      p. cm.
   ISBN 978-0-8261-0385-7 (alk. paper) — ISBN 978-0-8261-0386-4 (ebook)
1. Adlerian psychology.   2. Psychology—Religious aspects.   2. Adler, Alfred, 1870-1937.
I. Title.
BF175.5.A33J64   2009
201'.61501953—dc22   2009043445

Printed in the United States of America by Bang Printing.

*This book is dedicated to
my two year-old daughter, Annika Louise,
my devoted and encouraging wife, Kate, and
my loving parents, Anne Merete and Thor-Erik.*

Contents

Preface

Issues pertaining to religion, spirituality, and psychotherapy have gained prominence over the past three decades. Many psychotherapists have begun looking at ways of integrating spirituality into the therapeutic process. The terms "religion" and "spirituality" have come to mean different things, although the terms are very much related. Defining the two terms has proved to be a challenge. Religion is generally thought of as a shared belief system that involves communal ritual practices, whereas spirituality is about the individual's search for meaning, belonging, and a sense of connectedness with something beyond the self. Spirituality is generally thought of as having "to do with however people think, feel, act, or interrelate in their efforts to find, conserve, and if necessary, transform the sacred in their lives" (Pargament, 1997, p. 12). Adlerians acknowledge the role of cognitions, feelings, and actions in spirituality, and view spirituality as "conscious movement from a felt-minus to that of a fictional-plus" (Mansager, 2000, p. 385).

Religion and spirituality "appear to connote in the public's mind, institutional—public and individual—personal expressions of religious sentiments with transcendent realities" (Shafranske & Sperry, 2005, p. 14). Issues regarding religion and spirituality are normal aspects of people's everyday lives. Spirituality, spiritual problems, and religious practices are not solely the domain of clergy and pastoral counselors. They are important aspects of human functioning that involve cognitions, ethical convictions, and behavior, and they must be attended to in the psychotherapeutic process.

With the explosion of psychological literature on religion and spirituality in recent years, it is surprising and unfortunate that Adler's theories have been largely overlooked. There are some texts that address single approaches to incorporate spirituality and religion in psychotherapy. And a few texts are available that addresses different approaches, mainly psychoanalytic, Jungian, cognitive-behavioral, and interpersonal theories. Regrettably, Individual

Psychology has not been included in these texts. Given the relevance of Adler's system to contemporary practice and its friendly attitude toward religion, Adler's theories should be included in our attempts at integrating religion and spirituality in psychotherapy.

In attempting to understand patients, Adlerian practitioners conceptualize people in terms of psychological, social, and emotional, as well as spiritual development. Attending to religious and spiritual experiences is often thought of as being as important as addressing such issues as love, work, and social relationships. Religion and spirituality can be a great source of strength, healing, and adaptation. But sometimes religion contributes to dysfunction and psychopathology. Thus, spiritual experiences and religious beliefs are to be explored, understood, respected, and discussed in psychotherapy, regardless of the therapist's orientation.

There are several approaches to developing religious and spiritual competency as a therapist. The study of the world religions and issues pertaining to cultural diversity is probably the most important step toward such competency. Burke et al. (1999) pointed to the personal exploration of spiritual beliefs as another important aspect in this process. A third approach is the exploration of one's own personal spiritual and religious beliefs in relation to the theory of human nature by which one practices. This allows for greater understanding, appreciation, and respect for various religious and spiritual beliefs and practices. It also helps foster ideological consistency (Polanski, 2002) allowing the clinician to be fully integrated (Hart, 1971).

In order to really understand and appreciate a system of religion, one needs to understand it in relation to one's own philosophy of life. Thus, by comparing and contrasting the various world religions to Individual Psychology, the therapist can begin to understand and appreciate the various religions from the perspective of Individual Psychology. Furthermore, such study gives therapists a point of reference when they are working with clients. And it allows them to foresee certain areas that may complicate the therapy process, as well as permitting them to benefit from areas of compatibility. Other than some sporadic articles in Adlerian journals, there is no single text that systematically compares Individual Psychology to the various religions. *Religion and Spirituality in Psychotherapy: An Individual Psychology Perspective* is the first such book that describes, illustrates, and compares Adler's psychology to the world religions.

The purpose of this text is to examine religion and spirituality through the lens of Individual Psychology to help the Adlerian clinician understand and appreciate the religious dimensions in counseling. The book is not intended to cover the world religions and all their aspects thoroughly, and it cannot substitute for more intensive study of religion and spirituality. Nor is this text intended to provide a complete overview of Individual Psychology. But, it should contribute to an understanding of the application of Individual Psychology to working with clients of various religious backgrounds. Through the process of comparing and contrasting religious doctrines to Individual Psychology the reader will become acquainted with religious and spiritual practices from an Individual Psychology perspective.

This book will be of interest to two audiences. First, psychologists, counselors, and social workers interested in the integration of religion and psychotherapy, as well as scholars and advanced undergraduate and graduate students in the fields of psychology and religion. Therapists who are unfamiliar with Adler and Individual Psychology and who want to know more about his theories will find this book informative. Therapists will also find both theoretical and clinical information that is relevant to contemporary clinical practice. Second, this text will be useful to Adlerian practitioners and students of Adlerian psychology who want to know more about Adler's philosophy and its relationship to the world religions.

Chapter 1 presents an overview of the major developments in the field of psychology and the shift toward religious and spiritual integration in psychotherapy. Religion and spirituality have been recognized as important aspects of cultural diversity that need to be respected and understood. The changes in our field that have helped increase awareness of religious and spiritual issues as important factors in psychotherapy, and the need for religious competency among mental health professionals are discussed.

Chapter 2 briefly presents a biographical sketch of Alfred Adler and the theoretical principles of Individual Psychology. It is intended to familiarize the reader with the underlying assumptions of Adler's psychology.

Chapter 3 presents an Individual Psychology approach to working with religious persons. Given its eclectic nature, relevance to contemporary practice and positive view of religion, Adlerian psychology is applicable to working with people of faith. A case example illustrates how spiritual problems may be approached in Adlerian psychotherapy.

Chapter 4 compares and contrasts Individual Psychology with Biblically based Christian spirituality. A number of authors have addressed various aspects of Christianity and compared these to Adler's philosophy. Christian teachings are examined through the eyes of Individual Psychology.

Chapter 5 discusses Adlerian contributions to traditional pastoral counseling. Given the philosophical overlap between Christianity and Individual Psychology, Adler's psychology may be a particularly good fit for many pastoral counselors. The academic literature on pastoral counseling and Individual Psychology is reviewed.

Chapter 6 addresses the Jewish faith in relation to Individual Psychology. Several authors have pointed to the relational aspects of the Jewish tradition and compared these to Adler's social interest. Judaism places great emphasis on social connectedness and social responsibility and, similar to Judaism, Adler's Individual Psychology encourages people to strive for an ideal future in which peace and justice dominate. Similarities and differences between the two philosophies are discussed, and implications for therapy are presented.

Chapter 7 compares and contrasts Adler's theories to the all-encompassing ethical, spiritual, and social system of Islam. Its basic doctrines and the five pillars of faith are discussed. Implications for therapy are addressed, and a clinical case example illustrates an Adlerian approach to working with clients of the Islamic faith.

Chapter 8 reviews the doctrines of Hinduism, including the belief in karma and reincarnation, the goals of life, and the paths to God. A case example illustrates an Adlerian approach to counseling this population. Therapeutic issues are discussed.

Chapter 9 examines the teachings of the Buddha. Buddhism is probably the most popular philosophy of living that psychologists have attempted to integrate into psychotherapy. The four noble truths and the eight-fold path are examined from an Adlerian perspective. Issues relevant to counseling Buddhist clients are discussed along with the presentation of a case example.

Finally, chapter 10 discusses some broader ideas in relation to Individual Psychology, religion, and spirituality. The many areas that still need to be explored and developed by Adlerians are discussed.

Acknowledgments

I am grateful to Philip Laughlin, Senior Editor at Springer Publishing Company, who recognized the importance of this book. His advice and support have helped make this much-needed text a reality. I would also like to thank Gayle Lee, Production Editor at Springer Publishing Company, and Megan Washburn, Project Manager with Publication Services, Inc., for their assistance and professionalism.

I am thankful for the help and support of all the staff at the Samaritan Interfaith Counseling Center in Naperville, Illinois. Their encouragement and help is greatly appreciated. I would especially like to thank Rev. Jane Carlton, Rev. Howard Milkman, Jaimee Huseman, Sister Pat Kolas, and Dr. Scott Mitchell, who helped review the various chapters and provided helpful suggestions, insights, and advice that helped strengthen the book. I would also like to thank Dr. Erik Mansager, Poran Poregbal, and Marni Rosen who gave helpful suggestions, recommendations, and assistance along the way.

Finally, I remain grateful to my loving wife, Kate Johansen. Without her support this book would never have been completed.

Religion and Spirituality in Psychotherapy

An Individual Psychology Perspective

1 Religion and Clinical Psychology: Recent Developments

In recent years we have seen a renewed interest in psychology of religion. Religious institutions are also more accepting of psychological interventions, and they are recognizing the need to make behavioral health services available to their parishioners. The heightened interest in various aspects of the psychology of religion is evidenced by the increasing number of publications on the subject. In the years between 1900 and 1959, there were a total of 3,803 articles addressing religion and spirituality in the psychological literature. Between 2000 and 2006, however, 8,193 such articles were published (Bartoli, 2007).

We begin our discussion of Individual Psychology, religion, and spirituality by placing the psychology of religion and integration in historical context. In this chapter I will discuss the recent developments in our field that have contributed to the renewed interest in religion and spirituality. I will also discuss the need for religious and spiritual competency in our field, and some of the benefits clinicians stand to gain by understanding and appreciating various religious traditions. Finally, I discuss Alfred Adler's role in the integration movement.

THE PSYCHOLOGICAL STUDY OF RELIGION

According to Wulff (1998), the psychology of religion movement has been on the sidelines of psychology since its development. Yet efforts

1

to integrate psychology and theology have maintained a strong presence throughout the 20th century. The term *integration* to specify interdisciplinary efforts by psychologists and theologians was first used by Fritz Kunkel in 1953 (Vande Kemp, 1996). Kunkel, a major contributor to Christian education, founded the (Christian) Counseling Center at the First Congregational Church in Los Angeles in the 1940s. In 1952 he founded the Foundation for the Advancement of Religious Psychology. In a letter to William Rickel in 1953, he described his work as "the integration of Christianity and Psychology." This description was adopted by the editors of *Pastoral Psychology* in a biographical sketch of Kunkel in 1953 and later extended to Gordon Allport in 1955 (Vande Kemp, 1996). According to Vande Kemp (1996), integration was firmly established with the publication of Biddle's *Integration of Religion and Psychiatry* in 1955. In addition to the theoretical approaches by various psychologists, religion was the target of early scientists as well. Their early contributions are significant.

The psychological study of religion dates back to the very beginning of scientific psychology. Many of the early American psychologists had a strong interest in religion, and many studied theology along with philosophy and psychology. For instance, Granville Stanley Hall, the first president of the American Psychological Association, even worked as a preacher for a short period of time early in his career.

Two men are generally credited with founding the psychological study of religion in America: G. Stanley Hall and William James. Both men made significant contributions to the field and set the stage for further study in the area. According to Vande Kemp (1992) Hall and his students, particularly James H. Leuba and Edwin D. Starbuck, were surely the first Americans to attempt to study religion scientifically. Hall pioneered the empirical study of religious experiences by studying religious conversions, and his major religious contribution, *Jesus, the Christ, in the Light of Psychology* (1917), was an ambitious and controversial text.

Born in 1844 in Ashfield, Massachusetts, G. Stanley Hall graduated from Williams College in 1867 with a degree in philosophy. After graduation, he attended Union Theological Seminary in New York before he traveled to Germany to continue his study of philosophy. Upon his return to the United States, he worked as a tutor and studied with William James at Harvard University, where he eventually completed the first American Ph.D. degree in psychology in 1878. After receiving his doctorate degree, Hall traveled to Leipzig, Germany, where he studied with Wilhelm Wundt at his psychological laboratory. In 1881, Hall was invited to lecture at Johns Hopkins University. There, he opened his own psychological laboratory in 1883 and launched *The American Journal of Psychology* in 1887. Two years later he became the president of Clark University, where he eventually founded *The Journal of Religious Psychology* (1904). In 1892, Hall was appointed as the first president of the American Psychological Association.

G. Stanley Hall's contributions to psychology are many, but his contribution to the psychology of religion was in part marked by his leadership in religious psychology and his guidance of several other young psychologists that eventually led to the development of the Clark school of religious psychology (Vande Kemp, 1992). His students, James H. Leuba and Edwin D. Starbuck, continued the psychological study of religion throughout their careers. For instance, Leuba published extensively on the subject. In his books, *The Psychological Study of Religion* (1912) and *The Belief in God and Immortality* (1916), Leuba discussed the psychological development and function of ideas of and belief in God. He argued that belief in God was derived from a need to explain and provide support in life's struggles. Starbuck also wrote extensively on psychology and religion. Attempting to understand religious experiences firsthand, he used survey methods to study topics such as religious conversions, doubt, alienation, and substitutes for religious feelings.

In contrast to Hall and his followers, who emphasized a quantitative approach to understanding and studying religious experiences and behavior, William James took a very different approach, namely by studying religion using case studies. In his classic work, *The Varieties of Religious Experience* (1902), he defined religion as an individual's feelings, acts, and personal experiences. James was attempting to understand the uniqueness of religious practices and focused on peoples' religious and spiritual experiences in everyday life. In this classic work, James portrays the need for the spiritual aspect of human consciousness as a natural and healthy psychological function.

James is a significant figure in the psychological study of religion. According to the early historian James Bissett Pratt (1908), William James's book was the single most important contribution to the psychology of religion. Although he is probably best known for his masterwork, *The Principles of Psychology* (1890), *The Varieties of Religious Experience* remains one of the great classics of the psychology of religion (Wulff, 1991).

Between 1879, when Wilhelm Wundt opened the first psychological laboratory in Leipzig, and the publication of James' classic work in 1902, the doors had been opened, and opportunities for the psychological study of religion were ample. However, the psychology of religion movement soon began to dwindle. The *American Journal of Religious Psychology* was discontinued after Hall failed to find a new editor in 1915 (Vande Kemp, 1992), and the movement either followed the lead of experimental psychology or psychoanalysis, whereas the pastoral psychology movement took its own direction (Menges & Dittes, 1965; Vande Kemp, 1992). As American psychology moved toward behaviorism and attempted to establish itself as a science, religious and spiritual issues became increasingly insignificant. Matters that seemed to be more scientific were prioritized, and issues of faith, religion, and spirituality were put aside.

RECENT DEVELOPMENTS

The revitalization of religion and spirituality in psychotherapy is a result of several significant developments in the last half of the 20th century. The organization of professional societies and interest groups, the establishment of professional journals addressing theory, research, and practice of integration, the publication of textbooks that directly address religion and psychology, the inclusion of religion and spirituality in professional ethical codes, changes in our diagnostic system to include religious and spiritual problems, and the establishment of several advanced degree programs have all contributed to the renewed interest in religion and spirituality in the mental health professions. While acknowledging the rich historical tradition of the psychology of religion and integration, I will focus on a few key developments in this chapter.

Professional Organizations

The American Psychological Association's Division 36—Psychology of Religion—is one of the main organizations for psychologists interested in the psychological study of religion. The organization has its origins in the American Catholic Psychological Association (ACPA), which was founded in 1946. The ACPA was established in an effort to bring psychology to Catholics and to encourage Catholics to obtain doctorate degrees in psychology (Reuder, 1999). The organization eventually outgrew its original objectives and underwent a total reorganization in 1970. The name of the organization was changed to PIRI (Psychologists Interested in Religious Issues), and in 1976 it received division status with the American Psychological Association. In 1993, the membership voted to change the name to Psychology of Religion. Today, Division 36 works to promote psychological research of religion and spirituality, encouraging the incorporation of research into clinical and other applied settings.

In addition to Psychology of Religion, there are numerous other organizations that promote the study and integration of religion and psychology. The most notable organizations are the Association for Transpersonal Psychology, the Religious Research Association, and the Society for the Scientific Study of Religion.

The Association for Transpersonal Psychology was established in 1972 to encourage education, theory, and research application of transpersonal psychology. This branch of psychology examines the interface of psychology and spiritual experiences. It addresses the integration of psychological concepts and theories with religious and spiritual practices. Transpersonal psychology concerns itself with mystical states of consciousness, meditative practices, spiritual experiences, and the overlap of such experiences with pathological states such as depression and psychosis. The association has worked to promote dialogue between science and the religious and spiritual traditions and has worked to encourage the use of meditation in various health care settings. As for psychotherapy, transpersonal psychologists consider therapy a form of awakening to a greater identity that is facilitated through the enhancement of awareness and intuition. *The Journal of Transpersonal Psychology* publishes theoretical and scientific papers addressing the integration of psychology and spirituality.

The Religious Research Association was first organized as the Religious Research Fellowship in 1951. Today the group encourages research on various aspects of religion, including religious experiences, religion and family life, religious movements, dynamics of religious denominations, and ethnic religious groups. The organization consists of a broad group of interested individuals including social scientists, religious educators, and theologians. The organization's journal, *The Review of Religious Research*, publishes a variety of articles addressing religious issues.

Finally, The Society for the Scientific Study of Religion promotes social scientific research about religious institutions, as well as religious experiences. Founded in 1949, the society seeks to encourage dialogue between the fields of psychology, religious studies, sociology, international studies, gender studies, political science, and economics. Its publication, *The Journal for the Scientific Study of Religion,* is a multidisciplinary journal that publishes articles on the social scientific study of religion. Together, these and other organizations are working to promote psychological research of religion and spirituality and to apply that knowledge in various settings.

Professional Journals and Text Books

In addition to the journals mentioned above, several other integrative journals have been established: for instance, *Counseling and Values* (formerly the *National Catholic Guidance Conference Journal*), founded in 1956; *Journal of Religion and Health*, founded in 1961; *Journal of Psychology and Theology*, founded in 1973; *The Journal of Psychology and Christianity*, founded in 1982; and *The Journal of Psychology and Judaism*, founded in 1976. Two other journals that address the psychology of religion are also noteworthy: *The Journal for the Scientific Study of Religion*, founded in 1949, and *The International Journal for the Psychology of Religion*, established in 1991. These are just some of the journals available to psychologists who wish to publish material related to issues of faith, religion, spirituality, and psychology.

Given the increasing interest in issues surrounding religion and spirituality over the past decade, Psychology of Religion (APA's Division 36) recently published its inaugural volume of *Psychology and Spirituality* in February of 2009. The journal aspires to become an open forum for the advancement of the psychology of religion and to further our understanding of religious and spiritual phenomena in human development and behavior (Piedmont, 2009). The establishment of this new journal represents the latest major development in the field.

Numerous textbooks have been published addressing the integration of religion and psychology. Whereas some focus on religious issues in clinical psychology and psychotherapy, others address religion and personality theory, psychopathology, and psychometrics. A discussion of these publications is beyond the scope of this book; however, three recent texts deserve attention. First, the classic text, *The Individual and His Religion*, by Gordon Allport (1950), inspired a renewed interest in religion among psychologists and counselors. In his book, Allport describes how the individual may use religion in different ways. He distinguished between mature and immature religion, arguing that people can grow and mature in their religious development much as they mature in other areas of their lives. Although acknowledging the "neurotic function" of religious beliefs, he also recognized the healthy aspects of religion.

In 1996, the American Psychological Association published its first book on the topic of religion and clinical practice (Shafranske, 1996). The book, *Religion and the Clinical Practice of Psychology*, discusses the conceptual, cultural, and historical aspects of the psychology of religion. It goes on to discuss various psychotherapeutic approaches to working with people of faith. Finally, in 1999, the American Psychological Association published another important book in this area, *Handbook of Psychotherapy and Religious Diversity* (Richards & Bergin, 2006a). This text examines the many religious customs, beliefs, doctrines, rituals, spiritual practices, and healing traditions found within the world religions and discusses how these are relevant in clinical practice.

Professional Degree Programs

There are numerous master's degree programs and other nonaccredited programs throughout the United States. However, a number of accredited degree programs are now available to students interested in the integration of religion and psychology. The Graduate School of Psychology at Fuller Theological Seminary in Pasadena, California, was the first integrative doctoral program to receive APA accreditation in 1972. The school offers both doctor of philosophy and doctor of psychology degrees. The Rosemead Graduate School of Psychology at Biola University, also in California, received APA accreditation in 1980. The most recent integrative program to be accredited by the APA is that at Regent University in Virginia Beach, Virginia. Regent University offers a doctor of psychology degree program that aims to integrate a Christian perspective with clinical psychology. The program was accredited by the APA in 2002. Other doctoral programs (Psy.D.) include those at Baylor University in Waco, Texas, George Fox College Graduate School of Psychology in Newberg, Oregon, and Wheaton College in Wheaton, Illinois.

Ethical Responsibility to Maintain Competency in Religious Diversity

The multicultural counseling movement has had significant influence on the field of psychology, encouraging mental health providers to develop and maintain competency in cultural diversity and to develop skills to work effectively with clients of various cultural backgrounds. Multicultural counseling aims to include and address sociocultural, economic, and historical, as well as individual factors in the therapeutic process. Religious values, beliefs, and practices are part of this all-encompassing approach. Religion is an area with which mental health professionals are likely to be unfamiliar and an area in which stereotypic biases have been present and to some extent accepted in our field (Delaney, Miller, & Bisonó, 2007). As psychology continues to emphasize the importance of cultural competency, religious and spiritual issues are gradually getting more recognition as important aspects of the multicultural diversity discussion. Psychologists and counselors have a responsibility to understand, respect, and competently address religious diversity. This concept is emphasized in the ethical guidelines of psychologists, counselors, and social workers. The inclusion of religion as an aspect of diversity that mental health professionals need to respect and be competent in can be considered a major development in the field. The importance of religious competency was stressed in the American Psychological Association's ethical guidelines in 1992.

> Psychologists are aware of and respect cultural, individual, and role differences, including those based on age, gender, gender identity, race, ethnicity, culture, national origin, *religion,* sexual orientation, disability, language, and socioeconomic status, and they consider these factors when working with members of such groups. (italics mine)

> Where scientific or professional knowledge in the discipline of psychology establishes that an understanding of factors associated with age, gender, gender identity, race, ethnicity, culture, national origin, *religion,* sexual orientation, disability, language, or socioeconomic status is essential for effective implementation of their services or research, psychologists have or obtain the training, experience, consultation, or supervision necessary to ensure the competence of their services, or they make appropriate referrals. (italics mine)

The need to respect and understand religious diversity was also emphasized by the American Counseling Association's code of ethics in 1995. This concept remains an important aspect in the association's most recent ethical guidelines (ACA, 2005).

> Counselors do not condone or engage in discrimination based on age, culture, disability, ethnicity, race, *religion/spirituality,* gender, gender identity, sexual orientation, marital status/partnership, language preference, socioeconomic status, or any basis proscribed by law. (italics mine)

Finally, along with psychologists and counselors, the National Association of Social Workers (NASW) has also acknowledged the necessity of cultural and religious competency. Religion was identified as an aspect of diversity in the association's ethical guidelines in 1996. The most recent revision completed by the NASW Delegate Assembly in 2008 reads as follows:

Social workers should have a knowledge base of their clients' cultures and be able to demonstrate competence in the provision of services that are sensitive to clients' cultures and to differences among people and cultural groups.

Social workers should obtain education about and seek to understand the nature of social diversity and oppression with respect to race, ethnicity, national origin, color, sex, sexual orientation, gender identity or expression, age, marital status, political belief, *religion,* immigration status, and mental or physical disability. (italics mine)

The recognition of religion and spirituality as a type of diversity signifies the need for religious competency in clinical practice, but is also a sign of the shift toward inclusion and appreciation of religious issues in our field. In addition to the inclusion of religion in practitioners' Codes of Conduct, the shift from evasion to appreciation of religious and spiritual issues is in part a result of the introduction of the "Religious or Spiritual Problem" V-code in the diagnostic system. This V-code was in part an effort to call attention to the need for training and competency in religious and spiritual issues.

"Religious or Spiritual Problem" V-Code

When the DSM-IV was published in 1994, it included a new V-code designed to specifically address religious and spiritual problems. The introduction of this new code represented a major shift in the field, signifying the importance of recognizing and developing competence in issues of faith, religion, and spirituality. The justification for including this category in the new diagnostic manual was that the frequency of religious and spiritual problems was much higher than once thought. There was also a need to train psychologists in the areas of religion and spirituality, and there were concerns about how to address the ethics of cultural sensitivity related to religion and spirituality (Lukoff, 1998).

The creation of the "Religious or Spiritual Problem" V-code grew out of the Transpersonal Psychology movement's emphasis on spiritual emergencies (Lukoff, 1998). The Spiritual Emergence Network was founded in 1980, by Stanislav and Christina Grof (Prevatt & Park, 1989), in response to the lack of understanding and respect for spiritual issues in the mental health professions. Its members were concerned with how intense spiritual crises had a tendency to be conceptualized as a pathological process. As a consequence, the movement pushed for a new diagnostic category in the upcoming DSM-IV. The network's members believed that a new diagnostic category would draw attention to the importance of addressing spiritual issues in therapy. The initial proposal was entitled "Psychoreligious or Psychospiritual Problem." The definition of the proposed V Code stated the following:

> Psychoreligious problems are experiences that a person finds troubling or distressing and that involve the beliefs and practices of an organized church or religious institution. Examples include loss or questioning of a firmly held faith, change in denominational membership, conversion to a new faith, and intensification of adherence to religious practices and orthodoxy. Psychospiritual problems are experiences that a person finds troubling or distressing and that involve that person's relationship with a transcendent being or force. These problems are not necessarily related to the beliefs and practices of an organized church or religious institution. Examples include near-death experiences and mystical experience. This category can be used when the focus of treatment or diagnosis is a psychoreligious or psychospiritual problem that is not attributable to a mental disorder. (Lukoff, Lu, & Turner, 1992, p 680)

The proposal for the Psychoreligious or Psychospiritual Problem code was formally submitted to the Task Force on DSM-IV in 1991 (Lukoff, Lu, & Turner, 1992). It stressed the need to improve the cultural sensitivity of the DSM-IV and argued that the adoption of the new category would increase the accuracy of diagnostic assessments when spiritual and religious issues are implicated. Second, it would reduce the occurrence of iatrogenic harm from misdiagnosis of religious and spiritual concerns. Third, it would improve treatment of such problems by stimulating research. And finally, it would improve treatment of religious and spiritual problems by encouraging training in this area.

The proposal was accepted, but the title was changed to "Religious or Spiritual Problem." According to the DSM-IV, this V-Code represents problems involving religious or spiritual issues that may be the focus of clinical attention.

> This category can be used when the focus of clinical attention is a religious or spiritual problem. Examples include distressing experiences that involve loss or questioning of faith, problems associated with conversion to a new faith, or questioning of other spiritual values that may not necessarily be related to an organized church or religious institution. (American Psychiatric Association, 1994, p. 685)

The development and addition to the DSM-IV of this diagnostic category is a major contribution to the field, emphasizing the importance
of training in issues pertaining to religion and spirituality. Its inclusion in
the diagnostic manual also speaks to the need for the integration of these
factors in clinical practice. Nonetheless, there is still a need for training
psychologists in religious and spiritual issues. The need for such training
is especially important as the cultural and religious diversity of North
America continues to grow.

A NEED FOR RELIGIOUS COMPETENCY IN PSYCHOLOGY

In the *Handbook of Psychotherapy and Religious Diversity,* editors Scott
Richards and Allen Bergin (2006) called for greater competency in religious and spiritual diversity. They argued that religious diversity is a cultural fact, and that most mental health professionals will encounter it in
their work. They also opined that clinicians will develop more credibility
and trust with religious patients, leaders, and communities if they exhibit
religious competency. Third, they stated that, given the ethical obligation
to obtain such competency, therapists should develop specialized knowledge and training about various religious beliefs and practices. Last, they
felt that therapists could more readily access healing resources in religious communities to assists patients in the therapeutic process.

Religious Diversity in North America

The study and integration of religion is an important aspect of psychology. Religion and spirituality are relevant to our understanding of individuals as they constitute an important aspect of most people's lives.
The majority of people in North America profess a belief in a higher
power. In fact, 95 percent of adults in the United States say they believe
in God. Most adults also claim a religious affiliation (94 percent) and
report that religion is very or fairly important in their lives (85 percent).
Seventy percent of adults in the U.S. report membership in a church,
synagogue, or mosque, and 40 percent say they attend religious services on a regular basis (Gallup and Lindsay, 1999). Another important
factor that mental health professionals should pay attention to is the
apparent benefits of religious involvement. A significant development
in the field of psychology of religion is the increase in research linking
spirituality and religiosity to mental health. Many studies have found

positive correlations between religious involvement and improved mental health outcomes (Gartner, Larson, and Allen, 1991; Hackney and Sanders, 2003; Koenig, McCullough, and Larson, 2001; Larson et al, 1992; Payne, Bergin, Bielema, and Jenkins, 1991; Seybold and Hill, 2001). The reason for this positive relationship remains unclear, however (Miller and Thoresen, 2003).

The North American landscape is host to all the major world religions and to many smaller religious groups. Throughout the United States and Canada there are approximately 250 million Christians. Of these, there are about 74 million Roman Catholics, 95 million Protestants, and 6 million Orthodox Christians. There are about 40 million people who belong to other Christian groups. In addition, North America is home to almost 6 million Jews, over 1 million Hindus, 2 million Buddhists, and 2 to 4 million Muslims (Barrett & Johnson, 1998; Pew, 2008). The religious diversity within these religious groups is also significant. For example, the *Yearbook of American and Canadian Churches* (Bedell, 1997) listed over 160 different denominations throughout North America, most of which were Christian. The present diversity observed in North America is in part a result of the effects of higher education, media, world consciousness, and most important, immigration (Richards & Bergin, 2006b). People from a variety of ethnic and religious backgrounds, including Buddhists, Muslims, and Hindus, are immigrating to United States and Canada, a trend that is very likely to continue. These various religions and the numerous denominations represent tremendous diversity in terms of customs, cultural and religious beliefs, myths, rituals, worship, and healing traditions. Developing knowledge about these religions and their practices is the first step in developing more trust and credibility with people of various faiths.

Given the fact that most people in North America profess a religious faith, it is noteworthy that mental health professionals are less likely to be religious than the general population. According to Delaney, Miller, and Bisonó (2007) 48 percent of the psychologists surveyed described religion as unimportant in their lives, compared with 15 percent of the general population. On the positive side, the vast majority of the psychologists surveyed recognized that religion is beneficial (82 percent) rather than harmful (7 percent) to mental health.

In addition to the variation of religious beliefs, practices, and values found throughout North America, the prevalence of religious and spiritual problems in clinical settings is also noteworthy. In a survey of psychologists belonging to the American Psychological Association, it was found that 60 percent reported that their patients often expressed their personal experiences in religious language. The survey also found that at least one in six of their patients presented issues that directly involved spirituality or religion (Shafranske & Maloney, 1990). Another survey found that 29 percent of psychologists, psychiatrists, marriage and family therapists, and social workers agreed that religious issues were important in their work with all or many of their patients (Bergin & Jensen, 1990). In a more recent survey of psychiatrists, 49 percent reported that issues of spirituality came up *often* or a *great deal of the time.* Last, patient's loss of meaning or purpose in life was stated as the most important focus in treatment (Shafranske, 2000). Furthermore, one survey (Westfeld, 2001) indicated that people feel it is appropriate to discuss religious and spiritual issues in psychotherapy. Steere (1997) observed that Americans are beginning to seek answers to questions regarding meaning, purpose, and spiritual direction from sources outside religious traditions. Consequently, many individuals are likely to look to psychotherapists to help them find health, meaning, and wholeness.

Religion and spirituality are defining aspects of the cultural diversity that psychologists and counselors encounter in clinical practice. It is arguably the most important dimension of culture that forms the individual's beliefs, values, and behaviors (James, 1958; Krippner & Welch, 1992). Ignoring this aspect, therapists are, to quote Grizzle (1992), "operating with a vital value system and possibly even a member of the family, God, left at home and ignored" (p. 139).

Developing Credibility Among the Faithful

By maintaining a certain level of religious competency and exhibiting respect for religious and spiritual issues, therapists can begin to build trusting relationships with people of faith. Indeed, there is a need for psychologists and counselors to develop a sense of trust and confidence with parishioners and religious leaders. There is still a tendency for people of faith to be distrustful of psychotherapists. Historically, most systems of psychotherapy have taken either a neutral or a negative position toward religion and spirituality. Many prominent leaders in our field have been openly critical of religion, and their comments have by no means gone unnoticed. For example, Freud's psychoanalysis, which dominated psychology for most of the 20th century, has been very critical of religion. Freud, a lifelong atheist, rejected religion outright, calling it an illusion and a symptom (Freud, 1927). He argued that religion was derived from a child-like sense of helplessness. Religion, Freud opined, allows the individual to explain the unknowns of life, thus providing comfort and happiness. Despite these openly critical comments, however, Freud did acknowledge that only religion could answer questions about life's meaning and purpose. And some argue that Freud was not completely opposed to religion regarding its therapeutic implications (Corveleyn, 2000). Yet Freud's statements about religion have undoubtedly caused many people of faith to turn away from psychology and psychotherapy.

Albert Ellis also contributed to the denigration of religion when he opined that religion is neurotic (Ellis, 1976). According to Ellis's early writings on religion, a belief in God is an irrational belief that fosters dependency, anxiety, and hostility. Thus, religion creates and maintains neurotic and psychotic behavior. Ellis went on to argue that psychotherapists should not go along with the patient's religious beliefs. He viewed this as being equivalent to trying to help patients live successfully with their emotional illness, thus pathologizing spirituality. Like Freud, Ellis was highly critical of religion, stating that

> in a sense, the religious person must have no real views of his own, and it is presumptuous of him, in fact, to have any. In regard to sex-love affairs, to marriage and family relations, to business, to politics, and to virtually everything else that is important in his life, he must try to discover what his god and his clergy would like him to do; and he must primarily do their bidding. (Ellis, 1976, back cover)

It should be noted that Ellis (2000) later revised his opinion about religion and affirmed the positive aspects of religion and spirituality:

> Even dogmatic religiosity, which I believe to have distinct disadvantages, and which I formerly held to be almost always harmful to emotional health, can help many people. . . . Devout believers in Christianity, Judaism, and Islam sometimes hold some rational, self-helping beliefs that are quite similar to those favored by Rational Emotive Behavior Therapy (REBT), in Adlerian psychotherapy, and in other secular forms of therapy. (p. 279)

These and other antireligious comments, along with political disagreements between psychological and religious organizations, particularly Conservative Christian organizations (Lavin, 2009), have certainly created a level of distrust of mental health professionals among some. Psychotherapists have to be mindful of this lingering distrust as they move forward in their effort to connect with people of faith and their communities. By developing competency in religious diversity, we can continue to strengthen our relationship with the many religious groups throughout North America.

Developing such competencies not only allows therapists to adhere to their ethical obligations and practice within their boundaries of competence, but it also allows clinicians to better distinguish between spiritual problems and psychopathology (Lukoff, 1985). Furthermore, according to Richards and Bergin (2006c), such competency grants the therapist better knowledge of and access to various resources in religious communities. These factors contribute to the improvement of treatment and care provided by psychologists and counselors.

Accessing Healing Resources

Psychotherapists who are well connected in their communities can benefit their patients by adding ancillary services whenever they are needed. Psychotherapists should have knowledge of other medical, psychological, educational, and spiritual resources in their community. Clinicians who are connected with various religious groups can enjoy greater access to chaplains, pastoral counselors, shamans, imams, rabbis, and other spiritual healers. They may also have access to nurses, physicians, and psychiatrists who are comfortable working with people of faith. Furthermore, these clinicians may also enjoy greater access to youth leaders, congregational support groups, and other healing resources, such as herbal medicine and meditation groups that may be available in the community. Such ancillary services are invaluable to many patients, and a willingness of therapists to work together with these healers will greatly benefit patients.

Finally, attending to religious issues in psychotherapy can aid in the process of preserving and promoting mental health. Psychologists have traditionally focused on the negative aspects of religion, but religiosity, along with religious institutions, have several preventive functions. For example, problems such as drug abuse, violence, and lack of responsibility are frequently considered wrong or sinful by most religious institutions. Furthermore, religion often serves a significant function in coping during difficult life transitions and other tribulations. By incorporating methods of religious coping, psychotherapists can effectively use religion to help patients build, sustain, and restore their lives (Pargament, 1996).

INDIVIDUAL PSYCHOLOGY AND THE INTEGRATION MOVEMENT

Alfred Adler did not write much about religion and spirituality. Other than referencing religion in a few of his writings, Adler wrote only one paper directly on religion. This paper was written in collaboration with Ernst Jahn, a Lutheran pastor who wrote extensively on the integration of psychology and Christian pedagogy (Vande Kemp, 2000). Jahn had also written comprehensive critiques of psychoanalysis (1927) and Adlerian psychology (1931). In 1932 he became acquainted with Adler, and the two decided to write a book on the care of souls and Individual Psychology. Published in 1933, the book was soon seized by the Nazis and destroyed (Ellenberger, 1970). The book consisted of Jahn's essay "The Psychotherapy of Christianity," Adler's essay "Religion and Individual Psychology," and Jahn's "Epilogue." I will discuss Adler's essay in chapter three.

Vande Kemp (2000) discussed Adler's place in the integration movement and concluded that "Adler is only a minor figure in the psychology of religion" (p. 249). For example, in her review of the literature, Vande Kemp reported that her search of Religious and Theological Abstracts produced a mere 16 references to Adler, compared to 263 to Freud, 226 to Jung, 39 to Gordon Allport, and 22 to Carl Rogers. Furthermore, by 1984 Adler was mentioned as a significant figure in only 2 of 66 books on pastoral counseling in Vande Kemp's annotated bibliography (Vande Kemp, 1984; 2000). She reported that Adler was discussed by Zahniser in his book *The Soul Doctor* (1938), in which Adlerian theory, along with Freud's theories, were applied to case studies, and Cavanagh's 1962 text, *Fundamental Pastoral Counseling: Techniques and Psychology,* in which Adler was included in the group of contemporary psychologists he criticized.

Wulff (1991), in his historical review of the psychology of religion, argued that Adler's theories have received little notice in the literature. Though devoting full chapters to Freud, Jung, Erickson, and the object relation theorists, Wulff referred to Adler only as an influence on Victor Frankl and Theodore Schroeder.

Hood, Spilka, Hunsberger, and Gorsuch (1996) reviewed the empirical literature in the psychology of religion. Although they organized the conceptual and research information according to Adler's life tasks, they made "no references to other contributions by Adler, nor to Individual Psychology as a school of thought" (Vande Kemp, 2000, p. 249).

Adler was, however, a strong influence on some theorists, i.e., May (1940); Nuttin (1950/1962); and Progoff (1956). Yet his influence on the psychology of religion movement has been small. Vande Kemp (2000) concluded that

> Adler has had a significant influence on character education, a selective influence on the pastoral counseling movement, a negligible influence on the psychology of religion, and a minimal influence on psychology-theology integration. (p. 250)

As pointed out by Vande Kemp (2000), Adlerian psychologists and counselors have not contributed widely to the professional and academic literature on religion and psychology. However, Adlerians have discussed the issue of religion and spirituality among themselves for some time. Mansager and Rosen (2008) reported that their search of the literature resulted in 127 journal articles spread across 13 professional journals. The bulk of the articles were produced over the past two decades, but articles published as early as 1922 were reportedly found. *The Journal of Individual Psychology,* published by the North American Society of Adlerian Psychology (NASAP), has to date dedicated three issues to the topic of religion and spirituality. The first was a monograph published in 1971. Then in 1987, an entire issue was devoted to the topic of pastoral counseling. And finally the last issue to be devoted to religion and spirituality in its entirety was published in 2000.

The broadening of Adler's ideas on religion and spirituality began when Adlerians started to discuss spirituality as a life task. In the late 1960s Mosak and Dreikurs (1977/1967) argued that questions about the existence of God, immortality, and meaning were things every individual had to come to grips with. They asked the question: "Since the individual's relationship to the tasks of existence involve belief, conviction, and behavior, are these postures not also objects of psychological concern?" (p. 109). Their paper on the subject formed the basis for a discussion on religion and spirituality and spurred interests in these issues among Adlerian writers.

Although Adler never specifically identified a spiritual task, Mosak and Dreikurs (1977/1967) argued that he alluded to it in his writings. Therefore, they determined that Adlerians should be talking about the spiritual task in addition to the tasks of love, work, and association. They went on to discuss five subtasks included in the spiritual task: the individual's relationship to God, what the individual does about religion, man's place in the universe, issues around immortality and life after death, and the meaning of life. I will discuss the spiritual tasks as presented by Mosak and Dreikurs in more detail in chapter two. However, it should be noted that some Adlerians have strongly argued against the addition of the spiritual task. Gold and Mansager (2000) concluded that Adler made no reference or allusions to other life tasks beyond the original three. They argued that Adler had a deep appreciation for spiritual matters, however, and believed that religious and spiritual concerns were essential aspects of human life that Adlerians must attend to. It seems the addition of a spiritual task served to provide a context in which to discuss and address issues pertinent to religion, faith, and spirituality.

To conceptualize spirituality as a life task diminishes the significance and importance of spiritual experiences. Spirituality is more than a task that has to be dealt with, but rather an aspect of the human condition that may or may not be central to the original three tasks. For those who value religion and spirituality in their lives, spirituality can become a core aspect of work, love, and/or friendship. Thus, for these individuals spirituality becomes a central aspect around which life is organized. As such, it becomes part of everyday experiences. People may find the spiritual in their work, their relationship with those around them, in music, movies, sports, nature, and in every other human activity.

In their writings on religion and spirituality, Adlerian authors have addressed a variety of topics, such as the interface of spirituality and Individual Psychology, pastoral counseling (Baruth & Manning, 1987; Ecrement & Zarski, 1987; Huber, 1986; Mansager, 1987; 2000), the life tasks (Mosak & Dreikurs, 1977/1967; Gold & Mansager, 2000), the process of encouragement (Cheston, 2000), the political science of the Ten Commandments (Shulman, 2003), the "religious and spiritual problem" V-code (Mansager, 2002), and the interface of Individual Psychology and Christianity (Gregerson & Nelson, 1998; Jones and Butman, 1991; Kanz, 2001; Merler, 1998; Mosak, 1995, 1987; Newlon & Mansager, 1986; Saba, 1983; Savage, 1998; Watts, 1992; 2000), Judaism (Kaplan, 1984; Kaplan & Schoeneberg, 1987; Manaster, 2004; Rietveld, 2004; Weiss-Rosmarin, 1990), Buddhism (Croake & Rusk, 1980; Huber, 2000; Leak, Gardner, & Pounds, 1992; Noda, 2000; Sakin-Wolf, 2003), Confucianism (McGee, Huber, & Carter, 1983), Islam (Johansen, 2005), Hinduism (Reddy & Hanna, 1995), and Native American religions (Hunter & Sawyer, 2006; Kawulich & Curlette, 1998; Roberts, Harper, Tuttle-Eagle Bull, & Heideman-Provost, 1995/1998).

CONCLUSION

I have briefly discussed the complex and extensive history of the psychology of religion movement in America. I have also addressed psychology's heightened interest in issues pertaining to religion and spirituality as I presented the major developments that have helped our field be more attuned to religious issues in clinical practice. Along with the tremendous increase in professional publications on the subject, there have been a number of other important developments, including the inclusion of religion and spirituality as an aspect of diversity that therapists are obligated to respect; the inclusion of the Religious or Spiritual Problem V-Code; the development of numerous professional organizations that promote integration; and the establishment of degree programs that focus on integration. I have also noted how Adler's influence on the psychology of religion movement has been minimal. And although Adlerian writers have published extensively within their own circles, they have received little attention in the field.

2 Alfred Adler and the Principles of Individual Psychology

Dr. Alfred Adler was a general practitioner and psychiatrist in Vienna, Austria. Born in Penzing, a suburb of Vienna, on February 7, 1870, he was the second of six children in a middle class Jewish family. In his early childhood, Adler was a very unhealthy child, and he was confronted by death on several occasions. He suffered from rickets and later contracted pneumonia and became seriously ill. As an adult, Adler recollected his father being told by his physician, "Your boy is lost" (Orgler, 1939/1963, p. 16). In addition to being sick, Adler was also run over by a vehicle on two separate occasions. And when Adler was three, his younger brother died in bed next to him. As he grew older, Adler vowed to become a physician in order to overcome death (Adler, 1947). His early experiences certainly influenced his world view and also his theory of human nature.

Adler received his medical degree from the University of Vienna Medical School in 1895. He specialized in ophthalmology, but would soon transition to internal medicine, and later to psychology. Shortly after graduating he established a private practice in Vienna. He became interested in politics and began attending meetings of the socialist movement that was on the rise at the time. It was through these meetings that Adler met his future wife and socialist/feminist activist Raisaa Timofeyewna Epstein (Hoffman, 1994). The two married in 1897 and had three daughters and one son.

After he started his private practice, Adler's work changed to internal medicine. He noticed that many of his patients had problems that appeared to result from the social situations in which they worked and lived. And so in his first publication (Adler, 1898) he wrote about the health of tailors, and he noted how the social conditions in which people worked and lived had a significant influence on the illnesses they contracted.

In the fall of 1902, Sigmund Freud invited Adler to join his Wednesday evening discussion circle. Freud's seminal work, *The Interpretation of Dreams*, published in 1900, had been roundly criticized. In the midst of all this disparagement, legend has it that Adler published an article in a local paper strongly defending Freud's work. (This article has never been found.) Grateful for Adler's courage to defend his work, Freud reportedly invited Adler to join the Wednesday evening discussion circle (Mosak & Maniacci, 1999). These discussion groups became known as the Wednesday Psychological Society and were later called the Vienna Psychoanalytic Society. Adler became president of the society in 1910, but only a year later he resigned from the organization, in part because of Freud's pressures for uniformity and strict allegiance to his theory. After severing his ties with Freud, Adler went on to form his own group, initially called the Society for Free Psychoanalytic Research. The name was later changed to the Society for Individual Psychology, with the word *Individual* meaning "indivisible" (from the Latin word individuum), referring to the indivisible nature of the human personality and signifying the holistic approach to his theory.

In 1904 Adler converted from Judaism to Protestantism (Ellenberger, 1970). He was disgruntled with the Jewish faith limiting itself to one ethnic group rather than a more universal one. Despite his conversion to Christianity, Adler did not appear to be a religious man. His writings suggest that he could best be described as a humanist (Baruth & Manning, 1987). Although he wrote little on the issue of religion, he was far from skeptical of it. In fact, he believed that the idea of God was an idea of perfection that included being caring, loving, and helpful, and cooperating with others for the good of humanity (Baruth & Manning, 1987; Ellenberger, 1970).

During the First World War, Adler served as a physician for the Austrian Army on the Russian front. He was later moved to a children's hospital, but he saw firsthand the damage war could do. Shortly before the war, Adler had begun developing the social view of the neuroses. He and his coworkers maintained a primarily clinical focus, but Adler also demonstrated an interest in children, families, and education (Adler, 1914; Mosak, 1995). After the war he began to emphasize the importance of community feeling in his writings. He began setting up child-guidance clinics for Vienna's State schools. These were likely the first community outreach programs ever developed. Unfortunately, this psychoeducational movement was later suppressed when the fascists took over in Austria in 1934, followed by Hitler's Nazi Germany's forced annexation of Austria the following year. Adlerian family education and child guidance clinics were later opened throughout the United States, lead by Rudolf Dreikurs and his students (Dreikurs, Corsini, Lowe, & Sonstegard, 1959).

Following his first visit to the United States in 1926, Adler began teaching and lecturing in the United States more and more frequently. In 1929 he became an adjunct professor at Columbia University and started to shift the base of his operations from Vienna to New York. He later became professor at the Long Island College of Medicine in 1932. This was his first full-time academic position in the United States. Eventually, in 1935, he fled Europe and settled in the United States.

Adler continued to lecture throughout the United States and Europe until his death on May 27, 1937. He died of a heart attack in Aberdeen, Scotland, during a lecture tour in the United Kingdom. Over the course of his life, Adler published more than 300 books and articles. Most of his work was assembled by members of his groups and based on his lectures and notebooks. The books Adler wrote himself, he wrote as a psychoanalyst before the First World War—*The Neurotic Constitution* (1912/1983), and *The Practice and Theory of Individual Psychology* (1925/1959). Following the war, Adler published works such as *Understanding Human Nature* (1927), *The Science of Living* (1929a), *The Education of Children* (1930/1970), *What Life Should Mean to You* (1931/1958), and *Social Interest: A Challenge to Mankind* (1933/1964). These works were written primarily for the lay public, as were his lectures and public demonstrations.

Adler left us with a wealth of ideas and theories that are very much relevant today. The Adlerian Psychology movement is continuing to grow, and organizations such as the North American Society of Adlerian Psychology (NASAP), the International Association of Individual Psychology (IAIP), and the International Congress of Adlerian Summer Schools and Institutes (ICASSI) offer conferences, workshops, and publications on Individual Psychology.

Training in Individual Psychology is also becoming increasingly popular, and many universities and colleges throughout the world offer Adlerian training. Training institutes in New York, Chicago, Minneapolis, San Francisco, Fort Wayne, Vancouver, Montreal, and Toronto offers certificates in Adlerian counseling and psychotherapy. The Adler School of Professional Psychology, with campuses in Chicago, Illinois, and Vancouver, British Columbia, offers training at the Master's and Doctoral level in clinical and counseling psychology. As these and other schools continue to develop, Adlerian practitioners are growing in numbers and becoming part of mainstream practice, particularly in the United States and Canada.

THE PRINCIPLES OF INDIVIDUAL PSYCHOLOGY

Adler's theory is based on several philosophical principles such as holism, soft determinism, phenomenology, creativity, and teleology. These and other principles that make up the foundation of Adler's psychology will be discussed throughout the book as we compare and contrast his theories to different religions. These principles are briefly reviewed here for readers not familiar with Adler's theory.

All Behavior Occurs in a Social Context

Dr. Adler emphasized the point that people cannot be studied in isolation (Adler, 1929b). His theory views people as members of a social species, who live and develop in social groups, and whose survival depends on their engagement in reciprocal relationships. The establishment and maintenance of these relationships give meaning to our lives. Kurt Lewin's Field Theory parallels Adler's emphasis on the social context. According to Lewin

> The world, as experienced by the individual at any given point in time, is his [her] life space, which always includes both the person and his [her] psychological environment. . . . Behavior is always a function of this life space, which, in turn, is always a product of the interaction between the person and his [her] environment. (Lewin, in Schellenberg, 1978, p. 70)

Adler stressed that human behavior is best understood in a social setting, and any problem always has the potential of becoming a social problem (Mosak & Maniacci, 1999). For example, having a headache is a problem that belongs to me and me alone. The moment I decide to complain about the headache and stay home from work, it becomes a social problem. In trying to understand human beings, we have to consider their social context. As Adler (1927) put it, "In order to know how a man thinks, we have to examine his relationship to his fellow men. . . . We cannot comprehend the psychic activities without at the same time understanding those social relationships" (p. 34).

Although cultural and religious diversity is becoming increasingly popular as psychologists are calling attention to the importance of cultural competency, it is certainly not a new idea. Adler stressed this point at the very beginning of the 20th century, emphasizing the importance of understanding the person's social field. Mosak and Maniacci (1998) stated it this way: "One needs to know not only the person, but the person's social field; therapists need to be versed in more than psychology. Literature, myths, religion, ethnicity, history, movies, and the like all help to illuminate the person's picture" (p. 21).

Individual Psychology is a Holistic Psychology

Adlerians assume that the person is a self-consistent unit, that is to say, humans are indivisible. Holism can be conceptualized as "the whole is different from the sum of its parts" (Smuts, 1926/1961). People function as complete units in which each element influence the others. To Adler (1956), the concept of holism played a central part in his theory.

> Very early in my work, I found man to be a unity. The foremost task of Individual Psychology is to prove this unity in each individual—in his thinking, feeling, acting, in his so-called conscious and unconscious, in every expression of his personality. (p. 175)

Given this assumption, dividing a person or human experiences into different parts such as id, ego, and superego, conscious and unconscious, mind and body, ambivalence and conflict, approach and avoidance is meaningless (Mosak, 1995). When dividing a person into different units, we miss the whole picture. From an Adlerian viewpoint, people and their so called "parts" all move in the same direction.

For example, consider a client who says: "I know what I need to do intellectually, but I don't feel it in my heart." From an external point of view, this person appears to be stuck in a conflict between two parts of her personality. One might say she is conflicted over two separate elements, namely, her heart and her mind or her body and her soul. Adhering to the concept of holism, Adlerians would avoid conceptualizing her as consisting of separate elements, and rather look for the consistency of her movement. What she is really saying is, "I hear what you say, but I have no intention of changing."

Teleology

Aristotle (350 BC/1941) described four causes and wrote that, in order to understand the nature of anything, we need to know the material cause (i.e., what is it made of), the efficient cause (i.e., how it came to be), the formal cause (i.e., what shape or essence it is), and the final cause (i.e., for what purpose it is). Most psychological theories stress the first three causes. To Adlerians, however, it would be considered reductionistic (as opposed to holistic) not to emphasize all four causes. Therefore, Adlerians emphasize all four causes, particularly the final cause (Ansbacher, 1951; Mosak & Maniacci, 1999).

This teleological approach implies that human behavior, including symptoms, has a purpose. Adlerians stress the fact that all living things move, and that every movement must have a goal (Dreikurs, 1933/1989). As Adler put it: "The person . . . would not know what to do with himself were he not oriented toward some goal" (Adler, 1925/1959, p. 3). He went on to say that "we cannot think, feel, will, or act without the perception of some goal" (p. 3). This concept, that human behavior has purpose and is goal directed, is what distinguishes Individual Psychology from most other psychological theories. Emphasizing the final cause, Adlerians do not view people as pushed by causes, but rather believe that behavior is created by the individual and is not the direct result of preceding events.

Adlerians believe that people move in the direction of belongingness. We all want to belong, to feel important or significant. As the personality develops in the first few years of life, the individual establishes a subjective final goal that directs him or her as to what he or she should accomplish or be in order to belong (Adler, 1956). This final goal becomes the basic unconscious motivating factor throughout life. The goal is largely unconscious (i.e., unknown to the individual), yet it is self-selected according to the person's unique perception of an ideal state. Consider the story of John, a man in his late twenties, who had sought counseling with me a few years ago.

During his formative years, John concluded that the best way to feel important in his family was to get things. His parents would spoil him by giving him whatever he pointed his finger at, so John learned quickly that whenever he got something he felt important. For John, "getting" is the final goal. As he grew older, the goal became concretized in various ways. At school and later at work, he made a point of always being nice to others, hoping they would return the favor. He would always ask others to help him with homework as he perceived it as tedious and unnecessary work. He picked friends who were eager to help and give. Whenever people would ask him to contribute, he would distance himself from them, telling himself that they didn't see eye-to-eye.

According to Shulman (1985), Adler viewed the goal of belonging as both an inherent and potential factor in life:

> The tendency of human beings to form attachments (social feelings) was considered by Adler to be a fact of life. The striving of the human is always in some way connected with human bonding. Social interest is the expression of this tendency in a way that promotes human welfare. Some aspects of social interest are innate as in the infant's tendency to bond to its mother. However, social interest is a potential that must be developed through training in cooperation with productive endeavor. (p. 248)

The final goal is what motivates us through life. It is the fundamental motivating factor, and most other behaviors are organized such that we can continue pursuing this particular goal of belonging.

Moving From a Perceived Minus to a Perceived Plus

Movement toward the final goal is conceptualized as moving from a perceived minus situation toward a perceived plus situation. Adler (1956) used a variety of terms to describe the perceived plus situation: a real man, a will to power, perfection, completion, security, overcoming, and superiority. The terms Adler used changed as he developed his theory and moved from writing as a psychoanalyst early in his career to writing as an educator, social psychologist, and philosopher toward the end of his life (Mosak & Maniacci, 1999). When Adler spoke of striving for superiority, he meant striving for a more advantageous situation, not being superior to others. Striving for superiority, according to Adler, meant striving for significance, competence, and belonging. The various terms Adler used in his writings all describe the striving toward a subjective final goal.

According to Adler, striving toward a perceived plus situation falls into two categories, the useful and useless side of life. If the striving toward superiority is done for the person's own success and admiration, Adler considered the striving useless, and even typical of mental problems in extreme cases. On the other hand, if one's movement toward superiority is done for the purpose of solving life's challenges, showing cooperation and compassion, the striving is considered to be on the useful side of life (Mosak, 1995). Adler considered the contemplation of a god to be the concretization of the idea of superiority (Adler, 1987).

Adler evaluated people as well as organizations in terms of their social usefulness (1956). When he stated that he "would acknowledge as valuable any movement that guarantees the welfare of all as its final goal" (p. 463), he suggested that individuals, organizations, and social institutions all have a responsibility to care for the welfare of their communities and their communities' people.

Social Interest

The concept of social interest is the most important one in Adlerian psychology. It is particularly important in the discussion of religion and spirituality, as the concept is probably the point of greatest agreement between individual psychology and religions, particularly Christianity (Kanz, 2001).

Social interest, or *gemeinschaftsgefuhl*—meaning a "feeling of community"—is the feeling of having something in common with others, a feeling of belonging and connectedness to one's community. It is expressed in one's willingness to take responsibility for life's challenges and cooperate with others. "Social interest is expressed subjectively in the consciousness of having something in common with other people and of being one of them. . . . Expressed objectively it will show how far he is able to cooperate there" (Dreikurs, 1933/1989, p. 5).

Mental health is measured in terms of a person's degree of social interest. A willingness to cooperate and participate in the give-and-take of life in an effort to solve life's problems is considered characteristic of good mental health. On the other hand, placing one's own needs ahead of those of others and cooperating only to elevate oneself shows a lack of social interest and is considered a characteristic of mental illness.

The Creative Self

Our behavior is influenced not by genetic inheritance and the social environment, but by our opinion of it. People take an active part in their lives. They are not merely reacting to their environment. Our decisions are based on our biased apperceptions of the world. And so we tend to focus on the things that confirm our beliefs, and we block out information that is likely to create cognitive dissonance. This self-organizing principle is what Adler called the creative self. It is the creative self that determines the distinctive nature of our behavior. Thus, our actions are influenced by learning, making choices, and choosing between alternatives presented to us.

Soft Determinism

Another important philosophical assumption maintained by Adlerians is that of soft determinism. In the traditional philosophical debate over whether we are hard wired (determinism) or have free will, Adler concluded that neither is the case. Adlerians believe people are free to make their own choices within the limits of their environment and their biology.

Determinism is based on the idea that human behavior is causally related to past experiences and/or biological influences. Freud's psychoanalysis is a deterministic theory. On the other end of the spectrum is the concept of free will, suggesting that there are no causal connections at all. Assuming the middle ground, and advocating for soft determinism, Adlerians believe people have the power to choose their own direction, their own attitudes. People are determined by neither biology nor circumstance. Instead, we make our own choices based on our beliefs about ourselves, about others, and about the world, and on our interpretation of our current circumstances. In his book *Man's Search for Meaning*, Victor Frankl (1959/2006) gives a powerful and convincing argument for the idea that we are free to choose at least how we feel about something. In his book he tells of his experiences in four concentration camps during World War II and explains how one can choose to cope with suffering and even find meaning in it.

In discussing the issue of soft determinism, Mosak & Maniacci (1999) emphasized three important points to clarify the issue. First, choosing something does not always mean wanting it. If we find ourselves stuck "between a rock and a hard place," all our choices are perceived as undesirable. Making a choice in such a situation does not mean we wanted what we chose. In addition, sometimes choices are made unconsciously. We often make decisions without thinking about it. We frequently make split-second decisions, only to realize the implications at a later time. Second, freedom to choose is different from freedom of choice. That is to say, life does impose limits on our choices. Sometimes, we are left with only a few options from which to choose. And third, although Adlerians hold people responsible for their choices, they do not blame them for their decisions.

> Given the assumptions of holism, creativity, teleology, and soft determinism, people choose; they, and they alone, are responsible for their choices. They may not be aware of making the choices or of the consequences of their choices and many of the implications that those choices entail, particularly the social implications, but they are responsible for them. Adlerians do not believe that "the devil made me do it." (p. 19)

Beliefs

Our behavior is influenced by our beliefs (Adler, 1956). All of our experiences are screened through a schema Adler called the lifestyle, or style of life. The lifestyle encompasses our beliefs about ourselves, others, the world, and our idealized self (the final goal). The style of life has been equated with the ego, the self, and personality.

The lifestyle begins to develop and form early in life when experiences are limited and even before language has fully developed. It functions as a blueprint for action. It is the characteristic way in which we act, think, perceive, and cope with life's challenges. Mosak (1954) broke down the lifestyle into four basic components: self-concept, self-ideal, picture of the world (Weltbild), and ethical convictions of what we believe is right and wrong. Consider the lifestyle of a person suffering from an anxiety disorder.

Self-concept: I am inadequate

Picture of the world: Life is dangerous; others are there to protect me

Self-ideal: I must be in control

As our lifestyle develops preverbally, these beliefs are often out of awareness (i.e., unconscious). They are often represented in visual representations and images, intuitions, and affective states (Milliren & Clemmer, 2006). The lifestyle is the schema through which we filter incoming information. It represents the glasses that color our interpretation of the world. Therefore we do not see the world as it is; we see our subjective interpretation of it.

Behavior as a Function of Subjective Perception

Individual Psychology is a phenomenological psychology. We believe that our behavior results from our interpretation of our environment. The lifestyle colors our view of the world so that we do not see or sense the actual facts, but rather a subjective image of the situation (Adler, 1956). Of the individual Adler wrote, "We must be able to see with his eyes and listen with his ears" (1931/1958, p. 72). Therefore, Adlerian therapists are not concerned with the actual facts. We are concerned about the patient's interpretation of them. Thus, we construct our own reality, our beliefs, and final goals based on our interpretation of our experience. The quest to understand the subjective experience of patients is also one of the main assumptions of existential psychology (Yalom, 1980).

Individual Psychology as a Psychology of Use

In the quest to understand people, the Adlerian therapist is interested in what use people make of their history, heredity, environment, and experiences. Adler (1929a) stated that "it is not what one has inherited that is important, but what one does with his inheritance" (p. 37). Having been given exceptional intellectual abilities, a person may choose to use those abilities to create a new invention (the useful side of life). On the other hand, that person may decide to use those skills to mastermind a heist (useless side of life). Thus, what a person possesses is less important than what he or she does with it. The same is true for our disadvantages. Born with a disability, a person can choose to become a burden to his family, or he can decide to focus on the things he is able to do and contribute in any way he can.

Our emotions, memory, and cognitive processes can also be used in various ways (Mosak & Maniacci, 1999). For example, if we want to move toward someone, we may choose to remember all the nice things we know about that person. When we want to move away from someone, we may choose to use anger to display our displeasure, while remembering ways in which the person did us wrong. Concerning ourselves with how experiences, heredity, environment, and emotions are used, we focus on the person's motivations, decisions, and interpretations of events.

The Role of Emotions

If we are free to choose our opinions, we are also free to choose our emotions. Thus, emotions are something we control, not the other way around. The idea that passions can be overwhelming is not accepted by Adlerians. As Dreikurs (1967/1973) pointed out

> Disturbing emotions are not structurally different from positive and con-
> structive emotions. They are not irrational, only their rationale is not rec-
> ognized, particularly not by the individual himself. . . . To be sure, they all
> have a purpose. Whatever a human being is doing is purposeful. He uses
> all his qualities, be they physical or psychological, to achieve goals which he
> has set for himself. (p. 208)

Emotions are energizers of behavior: they produce movement. Just as our behavior is purposeful, so are our emotions. Thoughts alone do not produce behavior, but together with emotions they allow us to pursue our convictions, our goals. Emotions and thoughts affect each other. Emotions can be produced by thoughts, and thoughts can result from having various emotions. For example, if I think to myself that everyone will make fun of me during a presentation, I will have feelings of anxiety. On the other hand, if I am depressed, I will have negative thoughts. Adlerians hold people responsible for their own feelings. This understanding of thoughts, feelings, and behavior is certainly not unique to Adlerian psychology. Other theories, particularly Cognitive Behavioral Therapy and Rational Emotive Behavior Therapy, maintain similar views.

Optimism

Individual Psychology is an optimistic approach to living. Adler (1978) viewed people as neither good nor bad. He believed human nature was neutral. People have the ability to make their own choices, and, as a result, they can and do change for the better. People can take responsibility for themselves and their neighbor, learn to cooperate, and strive for a better society. Because we are not determined by heredity, past experiences, or our environment, we are free to decide how to cope with them, and we always have the potential to make our lives better.

The Tasks of Life

As we move through life we are faced with challenges with which we must all cope and to which we must find solutions. Adler (1958) identified three main challenges he called the life tasks: work, society, and sex. This concept was later expanded to include two additional life tasks: coping with oneself (Dreikurs & Mosak, 1977/1967) and the spiritual (Mosak & Dreikurs, 1977/1967). For Adlerians, these tasks consist of the problems each individual is confronted with and toward which each of us has to take a stand. Let us examine each one.

Work

We all have to work in order to survive. Therefore, we have to ask ourselves how and to what extent we are willing to put forth the effort needed to provide for ourselves and our families, and to contribute to society. Dreikurs (1933/1989) considered work to be the most important of all the life tasks. He defined work as "any kind of work which is useful to the community" (p. 92). Thus, work does not have to be considered a paying job, but it also includes the work of a homemaker, children's schoolwork, and participation in volunteer activities.

Society

Humans do not exist outside of society. We are all tied to each other in some shape or form. It is not a question of whether or not we belong socially, but of how (Mosak & Maniacci, 1999). We all play a role in the social community, and so we need decide to what extent we are willing to cooperate with other people. Our ability to survive (i.e., make our own food, shelter, care for our health, etc.) is limited unless we have the support of a community. How we go about finding a place of belonging in our families will set the stage for how we find a place in society. A child who has found a place of belonging by being the center of attention in her family will likely attempt to be the center of attention in her community as well.

Sex

Humans cannot reproduce without the cooperation of the opposite sex. In view of that, we all have to decide what kind of relationship we want with the opposite sex. Getting along with each other and reproducing requires a significant level of cooperation and effort, making the task of sex (also referred to as the task of love or marriage) the most difficult one. As Dreikurs (1933/1989) declared

> right fulfillment of the love task demands a maximum of social interest, because it involves the closest of all contacts between two human beings, tests their capacity for cooperation to the utmost, and destroys the distance which can always be preserved in occupational and social relationships. (p. 96)

Dreikurs went on to say that the love task is rarely fulfilled, in comparison with the other tasks. This task requires a significant amount of courage and cooperation.

The Task of Self

In addition to getting along and cooperating with others, we also have to deal or get along with ourselves. This task concerns our ability to reach a sense of inner peace and to be comfortable with who we are. Dreikurs and Mosak (1977/1967) argued that we have to realize that we have a place, simply by the nature of our existence. We need to come to terms with the reality that

> we are here to be useful, to contribute, not to prove our value. Only if we realize that we have a place in life, can we forget about finding one and become responsive to the needs of the situation and not to the needs of our prestige or our desires. (p. 104)

As with the other tasks, social interest plays a vital part in our success of getting along with ourselves. If we lack a sense of belonging, we will be ill fit to solve life's problems, and feelings of inadequacy will get in our way of accepting ourselves.

The Spiritual Task

In the 1960s, Mosak and Dreikurs (1977/1967) began exploring issues of faith and the meaning of life. The result was a series of publications addressing the five life tasks, with the last article addressing the spiritual. In their article, Mosak and Dreikurs argued that Adler alluded to the spiritual task on several occasions, although he never specifically mentioned it. They argued that issues of God, faith, and meaning are important to psychology and should be considered a life task that each of us has to contend with.

We are all faced with the question of whether or not there is a God. For those who deny the existence of God, questions about the meaning of life still remain. On the other hand, people of faith have to ask themselves what the nature of their God is. Is there only one God? What is our relationship with God like? Is there life after death? What is considered sinful? How do we communicate with God? Do we love God, or fear him? These and other questions are the ones included in the fifth life task. In addition to being called the spiritual task, it has also been referred to as *the existential, the search for meaning,* and *the metaphysical task.* Mosak and Dreikurs (1977/1967) discussed five aspects of the spiritual task and addressed the various challenges each of us is faced with.

The first aspect of the spiritual task involves the person's relationship to God. If we believe there is a God, what is the nature of that God? How and when do we call upon him? Do we pray? If so, do we pray regularly? Is God someone we visit only in church? For atheists, do they substitute for a belief in God? If so, what do they substitute with? And finally, how do we relate to other people who may or may not agree with our beliefs? Are we tolerant of them? Do we pity them? Do we attempt to convert them? All of these questions are part of what we have to contend with, consciously or unconsciously. Given the prevalence of religion in our culture, the issue of God is one we frequently encounter, and so we are confronted with the questions of God and our relationship to him.

The second aspect involves what the individual does about religion. Do we embrace religion and participate in religious practices with a sense of having a relationship with God, or do we identify with religion without a significant connection to God? Does religion imply that we have to go to church regularly? To what extent do we have to be involved in church activities and religious rituals? Does our religion involve missionary work? How do we define the goals of our religion? Is God there to protect us, or is it our job to serve him?

The third aspect of the spiritual task concerns our perceptions of our place in the universe. Each of us develops a theory of human nature, an image of man, that guides us toward a relationship with ourselves and others. Are we determined, or do we possess free will? Are we created in God's image? Are we basically good, basically bad, or burdened by original sin?

The fourth aspect involves questions of immortality and the existence of an afterlife. Questions about the nature of our souls, hell, damnation, and salvation become relevant here. If salvation is possible, what is required for its achievement? How do we avoid damnation? What behaviors will lead someone to be damned to hell? If there is no afterlife, how do we make our mark on this world? What happens when we die? Should we fear death?

Finally, the last aspect of the spiritual task deals with the meaning of life. Does life have inherent meaning, or does it possess whatever meaning we give it? This task overlaps the other life tasks, such as work, love, and friendship. For example, how much meaning do we place on our occupation, on our relationship with friends and family, and on our spouses? For Adler, life had no inherent meaning. He believed we create our own meaning of life. For Adlerians, any meaning bestowed on life that moves the individual in the direction of connecting with and caring for the welfare of others is considered a useful and worthwhile interpretation of the meaning of life.

View of Psychopathology

Because life is filled with challenges, it requires that we have courage. To Adlerians, courage means having the willingness to cooperate and share in life's struggles. To Adlerians, courage is not synonymous with bravery. Our willingness to engage in life despite our imperfections requires courage, which in turn depends of our degree of social interest and our lifestyle convictions.

Adler believed that, psychologically, healthy people move through life with courage and common sense, as they struggle to cope with the various tasks and challenges life puts forth. Nobody is perfect, and everyone experiences feelings of discouragement and inferiority at one time or another. Adler acknowledged that all of us are imperfect, and that we all experience failure at some point in our lives. In fact, Adlerians often talk about the importance of having the courage to be imperfect. Moving through life with such courage and common sense is what Adler considered to be the hallmark of a healthy personality.

On the other hand, psychopathology results when people believe they must be perfect and then justify their behavior as the only way to achieve this perceived perfection. Accordingly, Adlerians think of psychopathology as resulting from mistaken perceptions and a lack of courage. These mistaken beliefs are often unconscious and are associated with a perceived threat to self-esteem.

The person's faulty convictions are formed early in life and are part of what Adler called the lifestyle. All lifestyles have their strengths and their weaknesses. What makes a person's lifestyle dysfunctional is inflexibility. When a person is unwilling to adapt to the realities of the environment, and when problem-solving is self-protective, rather than task-oriented, the person is susceptible to psychopathology. In meeting the tasks of life, the person cannot cope effectively, because he or she puts his or her own needs ahead of the needs of the situation.

According to Adler's theory, symptoms (psychological or psychogenic) are "arranged" unconsciously to serve as an excuse for not meeting the tasks of life, or to safeguard self-esteem. For example, feeling inadequate about his abilities to do well in school and insisting on being able to do what he wants all the time, John developed severe stomachaches. The stomachaches served two purposes. On the one hand, he was able to stay home from school. On the other hand, he could tell himself that, had it not been for the stomachaches, he would have been at the top of his class.

Adler differentiated psychopathology along the dimensions of social interest. Faced with life's challenges, the neurotic patient takes a "yes, but" stance. The "yes," indicating a sense of social responsibility, and the "but" excusing him or her from that responsibility. The person communicates the idea that he or she wants to take responsibility, his or her intentions are good, but the person is unable to do so because of the symptom.

Whereas the neurotic patient shows a certain level of social interest, the psychotic patient exhibits very poor social interest by responding to the life tasks with "no." The psychotic person is conceptualized as having cut himself or herself off from society. In psychosis, common sense is discarded as the person distances himself or herself from others by creating his or her own reality and pursuing his or her goals for personal superiority. In discussing psychosis, Adler (1956) stated that

> Insanity is the highest degree of isolation; it represents a greater distance from fellow men than any other expression except, perhaps, suicide. But even insanity is not incurable if the interest in others can be aroused. It is an art to cure such cases, and a very difficult art. We must win the patient back to cooperation; and we can do it only by patience and the kindliest and friendliest manner. (p. 316)

The Adlerian conceptualization of psychopathology suggests that symptoms are an inadequate or socially useless way of meeting the challenges of life (Mosak & Shulman, 1967). They are purposeful (teleology), and they serve a variety of functions, all with the goal of safeguarding self-esteem.

THE PRACTICE OF INDIVIDUAL PSYCHOLOGY

Adlerians generally practice brief psychotherapy. Their approach is directive (frequently using psychoeducation), future-oriented, and eclectic. Adlerians frequently use cognitive and behavioral approaches. They also use existential, person-centered (Rogers, 1951), and solution-focused approaches in the therapeutic process. Given the integrative nature of Individual Psychology, Adlerians can make use of such a wide variety of techniques and still remain consistent with their theoretical orientation.

Dreikurs (1956) discussed four main phases of Adlerian psychotherapy, all of which are operating throughout the entire process of treatment.

1. Establishing an empathetic and egalitarian relationship between the therapist and the patient, a relationship in which the client feels safe and free to share their feelings and beliefs.
2. Understanding the patient's history, social context, and movement within that context. The therapist seeks to understand the lifestyle dynamics of the patient.
3. The therapist helps the patient develop insight into his or her own convictions and lifestyle goals.
4. The patient is encouraged to consider available alternatives to his or her problems and to move toward a change in behavior and convictions.

Relationship

Throughout the therapeutic process, Adlerians attempt to establish and maintain a safe, empathetic, and therapeutic relationship with the patient. The therapist informs the patient of the nature of the therapeutic process and seeks to align his or her goals with those of the patient. Mutual goal alignment communicates respect for the patient's needs and allows the patient and the therapist to work together. In Adlerian therapy, the role of the therapist and patient is seen as equal. Thus, the two parties are actively collaborating throughout the process. As Adler

(1956) put it, "psychotherapy is an exercise in cooperation and a test of cooperation" (p.340).

Lifestyle Assessment

The psychological investigation often consists of careful listening and gathering of data. Adlerians attempt to develop a complete and holistic understanding of the patient's beliefs, feelings, and perceptions. All data, including test data, are used in an effort to understand how they fit the individual's lifestyle.

When Adlerians believe the patient's lifestyle is a contributing factor to the presenting problem, they often complete a formal lifestyle interview. Some therapists use standardized forms for the collection of data (e.g., Powers & Griffith, 1987; Shulman & Mosak, 1988), whereas others collect the data through conversation with the patient.

The lifestyle interview consists of two parts: the family constellation and early recollections. The therapist gathers information about the patient's history and family of origin. Here, the therapist attempts to understand how the patient found a place for him or herself in the family. Thus, the family constellation provides an overview of how the client experienced his or her development and what the various influences were.

The second part of the lifestyle assessment consists of collecting early memories from the patient. Adlerians use early recollections as a projective technique, making it a unique feature of Adlerian practice. The early recollections provide information about the patient's lifestyle; self-concept, view of the world, expectations of other people, self-ideal, and ethical convictions. Given that people selectively remember incidents that fit their lifestyle, clinicians can get a glimpse into the client's subjective experience by interpreting a series of the patient's earliest memories. (For a thorough discussion on early recollections, see Clark, 2002.)

Insight

Having gathered information about the patient's history, social context, developmental influences, and lifestyle, the therapist helps the patient understand himself or herself. The patient learns about his or her lifestyle convictions and how mistaken beliefs and ideas lead him or her to act the way he or she does. Insight is seen as an important part of

the therapeutic process. Although change is possible without the development of insight, Adlerians aim to teach patients about themselves in
an effort to promote change and prevent additional problems in the
future.

Reorientation

Because Adlerians consider all patients to be discouraged, it should
come as no surprise that they always emphasize encouragement in the
therapeutic encounter. Encouragement to Adlerians is both an attitude
and a way of being (Carlson, Watts, & Maniacci, 2006). Adler (1956)
famously stated, "in every step of the treatment, we must not deviate
from the path of encouragement" (p. 342). Mosak (1995) described the
therapeutic process in terms of the Christian values of "faith, hope, and
love" (p. 69). These values are communicated and strengthened in the
patient, as the therapist sustains faith and hope that things can and will
improve, displays empathy and unconditional positive regard, and shows
that he or she cares about the patient.

Therapeutic change from an Adlerian standpoint involves changes
in behavior, feelings, attitudes, and motivations. The goals of Adlerian
therapy are to decrease feelings of inferiority, relieve symptoms, and
promote social interest. In addition to encouragement, Adlerians use a
variety of techniques and tactics to move the patient in this direction.

SUMMARY

In this chapter we have reviewed the biographical history of Alfred
Adler. We have examined his theory of Individual Psychology and various
principles that make up the foundation of his theory. We have discussed
the five tasks of life and how the spiritual task plays a significant role in
Adler's theory. Throughout the chapter, we have seen how Adler's philosophy has a religious quality, making it very friendly to most practitioners
and patients who value the importance of spirituality and religion in their
lives.

3 Adlerian Psychotherapy and the Religious Person

In the great and small religious movements; in the great achievements of philosophy, science, art, and political wisdom; as in the individual men and women who strive to penetrate the truth, of seek to refine and dignify the thought, emotion, sight, and hearing or mankind, consciously or unconsciously, there is expressed the most exalted ideal purpose: "Love thy neighbor." . . . I would acknowledge as valuable any movement which guarantees the welfare of all as its final goal.

—*Alfred Adler*

Adlerian psychology offers a unique, yet appropriate, approach to working with religious individuals. In this chapter, I present an overview of the discussions of religion and spirituality in the Adlerian literature, and a discussion of the application of Adlerian psychotherapy to religious persons along with a case illustration.

Most schools of psychotherapy have had either a neutral or a negative position toward religion. In contrast to these systems, Individual Psychology takes an optimistic and positive stance in regard to religion and spirituality. As one of the oldest and most relevant schools of psychotherapy today, it is arguably the most religion-friendly. The quote by Adler that begins this chapter points to Adler's positive view of religion. Adler was not concerned with the nature of a person's religion or with what god he or she worshipped, but rather with the consequences of the person's religious practices on the community as a whole.

Adler's theory of human behavior has resulted in models of practice that have had a broad impact on the fields of education, social science, family life, psychology, and psychotherapy. In regard to psychotherapy, his ideas and techniques have become the basis for most contemporary practices. Adler's work has influenced the development of several major psychological schools of thought, including Cognitive Behavior Therapy, Rational Emotive Behavior Therapy, Existential Therapy, Reality Therapy, Person-Centered Therapy, Constructivist and Social Constructionist perspectives, and Family Systems approaches (Watts, 2003).

Adlerian psychotherapy is usually brief and time-limited. It is also directive, present- and future-oriented, and integrative and eclectic (Carlson, Watts, & Maniacci, 2006). Adlerian practitioners have a long history of practicing short-term psychotherapy, and, consistent with current practices, many Adlerian therapists often limit psychotherapy to 20 sessions or fewer. Psychotherapy as practiced by Adlerians has often been misunderstood for focusing on past events. Although the patient's history is important, Adlerians spend time learning about a patient's past and collecting early memories in an attempt to understand the patient's current movement through life. They look to the past to understand what motivates the patient to move forward. Adlerians believe that the future predicates the way in which people remember the past and functions in the present (Manaster & Corsini, 1982). Accordingly, Adlerian therapy is present and future oriented.

Several authors have noted the tendency of Adlerian psychology to favor religion and spirituality. For example, Manaster and Corsini (1982) stated that "The most common Adlerian position toward religion is positive, viewing God as the concept of perfection. . . . For Adler, religion was a manifestation of social interest" (p. 63). Mosak (1995) stated that "Adler's psychology has a religious tone. His placement of social interest at the pinnacle of his value theory is in the tradition of those religions that stress people's responsibility for each other" (p. 59). The most essential principle of Adler's theory was social interest, which Adler equated with the obligation to "love one's neighbor as oneself" (Mosak, 1995). The sociological aspects of Individual Psychology along with the concept of social interest are central to most religions.

RELIGION AND THE IDEA OF GOD

Adler's (1933) essay "Religion and Individual Psychology," was written as part of a small book in collaboration with Ernst Jahn, a Lutheran minister. The main difference that emerged from their discussion was that from the perspective of Individual Psychology, God is an idea, whereas for the faithful, God is a reality. Starting with the principle that human striving is the essence of life and that people are constantly striving toward some goal as if it existed, Adler viewed the idea of God as being the ultimate representation or concretization of this final goal. People are constantly moving from a position they interpret as inadequate (a felt minus) toward a position of adequacy (a felt plus). Religious and spiritual experiences and practices are goals of striving, not a drive or an instinct. Constantly attempting to overcome and to find a place in the group, God, as a goal, points the way toward harmonic social living.

Adler believed that the meaning of life was serving mankind and developing a sense of community between people (Adler 1958/1931). Given that humans are socially embedded, the ultimate aspect of the final goal involves finding a place and sense of belonging in the community—of which religion plays a central role. Adler saw religion as helping to bind people closely to each other through worship and other religious practices. Thus, religion serves to further communal life and contribute to the survival of the individual and the larger group.

Recognizing that religion is not always used for the good of humanity, Adler (1933) argued that the contradictions between the actions of the religious power structures and their essential nature are in part responsible for the fact that a large number of people oppose religion. Adler also pointed to the frequent abuses of religion as another reason for people opposing it. In his essay he emphasized that any religious organization, along with other social movements, is considered valuable as long as its aim is directed toward the well-being of all people.

Although religion serves as a valuable force to promote social living and thus encourage wellness and health, Adler also recognized that religiosity can play a major role in the development and maintenance of neurotic behavior. In one of his earlier works, Adler said this:

> Some . . . people retreat into religion, where they proceed to do exactly as they did before. They complain and commiserate with themselves, shifting their burdens onto the shoulders of a benevolent God. They think only about themselves. It is therefore natural for them to believe that God, this extraordinary honored and worshipped being, is concerned entirely with serving them and is responsible for their every action. . . . They approach their god just as they approach their fellow human beings, complaining, whining, yet never lifting a finger to help themselves or to better their circumstances. Cooperation, they feel, is an obligation only for others. (Adler, 1927/1998, p. 214)

For Adler, God is an idea, a concretization of the ultimate striving found in each and every human being. He warned against the striving to be godlike, stating that God represents the ultimate ideal that no human being is capable of achieving. But he also valued certain aspects of religion, particularly its emphasis on social feeling. Adler was not concerned whether or not God could be proven scientifically. He considered God to be a "gift of faith," focusing rather on how the individual strives to overcome. Whether the individual's goal is God or something else is not as important as whether the individual contributes to the community and furthers communal life through his or her religious and spiritual actions. Thus, for Adler, the major purpose of religion is the facilitation of social cooperation.

Adler's Individual Psychology, being a secular form of therapy, has been criticized from theological perspectives (e.g., Ellerbrock, 1985; Fox, 1980; Rafford, 1972; Veltman, 1973; Wakley, 1995). For instance, Adler viewed all religions as a vehicle to assist in the facilitation of social interest, regardless of its doctrinal content. Adler has also been criticized for his disregard for God's actual or real role in people's lives and for his insistence that there is no intrinsic meaning to life. Another point of disagreement between Individual Psychology and religion is the issue of social equality. As Adlerians assign equal value to all people, including children and women (Dreikurs, 1971), their perspective may easily conflict with clients who maintain traditional religious values that emphasize the authority of men over women and of adults over children. I will point to these discrepancies in the upcoming chapters.

SPIRITUALITY

Adlerians have explored and expanded on the concept of spirituality (Brunner, 1996; O'Connell, 1987, 1997; Peven, 2004; and Cheston, 2000; Mansager, 2000; Slavik and Croake, 2001; Sperry and Mansager, 2007). For instance, Mansager (2000) explored the psychological study of spirituality and introduced Individual Psychology as a crucial collaborator in the field in the search for greater understanding of spirituality. He argued that Individual Psychology provides an adequate baseline for research examining the psychological movement of individual and communal spirituality. An important area of study for Adlerians has involved evaluating the relationship between spirituality and social interest. Social interest has been found to be positively related with healthy spirituality—spirituality via a healthy connectedness to other people—and negatively correlated with religious ethnocentrism and fundamentalism (Leak, 1992; 2006).

There are numerous definitions of spirituality mentioned in the psychological literature. But generally, spirituality is thought to deal with an individual's search for meaning and a sense of connectedness with something beyond the self. Cheston (2000) defined spirituality as the "seeking of a relationship with the creative power of the universe in an attempt to find meaning in life and to develop one's uniqueness as a human" (p. 297). Mansager (2000), discussing Adler's psychology and the study of spirituality, offered a holistic definition of healthy spirituality from an Adlerian perspective.

> Spirituality is the individual's conscious movement from a felt minus to that of a fictional plus, holistically experienced as a unifying factor not rooted in self-boundedness but in community feeling aimed at full participation in an apperceived perfect community. (p. 385)

From this perspective, spirituality coincides with movement—the individual's lifestyle. Its movement is characterized by living consciously focused on ultimate concerns. Thus, from an Adlerian perspective, spirituality is an innate capacity which can be developed, similar to a person's capacity to contribute to the community.

Mansager also outlined four critical criteria by which Individual Psychology measures spirituality and its relationship to wellness or illness. Spirituality is seen as contributing to an individual's wellness depending on (a) whether the person's striving toward ultimate concerns is self-serving or helps contribute to the community; (b) whether the individual's spiritual path is characteristically tolerant, open, judgmental, or prejudiced; (c) whether the individual's spirituality moves him or her toward a connection with others rather than leading to isolation and self-absorption; and (d) the degree that the individual's subjective ultimate value endorses the wellness criteria of striving, integration, and self-transcendence.

According to Slavik and Croake (2001), when addressing spiritual concerns in counseling and psychotherapy, Adlerians focus on movement and intentions. Feelings and spirituality are not viewed as independent of cognitions or other aspects of the individual. These are created to motivate and justify the individual's direction of movement. As Adler (1956) pointed out, the key to understanding another individual is the fictive goal. It is the fictive goal that coordinates all aspects of the lifestyle, including spirituality. Spirituality, then, is part of an individual's creative movement throughout life. And, as Adler (1933) pointed out, what an individual does with his religion (or spirituality) is what matters. As long as a person's spirituality or religion is used to move him or her toward others in a spirit of cooperation and tolerance, it may be considered psychologically healthy.

Being a psychology of use, Individual Psychology concerns itself with the way in which the individual subjectively perceives and adapts religion and spirituality to his or her approach to life. Adlerians seek to understand how faith and religion are used in meeting the tasks of life. For some, religion can be a source of comfort and healing. Many individuals find religion and spirituality in times of crisis and adversity. And people sometimes use them to resolve trauma or other life challenges. Generally speaking, religion and spirituality can be life-enriching in countless ways. But religion and spirituality can also be part of the problems in living. For instance, patients may be maintaining irrational or self-defeating beliefs that involve issues of religion and faith (i.e., "God will never forgive me," "God is punishing me, and there is nothing I can do about it"). Second, religious beliefs and practices may be used to elevate the individual's social status or achieve a subjective experience of superiority over others (i.e., "Nobody knows God as well as I do," "Because I'm Buddhist I am superior to these other people"). Religion and spirituality can be a tremendous resource for healing and optimal functioning, but they can also be part of the psychological problems—they can lead toward growth or result in one's decline (Pargament, 2007).

Ellis (2000) outlined a series of spiritual goals and values found in Adlerian Therapy, Rational Emotive Behavior Therapy, and Cognitive/Behavioral Therapy, which he viewed as favorable to mental health. Ellis pointed to the following goals and values—calling them profoundly meaningful, purposive, and spirited goals—as promoting wellness: (1) obtaining outstanding meaning or purpose in life; (2) unconditional other acceptance along with unconditional self-acceptance; (3) the courage to change life's difficulties, the serenity to accept that which cannot be changed, and the wisdom to know the difference; (4) maintaining high social interest and compassion for others; (5) maintaining significant optimism and being hopeful about the future; (6) taking responsibility for oneself and others; and (7) being one's authentic self despite what others may think. Ellis argued that these goals and values can be the aim of religious and nonreligious clients alike.

ADLERIAN THERAPY WITH PEOPLE OF FAITH

There are key aspects of Individual Psychology that make it useful in the treatment of religious patients, or patients with problems of a spiritual nature. First, its teleological aspects offer a unique approach to understanding spirituality. This concept is consistent with each of the world religions. Second, similar to most religions, Adlerians strongly believe in personal responsibility and the freedom to make choices. Third, Individual Psychology focuses on beliefs, convictions, and behavior. Likewise, many religious doctrines, parables, and teachings emphasize changing thoughts and actions. And finally, Individual Psychology views psychotherapy as being a process of learning. Let us look at each of these in turn.

Movement from a Felt Minus Toward a Fictional Plus

Pargament (1996, 2007) proposed that in order to effectively integrate spirituality in counseling and psychotherapy a major shift in psychological theory needs to occur. Psychologists need to understand spirituality as something humans search for. Individuals with a religious and/or spiritual inclination tend to view themselves as searching for the divine. They understand themselves as moving toward something beyond themselves. Thus, Pargament suggested that psychologists need to shift from a reactive view of human nature and understand people's behavior as goal-directed. Individuals attempt to find and maintain whatever gives them a sense of significance in living. Rather than being influenced only by our biology and our environment, Pargament argues, people strive to attain some future goal.

> The idea that individuals are involved in a process of "searching" rests on a critical, even radical, assumption: the assumption that people strive. . . . It conflicts with the major psychological theories of our time: psychodynamic, social learning, and biological. (p. 53)

Pargament goes on to say that people are born with a spiritual potential to seek the sacred in their lives. Thus every individual is seen as spiritual, although some are more motivated to seek the sacred than others. He concluded that the search for the sacred is a unique feature of human motivation and must be understood as teleological.

> From a clinical standpoint, it is important to take the search for the sacred seriously as a directing force in its own right. . . . Regardless of its roots, spiritual motivation is a part of what makes people unique. . . . Spirituality is, in short, a critical and distinctive dimension of human motivation. (p. 60)

Although this teleological premise conflicts with most psychological theories, the assumption that people strive is a basic tenet of Individual Psychology. According to Adler (1927)

> This teleology, this striving for a goal, is innate in the concept of adaptation. We can only imagine a psychic life with a goal towards which the movements which exist in the psychic life, are directed. (p. 28–29)

According to Adler, people strive toward a sense of belonging and significance. They strive toward what they perceive as being an ideal situation. Whatever the individual chooses as his or her ideal situation becomes the motivating force—the fictional final goal. In their efforts to understand human nature, Adlerians look at behavior as purposive striving toward the attainment of unique goals—both short-term and long-term goals. This assumption that individuals strive for the attainment of some goal (i.e., God, salvation, love, power, significance, etc.) is found in Christianity, Judaism, Islam, Hinduism, and Buddhism.

Consider the case of a woman in her early twenties complaining that everyone always "walks all over her." She finds it incredibly difficult to assert her opinion, and she can never find it in her heart to tell someone "no" when a person asks for her help. As a result she is feeling used, unloved, and angry. All her life she has made efforts to work hard and please others. She has concluded that doing these things makes her a good person in the eyes of God. From an Adlerian point of view, she is not behaving this way as a result of early childhood experiences, past traumas, or to fill some void, but because she believes that always being a good person and pleasing those around her will lead to salvation (subjectively perceived plus situation). She has concluded that life is about being good. Here, she finds a sense of significance and, in her own words, she feels "connected to God."

Pargament (2007) argued that the search for the sacred is a distinct feature of human motivation. Rather than being a result of unfulfilled childhood wishes, Pargament suggests that spiritual striving must be understood as a primary motivating factor. From the perspective of Individual Psychology, the fictional final goal is considered subjective and nonconscious. And the search for the sacred is conceptualized as a conscious effort to move from a felt-minus situation to a felt-plus situation. From a theological perspective however, the search for the sacred (i.e., salvation, Nirvana, unity with Brahman) is an objective reality. Experiences that restrict an individual in his or her search for this end goal are likely to result in a spiritual struggle or spiritual crisis.

According to Pargament, spiritually integrated psychotherapy must consider the individual as spiritually motivated—searching for the sacred. Adlerian psychology makes this argument for any individual, religious and nonreligious. But rather than searching for the sacred, Adler (1956) believed people strive toward a sense of belonging and significance. Whether an individual finds a sense of significance in connecting with God depends on the individual's creative movement throughout life.

In addition to adopting a teleological perspective of human nature, Pargament called for another change in perspective among psychologists. He argued that individuals must be understood as having freedom to choose. Individuals are not merely reacting to their environment, but are able to respond to it and influence it. Again, Individual Psychology maintains that people are free to make choices. Pargament pointed to two main reasons why such a shift in psychological theory is necessary. First, if we fail to see individuals as striving for goals or searching for the sacred, we miss the whole picture of the person. As important as biological and environmental factors are, psychology has to consider what people strive for in their lives. Second, without the freedom to choose, people are predetermined by environmental and hereditary restraints. Thus, the individual has no say in changing his or her life for the better. The assumption that individuals have the freedom to choose is optimistic and encouraging, suggesting that people are capable of changing and improving their circumstances.

Focus on Belief

Adlerian psychology is highly belief-oriented, and treatment focuses on the patient's basic mistakes (i.e., underlying assumptions and beliefs). Most religious individuals are familiar and comfortable with belief-oriented language. Thus the approach is well suited for the assessment and modification of all forms of beliefs, including religious and spiritual beliefs that may affect psychological functioning and spiritual health.

Adlerian therapy utilizes a wide variety of cognitive and behavioral intervention strategies. Similar to Cognitive Therapy and Rational Emotive

Behavior Therapy, Adlerians work at helping the patient understand the influence of thinking on behavior and emotion, helping the patient "catch himself or herself" by monitoring thoughts, beliefs, and assumptions, and challenging dysfunctional beliefs, thoughts, and assumptions. For example, cognitive disputations can be accomplished using scriptural or other religious evidence to argue against the patient's basic mistakes.

Tan and Johnson (2005) discussed two levels of cognitive disputation with religious clients in Cognitive Therapy: general and specialized. Such cognitive disputations are also used by many Adlerians. In generalized disputation, the therapist challenges the patient's beliefs without challenging his or her religious views. For example, a patient who is scared to assert herself and fearing God's wrath may be asked, "Where in the Bible does it say that it is sinful to feel angry?" In specialized disputation, a therapist may directly dispute a patient's dysfunctional or idiosyncratic religious beliefs or practices. Religious beliefs that are irrational or otherwise inconsistent with the patient's own religious culture can be challenged directly. Specialized disputations should be used only by therapists who are knowledgeable about the patient's particular religious tradition. For example, for a patient who is convinced his behavior is controlled by God and that his suffering is inevitable, a therapist may point out that the Bible says, "and if it seem evil unto you to serve the Lord, choose you this day whom you will serve" (Joshua, 24.15). "So it seems God grants us the freedom to choose our course in life; how is it that you don't have the same freedoms as the rest of us?"

The use of religious imagery may also be used as evidence against irrational beliefs, to offer comfort and support, or to alleviate anxiety. The incorporation of scripture readings or prayer in or outside of sessions may also be used, depending on the patient's needs. When asked why he had not yet followed through on his suicidal intentions, Joseph, a man in his mid-thirties, told his therapist he had always wanted to sit next to Jesus in heaven, but, were he to kill himself, he feared he would not be accepted into heaven. The therapist used the image Joseph had of himself sitting next to Jesus to counter the suicidal thoughts. Whenever he had thoughts of wanting to hurt himself, he was encouraged to picture himself sitting next to Jesus. This exercise reminded him of his reasons to continue living. And through continued visualization of being with Jesus, he also found comfort and support. He eventually used this imagery as part of his prayers as he imagined himself being with and talking with Jesus and being comforted by Him.

Therapy as a Process of Learning

Adlerian psychotherapy frequently makes use of psychoeducation and teaching. In fact, psychotherapy is viewed as a process of reeducation. Adlerians also integrate techniques from several other schools of thought into their work with patients. They frequently include cognitive, behavioral, solution-focused, existential, family systems, and person-centered approaches in their practice. Given the eclectic and integrative nature of Individual Psychology, therapists can make use of such a wide variety of techniques while remaining consistent with their theoretical framework.

The Adlerian model of change, along with theological inquiry, emphasizes a change of perspective for transformation. The process of growth and change is often very appealing and is easily accepted by religious individuals. Christian and Jewish traditions emphasize the development of self-examination, genuine insight, and change in behavior. Similarly, Buddhist and Hindu traditions stress the enhancement of insight that is accomplished through lifelong learning, duty, and right conduct. The Muslim tradition also emphasizes learning and spiritual growth through prayer, memorization of the Koran, and fasting.

From an Adlerian standpoint, the most important shift that needs to occur is a shift from concerns with oneself to a focus on others and the community—social interest. Adlerians certainly work toward the alleviation or reduction in symptoms and increased functioning in the life tasks, but the increase of social interest is seen as the hallmark of mental health. Through the development of insight, experimentation with new behaviors, cognitive restructuring of the basic mistakes, and ongoing encouragement, Adlerians work to give the patient a different perspective and the courage to move forward in life with a concern for others rather than herself or himself.

In terms of incorporating spiritual and religious material in psychotherapy, the Adlerian therapist moves comfortably between discussions about spirituality and psychological material in a clinically responsible and respectful manner. If spiritual issues are important to the patient, the therapist addresses these to the extent of his or her competency. Religious and spiritual issues are addressed if the patient presents with religious problems, or when the presenting problem is related to spiritual or religious issues. Although the Adlerian therapist strives to understand the patient's religious beliefs and practices, not every patient is seen as needing to address spiritual issues.

Tan (1996) delineated this movement between discussions of spiritual and psychological material when presenting two major models for integrating religion and spirituality in psychotherapy: implicit and explicit integration. Implicit integration refers to a covert approach in which discussions of religious and spiritual issues are not initiated by the therapist. Here, the therapist does not use religious and spiritual material or resources directly or openly. Explicit integration, however, is considered a more overt approach, where spiritual and religious issues are addressed directly and systematically. The therapist may draw upon religious material such as religious texts, referrals to religious communities, or other religious groups. Over the course of therapy, the therapist moves appropriately between implicit and explicit integration. Depending on the patient's presenting problem, needs, and goals for therapy, the Adlerian therapist moves along this continuum, addressing spiritual and religious issues when appropriate.

Indications and Contraindications

Issues relating to spirituality and religious beliefs should be assessed in counseling and psychotherapy. One might make an exception for crisis interventions, but even here spiritual issues may be critical. For instance, religious beliefs may keep someone from attempting suicide. But generally speaking, and given the vast number of clients who maintain a belief in God, therapists should inquire about religious beliefs as part of the assessment process.

Inquiring about religious and spiritual beliefs serves two very important functions in Adlerian therapy. First, if beliefs about spirituality and religion are not assessed, the therapist might miss an important aspect of the patient's life. He or she might fail to see aspects that contribute to the presenting problem or overlook an area of the patient's life that offers numerous resources for strength, comfort, and healing. Given that many people are reluctant to talk to therapists about religious and spiritual issues, they may not bring them up unless they are asked. Second, by asking about faith and related topics, the therapist indirectly informs the patient that he or she is willing to talk about these issues, thus inviting the patient to bring up concerns related to spirituality and religion. Patients who are hesitant to address issues of faith in therapy are more likely to talk about spiritual issues if they sense that the therapist is willing to have such conversations.

Spiritually oriented interventions can be used with patients who value religion and spirituality in their lives and who are willing to address such issues in therapy. When clients are unwilling to address spiritual issues, however, the therapist should not insist that they be addressed, nor should he or she use spiritually oriented interventions when religious issues are not relevant to the presenting problem. Patients often present with problems that are unrelated to the spiritual aspects of their lives. Consider Eila, a practicing Buddhist in his early thirties. After being promoted to a management position in the company he worked for, he developed a severe fear of public speaking. Given that his new job required him to give more talks, he sought therapy to help with his anxiety. Therapy was short term and consisted of Adlerian interventions along with relaxation exercises (which he was very good at, given his practice of meditation). Eila soon overcame his fear of public speaking and ended therapy. Other than a brief discussion of religious beliefs and practices during the interview process, no mention of spirituality was made or needed.

Another group of patients in which spiritually oriented interventions should not be used includes nonreligious people. Atheists or other patients who see little value in religion and spirituality are not likely to benefit from spiritual interventions. In fact, many might find it offensive or counterproductive and discontinue therapy as a result.

Adlerians working with children and adolescents need to be cautious in how they proceed with spiritual interventions in psychotherapy. If spiritual issues appear to be an important aspect of a child's life, the therapist should seek parental permission to discuss such issues with the child. In these cases the therapist needs to determine the religious values of the family and be clear on what the child's parents hope to teach their children in terms of religion. These values must be respected in the therapist's interactions with the child.

Therapists must always practice within the boundaries of their expertise and respect the patient's religious and spiritual beliefs and practices. Spiritual interventions should be used only in a clinically responsible manner for the benefit of the patient.

Issues Related to Diversity

Religious and spiritual beliefs are always maintained within a social and cultural context. Thus, Adlerian therapists working with religious persons must pay close attention to cultural factors and the patient's social context. Newlon and Arciniega (1983) discussed the need to respect cultural differences and integrate cultural considerations in Adlerian psychotherapy. They recognized that

> Counselors cannot operate without relevant cultural information when working with minority clients. They need to see the totality of a cultural group and its interacting systems. They must understand not only the culture of the clients they are serving, but their history, beliefs, values, and behaviors in an interacting, holistic sense. (pp. 133–134)

Therapists must also consider the patient's level of education and level of acculturation in order to have a full picture of the patient and his or her social context. Adlerians have discussed various cultural issues relating to African Americans (e.g., Brown, 1976; Gordon-Rosen & Rosen, 1984; Laird & Shelton, 2006; Perkins-Dock, 2005), South Africans (e.g., Brack et al., 2003), Asians (e.g., Carlson, & Carlson, 2000; Chung, & Bemak, 1998), Hispanics (e.g., Frevert, & Miranda, 1998; Martinez, 1998; Newlon, Borboa, & Arciniega, 1986; Zapata, & Jaramillo, 1981), and Native Americans (e.g., Kawulich, & Curlette, 1998; Nystul, 1987; Nystul, 1982; Roberts et al., 2003; Salzman, 2002; Roberts, et al., 1998).

In an effort to integrate cultural considerations, Newlon and Arciniega (1983) recommended that Adlerians address their own personal stereotypes regarding the various cultural groups, acquire knowledge regarding these groups, seek to understand their interactions with the dominant culture within their society, and attempt to understand and consider the effects of racism. These authors later argued that the Adlerian approach to psychotherapy is respectful to issues of cultural diversity.

Adlerian goals are not aimed at deciding for clients what they should change about themselves. Rather, the practitioner works in collaboration with clients and their family networks. This theory offers a pragmatic approach that is flexible and uses a range of action-oriented techniques to explore personal problems within their sociocultural context. It has the flexibility to deal both with the individual and the family, making it appropriate for racial and ethnic groups (Arciniega & Newlon, 1999, p. 451).

Last, for more information about cultural diversity, interested readers are referred to Sue and Sue (2008), who have detailed the many dimensions of multicultural psychotherapy. They address social, psychological, and political issues along with implications for counseling

African Americans, American Indians, Asian Americans, Hispanic/Latino Americans, and Arab and Jewish Americans.

Case Example

When 29-year-old William came to see me, he had suffered from depression for over a year. He decided to seek counseling after his roommate urged him to seek help. He was doubtful that therapy could help him and believed his depression would plague him for the rest of his life. William had struggled with depression ever since his late teens, but this past year had been particularly difficult. He had lost his job one year earlier and fallen into a "deep" depression. He had held a few odd jobs here and there, but he felt that his opportunity at having a real career was lost. William told me he had lost his job after a series of complaints from clients. He had reportedly failed to finish assignments and to complete legal documents accurately.

William had worked as a financial representative with an insurance company for four years. After struggling through college, he had joined the company and experienced significant financial success. He liked his work and said he enjoyed the company of his colleagues, but he never socialized with them outside of work. Instead he socialized with women he had befriended in college. His only male friend was his roommate. He said he felt more comfortable around girls because they were generally nice and certainly not as critical as his male colleagues.

When it came to women, William said he had dated on a few occasions, but he had found romantic relationships to be difficult. He told me that every romantic relationship he had been involved in ended when the girl decided to break up with him. This frustrated him and kept him from going out on further dates. He had no idea why his relationships with girls ended badly.

I asked William how he felt about God. He looked surprised when I asked him, and he told me that he was not a very religious person. In fact, "I never go to church," he said. "My parents did, but I never go." "Do you believe there is a God," I asked. "Sure I believe in God. I just don't think I have to go to church to see him." As our discussion about God and religion continued, William explained that he had a fondness for Buddhism. "I feel that the Buddhists are much less judgmental than the Church," he explained. We briefly discussed his religious beliefs and agreed to continue talking about his relationship with God in future sessions.

Diagnostic Impressions

William met diagnostic criteria for Major Depressive Disorder (APA, 2000). His depressive mood had been ongoing for over a year. Although he had experienced a few weeks of relief, he found himself falling back into a depressive state. He had gained a significant amount of weight over the past year—over thirty pounds, he had difficulty falling asleep, and he complained of chronic fatigue. Although there was no risk of suicide, he explained that he had thought about how dying would make things easier. He also experienced a lot of guilt and feelings of being sinful, and he thought that he probably deserved to die. When asked about his guilt feelings, he explained that he was a bad person. He was convinced he had been fired for making bad decisions at work. He also felt he had betrayed his colleagues and his roommate by not doing his job well.

William exhibited several dependent traits, such as fear of being alone and an excessive need to be taken care of, yet a diagnosis of Dependent Personality Disorder (APA, 2000) was not warranted.

Family Constellation

William's older sister, Katelyn, had moved away from home a few years earlier. After receiving her medical degree, she moved out of state to finish her residency in pediatrics. She and William had a close relationship. They talked on the phone at least once a month, and William admitted to feeling abandoned by her when she left for residency training. Feelings of abandonment were not new to William. When he was sixteen years old, his parents separated. Their divorce came as a complete surprise. He had always thought his parents' relationship was good. He never imagined they would leave each other. He said there were never any fights or arguments, although in the years following their divorce he had come to realize that there had not been much love between them either.

When he was growing up, William's family lived in an upper middle class neighborhood. His mother worked as a physician, and his father was in the financial business. When Katelyn was born, Mom had decided to work part time to spend time with the baby. She continued working part time for a few years, but five years later, when William was born, she gave up her career to focus on the children. A summary of William's family constellation reads as follows:

William grew up as the youngest child in a family of two children. He maintained the role of the youngest child throughout his childhood. He liked his position as the youngest child, as he felt privileged and admired. He always looked up to Katelyn, and she would compliment him on his achievements and protect him when he entered school. The feminine guiding line in William's family emphasized looking good, acting polite, and doing the right thing. People's perceptions of the family were of high importance. The masculine guiding line emphasized doing what you were told, doing the right thing, and never "messing up." The family values shared by both Mom and Dad included the importance of education, doing the right thing, and making sure people approved of you. William found a place for himself by being a good boy, never making mistakes, and being a good student. Katelyn found a place in the family by being a leader and an A student.

As William approached adulthood, he was faced with a series of challenges. His sister moved away to start her residency in pediatrics, leaving him feeling abandoned and alone. Shortly before his sister left the state, his parents separated, and his mother went back to work full-time. Having lived a life of safety and privilege, he found himself thrust into a world he was unprepared to handle.

William provided the following early memories as part of the lifestyle assessment:

Age 3

We had just moved into a new house. The neighbor came over and introduced herself. I remember thinking she was nice. I really liked her. I politely shook her hand, and she said I was a nice boy. I knew she would take good care of us.

Most vivid moment: feeling good.

Age 6

First grade. I remember sitting in the classroom and not knowing how to write my name. Everybody laughed at me. The boy next to me leaned over and asked me what my name was. I told him, and he showed me how to write it. I told him I liked him.

Most vivid moment: The teacher's face.

Feeling: I was scared someone would find out how dumb I was.

Age 6

Also in first grade. I remember this kid, (a boy) in school, who said my shoelace was untied. I didn't know how to tie it, so I turned around and ran. I must have stepped on the shoelace or something, because I remember I tripped and everybody laughed at me.

Most vivid moment: I just wanted to be home.

Feeling: embarrassed, stupid for not being able to tie my shoes.

Age 7

My friend's mom asked if I wanted to go to church with them. I said yes. I had never been to their church before. I remember it was bigger than ours. I felt so good being there, but then I messed it all up when I got in trouble for talking in church. I felt so bad, and my friend's dad was really angry at me. He told my parents, and I got in trouble.

Most vivid moment: Trying to say I was sorry.

Feeling: I messed up.

Age 8

Here's a good memory. I was playing with my cousins at my uncle's house. We had a barbeque, and it was really warm outside. My uncle showed us how to pitch. I remember thinking I wished he was my dad.

Most vivid moment: Learning how to pitch and playing with my cousins.

Feeling: Good.

William's early recollections were interpreted and summarized as follows:
      I am a bad and incompetent person. I create my own misfortunes. Even when things go in *my* favor, I mess it up. If people really got to know me, they would realize how incompetent I am. Because other people are competent, and I am not, I need people to take care of me. All I really hope for is to be liked and to be loved. In order to feel significant, I must be accepted and loved all the time. Therefore, I must act the way people want. I cannot allow others to see the true me.

Discussion of the Case

Despite intense feelings of inadequacy, William had managed to complete college and achieve occupational success. His firing confirmed his worst fear, however. From William's perspective, it confirmed that he was inadequate and that nobody liked him. After losing his job, William had lost all hope of being successful. Although he had made some attempts at working for other companies, he found himself either quitting, believing he was not good enough, or being fired for incompetence. He was reluctant to give up his depression, fearing he would have to make yet another attempt at going back to work. His depression protected him from further disappointments and failures. By remaining sinful and taking his punishment (i.e., his depression) from God, he also protected himself from going back on the social scene, where he risked rejection.

William spent our first few sessions complaining about his circumstances. Given his comments that therapy would not be helpful, I wanted to take time to build a solid relationship with him before trying to "fix things." Our discussions eventually led to Williams' goals for coming to therapy. His initial reasons for coming were to please his roommate, but he determined that he would use the time to learn about himself and find his way back to God. He told me that his spiritual connection with God was what had helped him through college, his parents' divorce, and his sister "abandoning" him.

Issues of religion and spirituality were explicitly integrated throughout William's psychotherapy. He wanted to talk about his relationship with God, and, despite some initial hesitations, he talked openly about his religious beliefs. William said he had "fallen away" from God and his religion. He felt he had sinned against God when he failed to follow through on his obligations at work. In order to maintain his depression and thus protect himself from failure, he concluded his sins were unforgivable.

In an effort to challenge and modify these irrational beliefs about sin, we talked about how God's forgiveness is given to everyone. I asked William, "What makes you so special that God will not forgive you? Surely, there are people out there that have committed more egregious sins than you have?" Given his insistence that he was more sinful than every other human being, we looked at what he stood to benefit from maintaining this belief. I wanted William to understand the purpose for his insisting on being unforgivable.

"Could it be that your suffering protects you?" I asked.

"Maybe" William said.

I continued, "If God forgives your sins, will you still feel depressed?"

"Probably not, I would feel a lot better," William responded.

I followed by asking "the question" (Dreikurs, 1967), "And if you were no longer depressed, what would be different in your life?" William thought about the question and told me he would be able to go back to work and not feel so bad about himself. It seemed to me he was protecting himself from going back to work, where he risked failure. "If it protects you, William, could it be that your suffering protects you from the possibility of failing and being fired again?"

Tears quickly filled his eyes as he looked down. "I just need to make sure no one leaves me again." This discussion was a major turning point in therapy. William was able to recognize the purpose of his depression and understand why he needed to see himself as a terrible sinner. Over the next few sessions, our discussions moved to focusing on his underlying assumptions and convictions. William began to recognize that his need to always be loved and accepted was problematic. I suggested to him that even God, perfect as He is, is not always loved and respected. How could he expect people to always accept him?

William gradually began to take action to change his life. He still felt he needed to ask for forgiveness and decided to discuss the issue with a pastor as well as with his meditation instructor. Through his discussions with them, he was able to ask for God's forgiveness and feel that he had received it. His meditation instructor was particularly helpful by encouraging him to take a more active part in the temple. This allowed him to focus on how he could be of service to others, rather than focusing exclusively on himself.

By spring, William's depression had lifted, and he had found the courage to pursue another job in the insurance business. He immediately encountered some challenging moments after interviewing for two jobs and not being hired. But with the support of therapy and people at the temple, he continued to seek employment. We decreased the frequency of our visits, and after a few months, William decided to end therapy, feeling he could manage on his own.

The last time we talked, William had made several significant changes in his life. He had found a new job and told me he was getting good feedback from his employer. He had also started going to church, while practicing Buddhist meditation at the same time. He felt that both gave him a sense of direction in his life, and he felt a strong sense of belonging, both at church and in the temple. When I asked him to tell me the most important thing he had learned over the past year, he said he now knew that God loved him no matter what he did or how he lived his life. Knowing the grace of God, he found the courage to meet the challenges that faced him at work. He still felt hesitant mingling with colleagues, but told me he had made good friends through church and temple.

Comment

William's story illustrates several important points. It demonstrates the interplay between psychological and religious issues. It shows how religious and spiritual beliefs and practices play into the individual's striving for significance. William found a sense of significance through the acceptance and love of other people. His misperceptions regarding God, sin, and forgiveness had served to maintain his "illness" in order for him to protect his self-esteem.

This case also illustrates the importance of assessing for religious beliefs and letting patients know that discussions around religion and spirituality are welcomed. William came to therapy very reluctant to speak of God, yet religion became a major theme in his psychotherapy. His story also illustrates the benefits of using a patient's spiritual relationships, religious leaders, and congregations as a valuable resource in treatment. It was in active participation through church and temple that William increased his sense of belonging—social interest. Here he found people to care for and work with, which gave him a sense of being useful and welcomed.

William's religious beliefs were unique in that he combined Christianity with Buddhism. He avoided church because he felt judged and feared that he would be rejected. In Buddhism he found a tolerant and nonjudgmental approach to living that allowed him to feel accepted. Again, we see how religious and spiritual values are consistent with the style of life. William returned to church only after knowing that God would accept him.

SUMMARY

In this chapter I have discussed the integrative, eclectic, and flexible nature of Adler's theory and its generally positive view of religion and spirituality. I have reviewed Adler's essay on religion and Individual Psychology and discussed an Adlerian definition of spirituality. There are key aspects of Adlerian therapy that make it useful in the treatment of religious patients: its teleological aspects, its emphasis on personal responsibility and freedom of choice; its focus on beliefs, convictions, and behavior; and the view of therapy as a process of learning. A case example illustrating an Adlerian approach to working with a religious client was presented.

SUGGESTED READINGS

Pargament, K. I. (2007). *Spiritually Integrated Psychotherapy: Understanding and Addressing the Sacred.* New York: Guilford Press.

Shafranske, E. P. (Ed.). (1996). *Religion and the Clinical Practice of Psychology.* Washington, DC: American Psychological Association.

Sperry, L. (2001). *Spirituality in Clinical Practice.* Philadelphia, PA: Brunner-Routledge.

Sperry, L., & Shafranske, E. P. (Eds) (2005). *Spiritually Oriented Psychotherapy.* Washington, DC: American Psychological Association.

4

Theories of Adler and the Christian Faith

In everything do to others as you would have them do to you; for this is the law and the Prophets.
— *Jesus of Nazareth*

Christianity emerged as a religious movement in the Greco-Roman area shortly after the crucifixion of Jesus of Nazareth around 30 CE. Jesus's followers set out to preach his message of loving God and one's neighbor. Over the next several centuries, Christianity grew into what is today the largest religion in the world, with nearly two billion followers.

Christianity is a monotheistic religion, centered on faith in one God. Although Christians believe in the Trinity, that there are three equal persons in God—the Father, the Son, and the Holy Spirit—they believe that the divine nature of God is one. Christians believe that God became incarnate—fully human—in Jesus of Nazareth.

There are over four hundred Christian denominations worldwide (Hale, 2003). Roman Catholicism, Protestantism, and Eastern Orthodoxy are the three primary groups. The largest of these groups is Roman Catholicism. These denominations represent a wide range of different beliefs and practices. Issues such as abortion, women's ordination, and homosexuality are widely debated across denominations, as well as within the various congregations (Hale, 2003).

Given the wide range of beliefs and practices within the Christian tradition, biblically based Christian spirituality will be used as the basis for comparing Adler's theory to Christian spirituality in this chapter. According to Collins (1998), biblically based Christian spirituality

> involves personal intimacy with God, a process of being conformed to the image of God for the sake of others. The spiritual journey is an ongoing experience of being shaped by God toward wholeness. . . . Christian spirituality is compassion oriented. It reaches out to the poor, the hungry, the needy, the sick, the victims of violence and the perpetrators, the down-and-outers in poverty-entrenched neighborhoods, and the up-and-outer suburbanites who often are too proud or self-sufficient to admit their neediness. Christ modeled concern for the needy, care for those in distress, and a willingness to come alongside people in their times of pain and confusion. He was deeply concerned as well for people who didn't know him, and he instructed his followers, as a last word of admonition, to go into the world and make disciples. (pp. 91, 190)

Watts (2000) discussed biblically based Christian spirituality and Adlerian psychotherapy using the following definition adopted from Croucher (cited in Collins, 1998):

> Christian spirituality is about the movements of God's spirit in one's life, in the community of faith, and in the cosmos. . . . It is concerned with how all realities relate, enlivened, enlightened, empowered by the Spirit of Jesus. [It is] the dynamic process whereby the Word of God (Bible) is applied by the Spirit of God to the heart and mind of the child of God so that she or he becomes more like the Son of God (Jesus). (p. 91)

Those individuals who have adopted this biblically based perspective share a number of core beliefs (Watts, 2000): (1) Humans were created by God to have a relationship with him and with fellow human beings; (2) God became incarnate and offers the forgiveness of sins through faith and following Jesus's teachings; (3) the Word of God is given to us through the Bible, which serves as the ultimate guidebook for spiritual truth; and (4) the Church is the body of Christ's followers, who are called together to worship, to love one another, and to minister to the world of fellow human beings, all of which are created in the image of God.

Of the major world religions, Christianity is particularly compatible with the concepts of Alfred Adler's Individual Psychology. Adler's notion of human nature, the tasks of life, teleology, and soft determinism are consistent with Biblical teachings. Other concepts of Individual Psychology, such as striving for superiority and the role of encouragement in the therapeutic encounter are also consistent with Christian values (Kanz, 2001; Watts, 2000). And finally, the most important of Adler's concepts, social interest, "may be the point of greatest agreement between Christianity and Individual Psychology" (Kanz, 2001, p. 347). Adler's psychology is one of the most adaptable schools of psychotherapy for working with Christian clients. According to Jones and Butman (1991)

> There is more compatibility between Christianity and Adlerian conceptions than with . . . most other systems of psychotherapy. . . . In [Adlerian psychology], we find an approach that respects human responsibility, rationality, individuality, social interconnectedness, and capacities for change. It is a view that has received scant attention from religious counselors over the years. . . . (p. 243)

Given the tremendous overlap between Christianity and Individual Psychology, Adlerians can feel comfortable working with people of the Christian faith. As long as Adlerian therapists remain knowledgeable about Christian values and traditions, and are open to incorporating the Bible into therapy, they can work collaboratively and effectively with Christian clients.

HISTORY AND TEACHINGS OF CHRISTIANITY

The story of Jesus of Nazareth is preserved mainly in the New Testament of the Bible. The gospels of Matthew, Mark, Luke, and John tell the story of Jesus's birth, life, death, and resurrection. The gospels are intended as a declaration about the "Kingdom of God" and about Jesus as Son of God and savior of civilization (Hale, 2003). Christians believe that Jesus was begotten by the Holy Spirit, and conceived by a virgin named Mary. Jesus is believed to have been born during the reign of Herod the Great, who ruled Judea from 37–4 BCE (Hale, 2003).

The birth of Jesus was surrounded by a series of miracles and mysterious events, yet Jesus's life went almost unnoticed until he reached the age of 30. Little is known of his early life. According to the gospels, the angel Gabriel appeared to Mary and announced that she would conceive a divine child through the Holy Spirit. "And behold, thou shalt conceive in thy womb, and bring forth a son, and shalt call his name JESUS" (Luke, 1. 31). At the time of Jesus's birth, a group of shepherds abiding in the field were approached by an angel of the Lord telling them, "for unto you is born this day in the city of David a Saviour, which is Christ the Lord" (Luke 2. 11).

A significant event narrated in the gospels is the story of Jesus's baptism by John the Baptist. John was proclaiming that people should turn from sin and allow themselves to be baptized with water. Water was seen as a sign of purification. The baptism of Jesus marked the beginning of his ministry. Jesus took on twelve disciples, also known as apostles, who followed him during his ministry in Judaea and Galilee. His disciples continued to preach the belief in Jesus as Son of God and redeemer of humankind after his death (Hale, 2003).

Over the course of his ministry, Jesus developed a flock of followers who believed him to be the son of God. The religious rulers, however, were challenged by his teachings and set out to accuse him of blasphemy. He was eventually tried and found guilty of blasphemy, a crime punishable by death under Jewish law. Jesus was executed by crucifixion by the Romans at Jerusalem between 29 and 33 CE. Christians believe that Jesus rose from the dead after three days and visited his disciples on several occasions before ascending into heaven.

Shortly after the crucifixion and death of Jesus, a small group of Jews began to proclaim that he had been resurrected. Although Christians view Jesus's birth and ministry as significant events, his death and resurrection and the mysteries surrounding his resurrection marks the birth of Christianity. Paul tells the Corinthian converts about the Easter faith that formed the basis for the infant Jerusalem Church (Parrinder, 1985):

> Christ died for our sins according to the scriptures; and that he was buried, and that he rose again the third day according to the scriptures: and that he was seen of Cephas (Peter), then of the twelve: after that, he was seen of above five hundred brethren at once; of whom the greater part remain unto this present, but some are fallen asleep. After that, he was seen of James; then of all the apostles. And last of all he was seen of me also, as of one born out of due time. (Corinthians 15. 3–8)

In the years following the death of Jesus, most of his followers were Palestinian Jews. But over the next two decades, the Christians began preaching to the gentiles (non-Jews), which caused Christianity to flourish (Hale, 2003). As Christianity continued to spread, Christians were faced with a series of obstacles. Many Christians refused to acknowledge the Roman emperor as a god, which was required by law. They also refused to sacrifice to the Greco-Roman deities. As a result, many Christians were tried for treason and martyred. Persecution of Christians continued for the next three centuries, until the Roman emperor Constantine declared tolerance for all religions in 313 CE. Seventy-nine years later, in 392 CE, Theodosius I declared Christianity the sole religion of the empire (Hale, 2003).

Over the course of two millennia, the Christian tradition has developed into several groups, or denominations. The primary Christian denominations are Roman Catholicism, Eastern (including Greek) Orthodoxy, and Protestantism. In general the Catholic Church subscribe to the authority of the Pope (the bishop of Rome). The Pope is the head of the Church, with supreme jurisdiction by Divine Law over the universal Church. The worship of Catholics is liturgical and focuses on seven sacraments—baptism, Holy Communion, confirmation, penance, matrimony, priestly ordination, and extreme unction (blessing of the sick). The worship of saints plays a major part in Catholic practice (Hale, 2003). There are about 1 billion Catholics worldwide and approximately 74 million in North America (Barrett & Johnson, 1998).

As with Roman Catholicism, Eastern Orthodoxy maintains a strong historical continuity with the early church (Hale, 2003). But the Eastern Orthodox church is governed by bishops, patriarchs, and councils, rather than by the Pope. As opposed to Catholic priests, Orthodox priests may marry if they do so before they are ordained. Their worship also centers on the sacraments and is known for their use of sacred images (icons and relics) as aids to spirituality (Hale, 2003). There are approximately 220 million members of the Orthodox Church worldwide, of whom about 6 million reside in North America (Barrett & Johnson, 1998).

The break between the Roman Catholic Church and the Eastern Orthodox Church was a result of cultural differences between the Greek-speaking East and the Latin-speaking West (Hale, 2003). The break was a gradual process, but it came to a head in 1054 over the question of allegiance to the Roman papacy.

Protestantism dates back to the sixteenth century, when Martin Luther (1483–1546) and his followers rejected many of the practices of the Roman Catholic Church. As with Eastern Orthodox Christians, Protestants reject the authority of the Pope and believe that the authority lies with the Bible. There are approximately 360 million Protestant Christians throughout the world, and approximately 95 million have made North America their home.

In 1517, Martin Luther, the leader of the German reform movement, from Wittenberg, Germany, publicly posted 95 statements criticizing Rome. This marked the beginning of a reform movement that lead to the break from Catholicism in only a few years (Hale, 2003). The break from Rome led to the development of a new group of Christian believers, Protestants. The name "Protestants" evolved from the protests of Luther's movement against the Roman Church.

Protestantism advocates the power of scripture over the priestly hierarchy of the Roman Church. They reject the authority of the Pope and believe that the Bible is the chief authority on spiritual matters. Compared to Catholics, Protestants recognize only two sacraments, baptism and the Lord's Supper. There are numerous Protestant denominations throughout North America. The major Protestant churches include Lutherans, Baptists, Presbyterians, Methodists, Mennonites, Mormons, Jehovah's Witnesses, and Christian Scientists (Hale, 2004). Each of these denominations differs in beliefs and practices.

THE BIBLE AND CHRISTIAN VALUES

The Bible, sometimes called "scripture," is the holiest text in Christianity. The word Bible means "book," and Christians believe it is the book of God's words to mankind. The Bible consists of 66 books written by many different authors at different times in history. However, Christians believe that its authors were guided by God, so that everything they wrote was God's will.

The Bible has two main parts, the Old Testament and the New Testament. The Old Testament is accepted as Scripture by both Jews and Christians. It discusses the creation of the universe and the creation of human beings. It goes on to address the history of God's chosen people and how God came to create the nation of Israel. The New Testament is accepted by Christians as the story of the arrival of Jesus, the Messiah. It tells the story of Jesus's birth, life, death, and resurrection. The Bible is open to a wide range of interpretations, thus creating the variability in Christian beliefs and practices. Let us examine, however, some of the basic Christian beliefs.

The basic Christian beliefs and ethics can be found in the Ten Commandments and the teachings of Jesus (Hale, 2004). According to the Bible, Moses received the Ten Commandments from God on Mount Sinai (Exodus, 20.2–17). These commandments cover the basic obligations the individual has to God and to his fellow men. They discuss the individual's relationship to God, parents, spouse, and community. The Ten Commandments are as follows:

1. Thou shalt have no other gods before me.
2. Thou shalt not make unto thee any graven image, or any likeness of any thing that is in heaven above, or that is in the earth beneath, or that is in the water under the earth: thou shalt not bow down thyself to them, nor serve them: for I the Lord thy God am a jealous God, visiting the iniquity of the fathers upon the children unto the third and fourth generation of them that hate me; and showing mercy unto thousands of them that love me, and keep my commandments.
3. Thou shalt not take the name of the Lord thy God in vain; for the Lord will not hold him guiltless that taketh his name in vain.
4. Remember the Sabbath day, to keep it holy. Six days shalt thou labour, and do all thy work: but the seventh day is the Sabbath of the Lord thy God: in it thou shalt not do any work, thou, nor thy son, nor thy daughter, thy manservant, nor thy maidservant, nor thy cattle, nor thy stranger that is within thy gates: for in six days the Lord made heaven and earth, the sea and all that in them is, and rested the seventh day: wherefore the Lord blessed the Sabbath day, and hallowed it.
5. Honour thy father and thy mother: that thy days may be long upon the land which the Lord thy God giveth thee.
6. Thou shalt not kill.
7. Thou shalt not commit adultery.
8. Thou shalt not steal.
9. Thou shalt not bear false witness against thy neighbour.
10. Thou shalt not covet thy neighbor's house, thou shalt not covet thy neighbor's wife, nor his manservant, nor his maidservant, nor his ox, nor his ass, nor any thing that is thy neighbour's.

The Ten Commandments provide the foundation for Christian ethics. However, in the gospel of Matthew, Jesus goes on to broaden the commandments provided in the Old Testament. Jesus speaks to a group of followers on a hillside about the ethical foundations of Christianity. In the so-called Sermon on the Mount, Jesus broadens the commandment against adultery to include lustful desires. He also broadens the commandment not to kill to include the nurturing of anger against others.

And the commandment not to take the Lord's name in vain is expanded to include swearing by heaven and earth, and by oneself. Jesus also teaches people to love their enemies and to "turn the other cheek."

In his sermon, Jesus outlines nine blessings for right behavior, also referred to as the Beatitudes (Matthew 5.3–12). These blessings reflect the Christian values of purity of heart, humility, simplicity, mercy, and peacemaking. Instead of requiring his followers to obey these rules, he suggests that these are values that people should aspire to. Finally, what many consider the most important Christian value is revealed in the gospel of Matthew: "love your neighbor as yourself." Jesus is asked by a lawyer what the greatest commandment is. Quoting the Old Testament, Jesus says to him

> Thou shalt love the Lord thy God with all thy heart, and with all thy soul, and with all thy mind. This is the first and great commandment. And the second is like unto it, Thou shalt love thy neighbour as thyself. On these two commandments hang all the law and the prophets. (Matthew 22. 37–40)

Christianity is a peaceful religion, promoting respect for other people, honesty, humility, and forgiveness. It values personal responsibility and freedom of choice. It emphasizes the importance of working together with fellow human beings and caring for oneself as well as for others. Therefore, Christian beliefs are very much in line with Adler's Individual Psychology.

PHILOSOPHY OF HUMAN NATURE

The philosophical assumptions of soft determinism, teleology, striving for superiority, holism, and social interest are all consistent with biblically based Christian spirituality. Watts (2000) discussed these philosophical assumptions and concluded that the Adlerian approach to psychotherapy is amenable to working with clients who hold a biblically based view of Christian spirituality. Furthermore, Kanz (2001) discussed the applicability of Adlerian psychology for working with conservative Christian clients. Comparing Adler's philosophical assumptions to Christian beliefs, he also agreed that there is tremendous overlap between Christianity and Adler's theory, making Adlerian psychotherapy applicable to working with Christians.

Soft Determinism

Adler (1956) embraced the philosophical assumption of soft determinism. This concept stresses that people choose the course of their lives, as opposed to their behavior being "determined" by external and internal forces. People's lives are constrained by circumstance, but they have free will to decide how to respond to those circumstances. Christians tend to believe that they are free to choose their own path in life. Many Christians think that they must be responsible for their own choices. And some feel they have made choices that were wrong, immoral, or bad, giving rise to feelings of guilt. The belief that people have to be responsible for their own choices may be an issue that leads some Christians to seek psychotherapy (Kanz, 2001).

The idea that individuals are responsible for their own choices and have freedom to choose is consistent with biblical teaching. According to Milne (1982), "scripture assumes the power of voluntary, responsible choice belongs to all people, Christians and non-Christians alike" (p. 110). There are many examples in the Bible that suggests that people have freedom to choose. For example, the story of Adam and Eve in the book of Genesis implies people's freedom to make decisions. In the story, Adam and Eve chose to eat from the Tree of Knowledge of Good and Evil, thereby condemning themselves to a painful and strenuous life (Genesis 3).

The theory of soft determinism and personal responsibility is also evident in several other stories throughout the Bible. In Deuteronomy (30.19) God says " . . . I have set before you life and death, blessing and cursing: therefore choose life, that both thou and thy seed may live." Joshua also suggested that individuals have free will: "And if it seem evil unto you to serve the Lord, choose you this day whom you will serve" (Joshua, 24.15).

Teleology and Striving for Superiority

The concept of teleology sets Adlerian psychology apart from most other schools of psychotherapy. This idea, that humans are motivated by some future goal, rather than influenced by past events, is referred to as the guiding self-ideal, or goal, of perfection (Adler, 1956). Christian theology is also teleological in nature. Christians believe that there is a future goal for which people strive. This ultimate goal both guides and motivates the individual. For most Christians, this ultimate goal is salvation. In the gospel of John, Jesus teaches, "for God so loved the world, that he gave his only begotten son, that whosoever believeth in him should not perish, but have everlasting life" (John, 3.16).

Adler (1987) stated that the belief in God was in fact a way of making the goal of perfection tangible. He contended that the idea of God

> is the concretization and interpretation of the human recognition of greatness and perfection, and the dedication of the individual as well as of society to a goal which rests in the future and which enhances in the present the driving force toward greatness by strengthening the appropriate feelings and emotions. (p. 523)

In terms of teleology, the difference between Adlerians and Christians is that Adlerians view the ultimate goal as being subjective and nonconscious. Christians, however, are likely to believe that salvation is an objective reality, one in which they are very much aware. Life struggles that are interpreted as impeding the goal of salvation are likely to lead many Christians to seek counseling and psychotherapy. Thus, salvation, or eternal life, becomes the ultimate goal for many Christians.

Holism

Adlerians strive to understand patients from a holistic perspective rather than from a reductionistic point of view. Thus, reducing an individual to various parts such as body and soul, mother and wife, good and evil, or conscious and unconscious is useless. So from the Adlerian perspective, people function as self-consistent units in which each element influences the others. This holistic approach is also evident in Christianity. Jesus's greatest commandment, "Thou shalt love the Lord thy God with all thy heart, and with all thy soul, and with all thy mind" (Matthew 22. 37), is suggestive of a holistic approach (Carlton, personal communication 2008). Throughout history, Christians have tended to view the soul and the body as separate. However, this dichotomy has shifted to an emphasis on the unity of individuals (Milne, 1982).

Social Interest

The strongest area of common ground between Individual Psychology and biblically based Christian spirituality is their relational perspectives (Watts, 2000). Biblically based Christian spirituality is a relational spirituality. The importance of relationships is addressed repeatedly in Scripture. According to the Bible, people have a three-fold relational responsibility: to God, to fellow human beings, and to themselves.

Adler (1956) emphasized the value of understanding people in their social context. He believed that people develop in social groups and strive to find their own sense of belonging, constantly being in relationships with others. Adler used social interest (feeling of community) as a measure of mental health. By placing social connectedness at the center of his psychology, his theory is consistent with Christianity, which also stresses social relationships and social responsibility. The individual's relational responsibilities are particularly evident in the Ten Commandments.

The Ten Commandments focus on relationships. The first four commandments address the individual's relationship to God, and the remaining six address the individual's relationships to other people. Shulman (2003) discussed the sociopolitical nature of the Ten Commandments. He argued that the Ten Commandments, whether revealed by God or created by Moses, are an astonishing set of rules for establishing a people and securing their survival.

According to Shulman (2003) there are five major factors that allow any group of people to function and endure. The first thing any group, family, or society needs is a code of conduct that regulates the relationships between the members. Such a code is necessary in order to maintain stability and stick together. Second, what holds any group together and allow it to endure is mutual respect. For members to get along harmoniously each member must view the others as worthy human beings. The third thing that allows groups to function is that its code of conduct and the mutual respect between members provide limits on unrestrained competition between individuals. Fourth, individuals need to feel that they are fully participating members of the group. As soon as individuals start feeling as if they are not participating members, they will become discouraged about their value and their contributions to the group. As a result, they are likely to take less seriously their obligations to the group and even withdraw from cooperative participation. Finally, the group's existence and the certification of membership must be affirmed and reinforced on a regular basis. Regular rituals and ceremonies allow members to feel part of the group, and they affirm the existence of the group. Any group, be it a church, an ethnic group, a marriage, or a professional organization, needs to be recognized through rituals such as regular meetings of one kind or another. Shulman examined the Ten Commandments from a psychosocial point of view and argued that the commandments provide the essential structure needed for any group or society to function and endure.

The first four commandments deal with the individual's relationship to God, and they provide a central reference point for the group. Shulman (2003) argued that such a reference point, a central theme or purpose as expressed in the First Commandment, is necessary for the establishment of any group or community. Once a community has a central focus (e.g. God), this centrality must not be diminished, as dimming of focus puts the community in danger of destruction. Thus, the Second Commandment instructs people not to build any idols. The Third Commandment orders the individual not to misuse the name of the Lord. From a psychosocial viewpoint, Shulman argued that this commandment is a warning against misconstruing the nature of the purpose of the group. He stated that if the centrality of the group is used for meaningless ends, it risks becoming less relevant to the members of the group. As a result, the group stands to loose its central focus and is in danger of collapsing. Finally, the Fourth Commandment instructs the individual to keep the Sabbath day holy. The social value of this commandment, according to Shulman, is its ability to strengthen the social pattern. It creates a regular ritual in which the group members are asked to put aside their labors and affirm and remember the central focus of the group.

The remaining commandments deal directly with the individual's relationship to his or her fellow human beings. The Fifth Commandment concerns itself with the individual's responsibilities to his or her parents. The focus on parents, rather than on priests or other authority figures, points to the hierarchical tradition of the time and the idea that the family is the main social unit. The remaining commandments deal directly with the person's responsibilities toward other people. The actions prohibited in these commandments are socially disruptive and result in conflict within the group. The commandments are not concerned with factors external to the group, but rather with its internal dynamics. They emphasize the responsibilities of each individual member and provide limits to certain behaviors that are likely to disturb the social pattern and its focus on God.

The Tenth Commandment, "Thou shalt not covet thy neighbor's house," not only prevents internal disruptions in a group, but it also limits competitive behavior. Adler (1956) viewed social cooperation as an indication of mental health. It is cooperation, not competition, that unifies a group. Shulman argued that the Tenth Commandment attempts to insure social stability by decreasing competition among individuals.

> Envy itself disturbs harmony. It is a disjunctive and discordant feeling. It leads to alienation rather than a feeling of belonging. The envious person feels inferior rather than equal and becomes more concerned with compensating rather than with contributing; more interested in whether he "gets" than in whether he can perform a useful act. In its most basic essence, envy leads to antagonism and invites self-seeking rather than group productive behavior. (p. 170)

The Ten Commandments provide a set of guidelines for Christians whose purpose it is to maintain harmony and peace within society. The concept of social interest includes factors such as empathy and concern for the welfare of others. Adler (1956) conceptualized the concept as the ability "to see with the eyes of another, to hear with the ears of another, and to feel with the heart of another" (p. 135). Thus social interest involves the ability and willingness to focus on others and to cooperate with the members of one's community. Kanz (2001) argued that Christianity reflects similar ideas and that there is a clear fit between Individual Psychology and Christianity in terms of social interest. For example, Jesus taught that people should be both concerned for each other and useful to each other.

> Then shall the righteous answer him, saying, Lord, when saw we thee a hungred, and fed thee? or thirsty, and gave thee drink? When saw we thee a stranger, and took thee in? or naked, and clothed thee? or when saw we thee sick, or in prison, and came unto thee? And the King shall answer and say unto them, Verily I say unto you, Inasmuch as ye have done it unto one of the least of these my brethren, ye have done it unto me. (Matthew, 25. 37–40)

So, along with teleology, soft determinism, the emphasis placed on personal responsibility, and the concept of holism, there is a clear fit between Individual Psychology and Christianity in terms of social interest. Both place human relationships at the center of understanding human nature, and they emphasize the importance of relating and cooperating with one's fellow human beings.

The Life Tasks

There are certain life tasks that each of us has to deal with. We all have to take a stand on the problem of work, how to get along with others in our society, sex, marriage, and relationships to members of the opposite sex, the existence and nature of God, and getting along with ourselves. The concept of the life tasks is readily applicable to Christianity.

As I discussed above, getting along with our fellow human beings is very important to Christians, and it is emphasized throughout Scripture. But for Christians, work is also particularly important. Christians tend to value the importance of work and of finding one's vocational place. For many Christians it is not enough to find work that is personally satisfying, work also needs to be compatible with their Christian values. Scripture teaches that the individual needs to contribute through work. For example, the Fourth Commandment assumes that people have to work and thereby contribute to the community. "Remember the Sabbath day, to keep it holy. Six days shalt thou labour, and do all thy work: but the seventh day is the Sabbath of the Lord thy God" (Exodus, 20.8–10). In addition, St. Paul writes in 2 Thessalonians that those who will not work should not be provided with food (3:10). Thus work is recognized as an essential part of living in a community of fellow men.

Sex and marriage are also important for Christians. Many Christians believe that one should seek out a partner of the opposite sex for marriage. Scripture suggests that marriage should be between a man and a woman. "Therefore shall a man leave his father and his mother, and shall cleave unto his wife: and they shall be one flesh" (Genesis, 2.24). Finally, Christians strongly believe in marriage to only one partner, as emphasized in the New Testament. From an Adlerian perspective, the goal of this life task is to learn how to cooperate with and relate to others of the opposite sex. Failure, or unwillingness, to do so is likely to cause conflicts and interpersonal problems. Kanz (2001) suggested that issues of sex and marriage that are likely to bring Christians into therapy include dealing with infidelity, being attracted to a person of the same sex, and no longer feeling in love with one's spouse.

The spiritual task is particularly important for Christians. This task involves one's relationship to God, what one does with religion, immortality, how the person perceives his or her place in the universe, and the meaning of life. Feeling as though they have lost their faith, feeling angry with God, feeling abandoned by God, or feeling a lack of meaning are spiritual issues Christians may bring to therapy. Adlerian therapy allows for discussions of these topics and acknowledges the phenomenological experience of the client in a nonjudgmental way.

Finally there is the existential task of coping with oneself. Christian clients may come to therapy to address concerns about being "sinful" or unworthy of God's love. For clients who struggle to find their place in God's world, therapy may be helpful in providing support and guiding the individual toward a sense of who he or she is and what his or her life's purpose is.

Adler's notion of the tasks of life fits well with biblically based Christian spirituality. When Christians seek the services of a psychotherapist, they are likely experiencing a problem in one of the life tasks. Knowing the patient's cultural and religious influences and values in regard to work, friendship, sex and marriage, and God, puts the psychotherapist at an advantage in moving forward in the therapeutic process.

APPLYING INDIVIDUAL PSYCHOLOGY TO PSYCHOTHERAPY WITH CHRISTIAN CLIENTS

Adlerian psychotherapy consists of four main stages or phases. The first and most important of these is the therapeutic relationship. Adlerian psychotherapists focus on the development of a respectful and egalitarian relationship with patients. The therapeutic relationship is equal and respectful throughout the process. It is based on Adler's conception that all people are equal and worthy of respect and dignity. This idea is consistent with Biblically based Christian spirituality, which views all people as created in the image of God. Thus all people are equal in the sight of God (Grenz, 1994), and therapists should relate to clients in an egalitarian fashion (Watts, 2000).

Mosak (1995) discussed three factors—variations on the Christian virtues of faith, hope, and love—that he believed are necessary, yet not sufficient, for psychotherapy to be effective. For Mosak, faith is the idea that the client must be confident that the therapist is able to help him or her. Hope involves the maintenance of a positive and optimistic view of the future and helping the client develop a similar hopeful attitude. Finally, love, according to Mosak, refers to the idea that the client knows and feels that the therapist cares.

A concept that goes hand in hand with these three factors is the process of encouragement. Encouragement is vital to all psychotherapy. Adler (1956) famously stated that "in every step of the treatment, we must not deviate from the path of encouragement" (p. 342). Adler viewed patients as discouraged as opposed to being sick. Therefore, encouragement is used as a therapeutic tool throughout the entire therapeutic process. Encouragement involves communicating respect for and confidence in clients. It also involves focusing on strengths and assets and helping clients focus on their efforts and progress. According to Watts (2000), "encouragement is the therapeutic modeling of social interest, and it is both an attitude and a process of facilitating growth" (p. 324). Watts went on to argue that the process of encouragement in Adlerian psychotherapy is consistent with Biblically based Christian spirituality and stated that the Bible routinely focuses on encouraging or "building up" other people.

The Bible teaches self-examination as an important part of living. The idea of self-examination and cognitive interventions is yet another point of philosophical overlap between the biblical perspective and Individual Psychology. "Adlerian psychotherapy shares the biblical perspective between cognitive/verbal intervention on the one hand, and the importance of action on the other. The Bible and Individual Psychology suggest that genuine insight or cognitive change always leads to behavioral change" (Watts, 2000, p. 323).

Finally, some Adlerian therapists incorporate parables (Pancner, 1978) and religious allusions (Mosak, 1987) into therapy. Jesus frequently used parables as a way of teaching his followers. In a similar fashion, many Adlerian therapists use parables and other stories to teach a lesson, make interpretations, or explain a concept.

> In psychotherapy, patients find it easier to grasp concepts, rules for living, and new ways of looking at life through the medium of stories. Stories are easier to remember and less threatening than direct confrontation and can be shelved and later reexamined as the patients deal with all aspects of their therapy. (Pancner, 1978, p. 19–20)

Mosak (1987) suggested the use of religious allusions as one approach to dealing with religious issues in psychotherapy. He discussed the use of biblical stories and how these stories can be used to teach lessons, offer interpretations, or get past sticking points in therapy. He recommended that therapists who set out to use such tactics have a firm grasp of the sources from which the stories are drawn and of the patient's religious knowledge and beliefs.

Despite the vast overlap between the Christian faith and Individual Psychology, there are important differences. The various differences will depend on the particular denomination of the client, along with other cultural factors. Thus, therapists would be wise to know and understand the unique differences in beliefs and practices found among the various Christian denominations. Some general differences should be noted. For example, the equality between men and women emphasized by Individual Psychology is often contradictory to conservative Christians. Many conservative Christians view the man as being the head of the household. Also, some conservative Christians consider themselves inherently sinful and evil in some fashion. And finally, some Christians perceive biblical truth to be the only and absolute truth. Thus for these individuals, the Bible is not open to creative interpretation (Kanz, 2001).

Adlerian therapists can be comfortable working with Christian clients, as long as they remain knowledgeable about the spiritual diversity within the Christian faith. Issues regarding sexuality, marriage and divorce, abortion and birth control, alcohol, and suicide and euthanasia are important issues that also vary within the different denominations. It is important that therapists remain knowledgeable about these and other moral issues. Therapists should be open to incorporating the Bible into therapy and should show interest and respect for spiritual and religious issues. Many therapists emphasize the importance of asking about God and religion in the assessment process. In this way a therapist lets the patient know that he or she is interested in the subject and willing to address issues related to religion and spirituality.

Case Example

Ann, a 38-year-old Christian woman, came for therapy due to anxiety and depression. She had struggled with symptoms for the past 17 years. She worried about day-to-day problems, her health, her two sons' success in school, and whether or not her sons might go crazy, given a family history of mental illness. A second presenting problem involved her dissatisfaction with work. She hated her job and shamefully admitted that the job she had was really intended for others—for less intelligent people.

Emotionally, Ann felt hopeless, sad, and worried. She said she was tired of always worrying and needed it to stop. She experienced several physiological symptoms including low energy, difficulty falling asleep, muscle tension, hyperventilation, and occasional shaking.

Interpersonally, Ann got along well with people. She was well known in her Church and often volunteered with various projects in her community. Although she appeared very outgoing, Ann described herself as very shy and socially anxious. She felt a strong need to make sure people liked her, and she would spend hours ruminating about whether or not her interactions with others had led them to detest her. Despite all her social networking, she complained that she did not have any close friends.

Ann had been in therapy multiple times over the past 17 years. She had had a difficult time finding a therapist that she liked. She complained that psychologists did not appreciate her faith. Over the years, only one therapist had been able to help her, but he had retired after working with Ann for a year. This therapist, Ann reported, had appreciated the importance of her faith. In terms of work, Ann felt that her depression and anxiety had kept her from following her dreams. She was not sure what she would have pursued had it not been for her anxiety, but she felt that that she would have made it big had it not been for all her suffering. She felt she was meant for something great.

Ann's lifestyle was characterized by a need to control, a need to be liked, and a need to do something great with her life. She believed that if people did not like her, it would be catastrophic. So, if she managed to maintain control of a conversation by dominating it, she felt she might secure people's approval. She viewed other people as being judgmental and mean, yet she feared being alone in this world. It seemed to the therapist that Ann was using her "illness" to control her family and to avoid having to face the life tasks. Her symptoms also provided her with an excuse for her failure to achieve "greatness." Moving forward, they also safeguarded her self-esteem by protecting her from the possibility of failure.

Ann's problems began in college. Her boyfriend had ended their relationship, and she found herself alone and disapproved of. Because of the grief resulting from the breakup, she failed several classes and concluded that she was not smart enough to graduate from college. She took a job at a clothing store, where she has worked ever since. After a few years she married and had two children. Ann always regretted her decision not to finish college. Her desire to pursue a higher education and to become "great" had been put on hold while she raised her children. She always knew that she would have to go back to school in order to achieve her goals.

Ann told her therapist that her husband was very supportive of her. They had a close relationship, and Ann was very satisfied with the life they shared. Her husband was a very religious man and also very involved in their church. Despite her commitment to the church, Ann felt that her faith was weak. She hoped there was a God, but did not feel certain. She had somehow lost her connection with God over the years and felt abandoned by Him. She could not understand why God would make anyone suffer the way she had suffered for almost half her life.

People's relationships with God are consistent with their style of life. Thus, their way of relating to others may sometimes fit with the way they relate to God. This was the case for Ann. She often wondered whether the Lord approved of her, and she viewed God as mean and judgmental. She frequently questioned whether or not God liked her and routinely pointed to her "bad" behavior to prove that she was unacceptable in the eyes of God.

Psychotherapy with Ann was difficult. In developing a strong therapeutic alliance with her, her therapist made an effort to show appreciation and respect for her religious beliefs. Many of the initial sessions were spent talking about faith and God. Ann brought in some of her religious readings and shared them in session.

The therapist's strategy was to curtail Ann's need to achieve greatness through education and work. Ann also needed to accept that she could not be liked by all people all the time, and that failure was part of being human. By addressing her religious values and beliefs throughout treatment, the therapist was able to maintain a therapeutic alliance and challenge her beliefs as she examined her faith. In her discussions about her faith, Ann gradually began to recognize that God accepted her no matter who she was or what she did. As she began to accept the grace of God, she became increasingly comfortable around others and did not feel as if she had to be liked by those around her all the time. This, in turn, also allowed her to question her need to achieve greatness and find the courage to take on new responsibilities in church without worrying about failure.

Ann eventually concluded that her success in raising respectful and successful children was a reflection of "greatness." She found that she could be at peace with who she was and that her need to be approved of was satisfied in her relationship with the Lord. Toward the end of her psychotherapy, she commented to her therapist that she no longer felt like a competitor among her friends. Her sense of belonging and her willingness to cooperate had significantly improved. Ann's anxiety and depression eventually subsided as she no longer needed to protect herself from failure.

SUMMARY

Christianity is a monotheistic religion centered on faith in one God. There are over four hundred Christian denominations worldwide (Hale, 2003), all of which differ in terms of their beliefs and practices. The three main denominations are Roman Catholicism, Protestantism, and Eastern Orthodoxy. In this chapter, Individual Psychology was compared to biblically based Christian spirituality.

The philosophical assumptions of teleology, soft determinism, striving for superiority, holism, and social interest are all consistent with biblically based Christian spirituality. Adler's notion of the life tasks is also consistent with this perspective. In terms of psychotherapy, Adlerians view the process of encouragement as essential to all treatment. They also emphasize cognitive and behavioral change as an important goal in therapy. These approaches are also consistent with biblically based Christian spirituality. Therefore, Adlerian therapists can feel comfortable working with Christian clients, remembering that there are vast differences among the various denominations. Individual Psychology therapists should maintain knowledge about the spiritual diversity among Christians and show interest and respect for spiritual issues. Therapists working with Christian clients should also be open to incorporating the Bible into therapy.

SUGGESTED READINGS

Hale, R. D. (2004). *Understanding Christianity: Origins, Beliefs, Practices, Holy Texts, Sacred Places.* London: Duncan Baird.

Hamm, D. (2008). *Christianity: An Outline of Salvation and the Christian Life.* CA: Create Space Publishing.

Smith, H. (1991). *The World Religions.* NY: Harper Collins.

5 Adlerian Contributions to Pastoral Counseling

Rooted in Christian theology, pastoral counseling is a unique approach to helping individuals that integrates religious and spiritual resources with clinical psychology. When psychology was first introduced and integrated in pastoral counseling, Freud's psychoanalysis dominated the field. Although pastoral counseling is still heavily influenced by psychoanalytic theory, several authors have addressed the integration of other psychological approaches to traditional pastoral counseling, including Cognitive Therapy (Carter, 1986; Parsons & Wicks, 1986), Family Therapy (Olsen, 1993), Gestalt Therapy (Knights & Koenig, 2002), Jungian psychology (Erickson, 1987; Hunt-Meeks, 1983; Sneck, 2007), Rational Emotive Behavior Therapy (Ellis, 1984; Lawrence & Huber, 1982; Wessler, 1984), and Solution-Focused Therapy (Kollar, 1997). Similarly, Adlerian practitioners have offered therapeutic insights and counseling techniques to complement the field of pastoral counseling (Anderson, 1971; Baruth & Manning, 1987; Ecrement & Zarski, 1987; Hart, 1971; Huber, 1987; Mansager, 1987; Oden, 1971; Sperry, 1987). Though recognizing the many voices that have contributed to pastoral care, this chapter examines the contributions made by Adlerians.

In chapter four I addressed the common themes of biblically based Christian spirituality and Individual Psychology. Given the theoretical and philosophical harmony between the two, pastoral counselors will find a comprehensive psychological theory that can easily and appropriately be incorporated into their care of people. Adler's Individual Psychology is a psychodynamic and cognitive/behavioral framework that maintains an optimistic, future-oriented, and directive approach—an approach to counseling and psychotherapy that is very much relevant to pastoral care.

This chapter addresses the contributions of Individual Psychology to the process of pastoral counseling. Of these various contributions, maybe the most important is the personal integrity Individual Psychology offers the pastoral counselor (Hart, 1971). Contrary to psychoanalysis and other theoretical approaches, pastoral counselors can utilize Adler's theories without having to shift between a psychological and theological mode, thus maintaining personal integrity. The life tasks are discussed because they provide a structured framework pastors can utilize in counseling. Finally, the four phases of Adlerian therapy are discussed in the context of Christian teachings and the four functions of pastoral care.

PASTORAL COUNSELING

Christian soul care and the spiritual counsel provided by pastors date back to the early days of the church. Pastors have always been involved in providing spiritual and psychological care to parishioners. Soul care has historically been understood to involve nurture and support, as well as healing (Benner, 2007). The word "soul" refers to the whole person, reflecting a holistic approach to counseling.

What we consider pastoral counseling today is very different from earlier understandings of soul care. Pastoral counseling has been narrowed by the clinical approaches offered by other helping fields, particularly psychology (Benner, 2007). According to Holifield (1983), contemporary pastoral counseling dates back to the beginning on the twentieth century, when a group of New England pastors began to integrate psychotherapeutic approaches to pastoral care. Because Freud's theory of psychoanalysis dominated the field at the time, psychoanalytic theory was incorporated into Christian soul care, a trend that continues to this day, despite obvious disagreements between the two philosophies.

Pastoral counseling is viewed as a specialized form of Christian soul care. However, pastors, Christian counselors, and psychotherapists often have different definitions of what constitutes pastoral counseling. Benner

(2007) offers a sound definition, as he distinguishes among five different forms of soul care: Christian friendship, pastoral ministry, pastoral care, pastoral counseling, and spiritual direction. These approaches form a continuum of specialization, moving from broad and least specialized (Christian friendship) to narrow and highly specialized (pastoral counseling and spiritual direction).

The broadest and least specialized form of Christian soul care is friendship. People may not consider themselves as offering soul care when they offer support, love, and encouragement to others, yet this is an essential part of Christian fellowship. A slightly more specialized form of care is pastoral ministry. Pastoral ministry involves activities such as teaching, preaching, community service, and other activities that bring people into contact with God. Pastoral ministry may also include pastoral care and counseling (Clinebell, 1984).

Pastoral care is broader and less specialized than pastoral counseling. "Pastoral care refers to the total range of help offered by pastors, elders, deacons, and other members of a congregation to those they seek to serve" (Benner, 2007, p. 19). Thus, it may involve comforting someone in grief, visiting the sick and dying, and supporting, encouraging, and nurturing people who are struggling with life's challenges.

Another aspect of Christian soul care is spiritual direction. Spiritual direction is a process in which an individual seeks to gain a deeper relationship with God by meeting with others for prayer and conversation focused on faith development. Although both pastoral counseling and spiritual direction share the focus on faith development, their approaches are different. Pastoral counseling attempts to help individuals reach mature faith. Spiritual direction however, seeks to deepen that mature faith (Shea, 1997).

According to Benner (2007), pastoral counseling differs from other pastoral care activities in several ways. First, pastoral counseling is initiated by the parishioner, not the pastor. Second, it tends to be more problem focused. Third, it involves the development of an ongoing relationship and therefore it usually involves more time than other pastoral care activities. Fourth, it involves a high level of involvement and responsiveness on the part of the parishioner. And finally, biblical instruction or the use of biblical allusions is not appropriate until after the pastor has heard the parishioner's story. In pastoral care however, biblical precepts are sometimes introduced immediately.

Pastoral counseling is rooted in Christian theology. Thus, in addition to psychological science, its approach to helping individuals and its philosophy of human nature is also rooted in Biblical teachings. Given the significant overlap between biblically based Christian theology and Individual Psychology, Adler's theories can contribute to pastoral counseling in numerous ways. In addition to philosophical congruence, the clinical approaches of Adlerian psychotherapy offer yet another set of contributions to the process.

The Theoretical Framework of the Pastoral Counselor

Rudolf Dreikurs (1960/1987) argued that therapists should adhere to some psychological theory. He stressed the importance of maintaining a set of underlying assumptions about human nature, a theory that guides the therapist through the process of understanding, relating to, and helping patients. But it is also important that this theory be consistent with one's outlook on life in general, including one's faith, spirituality, and religion.

Given the increasing focus on eclecticism in the current practice of psychology, many practitioners are becoming increasingly diverse in their approaches. Some are even critical of schools of psychotherapy, viewing them as dogmatic and outdated. Dreikurs (1960/1987) countered this argument by pointing out that everyone has a theory of human nature, and even those who consider themselves eclectic have a theory, namely that of eclecticism. When we adhere to a school of psychotherapy we benefit from having its strengths and its weaknesses exposed and criticized. It gives us a solid framework from which to understand and further examine human behavior and human experiences.

Since the integration of psychological concepts to pastoral counseling began in the early twentieth century (Holifield, 1983), pastors have searched for a school of thought that is consistent with their theology. Some pastoral counselors have distanced themselves entirely from psychology, and restricted themselves to offering biblically based spiritual counseling. In his book *Strategic Pastoral Counseling*, Benner (2007) argues that pastoral counseling can benefit from the contributions of psychology, while at the same time maintaining its unique pastoral components.

> Pastoral counseling can be both distinctly pastoral and psychologically informed. This occurs when it takes its identity from the rich tradition of Christian soul care and integrates appropriate insights of modern therapeutic psychology in a manner that protects both the integrity of the pastoral role and the unique resources of Christian ministry. (p. 14)

Individual Psychology allows for such integration. It offers a theoretical framework that is consistent with the minister's Christian values and beliefs. The overlap between Adler's psychology and Christian philosophy is clear. And given this compatibility, Individual Psychology can contribute to the personal integrity of the pastoral counselor, "perhaps its most important contribution" (Hart, 1971, p. 37).

Hart (1971) discussed the considerable common ground between Adler's psychology and Christian theology and emphasized the importance of personal integrity among counselors, particularly pastoral counselors. He contended that

> If the pastoral counselor is a man divided within himself, allotting one compartment of his inner being to "theology" and another to "psychology" and closing one compartment door when it becomes time to open another, he is not a truly integrated person. He will be somewhat defensive and, as a consequence, less open to others in counseling situations. (p. 37)

Over the past century, pastoral counseling has adopted theories and clinical approaches from Freud's psychoanalysis, and psychoanalytic theory continues to play an important role in the pastoral counseling field today (Sperry, 1987). This trend is perplexing, given its unfavorable stand toward religion. Grant (1984) pointed to several inconsistencies between Christian theology and psychoanalysis that create a philosophical dilemma for pastoral counselors. Grant noted that the psychoanalytic view underestimates the value of community relationships in the healing process. Instead, it emphasizes the importance of the therapist-patient relationship, viewing it as a primary source of patient healing. He also pointed to the lack of equality between the therapist and the patient and the focus on the omniscient position of the therapist. However, pastoral counseling has not relied solely on psychoanalysis. Other therapeutic approaches have had a significant impact on the field, particularly Carl Rogers, family systems, and Heinz Kohut's self psychology (Miller-McLemore, 1993). Although these and other schools of psychotherapy are likely to be more consistent with Christian theology than is psychoanalysis, Individual Psychology offers pastoral counselors a contemporary and holistic philosophy that is congruent with their religious outlook. There is more agreement between the essentials of religion and Individual Psychology than between the essentials of religion and any other psychological theory (Blumenthal, 1964). (See Sperry [1987] for suggestions for an integrative training program for seminary students in Adlerian psychology and counseling.)

The Counseling Process

The process of Adlerian psychotherapy and pastoral counseling has been discussed extensively (Anderson, 1971; Baruth & Manning, 1987; Ecrement & Zarski, 1987; Hart, 1971; Huber, 1987; Mansager, 1987; Oden, 1971; Sperry, 1987) in an attempt to compare and contrast the two approaches. Several authors have also discussed how Adlerian psychology can be incorporated into pastoral care. We will review the most significant contributions here.

Adlerian therapy is very much in line with contemporary practices. It is structured, directive, future oriented, eclectic, and usually short-term. These aspects should make the practice of Adler's psychology appealing to pastoral counselors. In practice, Adlerian therapists focus on building a safe, trusting, and egalitarian relationship with the client. They attempt to develop a holistic understanding of the client, and in addition to looking at symptoms and the presenting problems, they take the client's social relationships and spiritual beliefs into consideration. Finally, given the eclectic aspects of Adlerian psychology, techniques from other approaches, such as cognitive behavioral theory, existential psychology, and family systems theory can easily be integrated into Adlerian practice.

Structuring the Counseling Process

Adler's concept of the life tasks (work, association, and love) can be used to provide structure for the counseling process. Pastoral counselors can use the life tasks to structure therapy by obtaining information from each of the life tasks (Baruth & Manning, 1987). The tasks of life represent areas with which we all must cope. The extent to which an individual successfully meets the tasks of life is a measure of his or her social interest. When the demands of any particular life tasks go beyond the individual's willingness to cooperate, the individual becomes discouraged and may develop various ways of distancing him or herself (i.e., symptoms) to protect his or her self-esteem. When people seek counseling, it is most often because they are struggling with challenges in one of the life tasks. Therefore, the pastoral counselor can quickly assess the client's functioning by reviewing each task and then work toward finding solutions and ways of coping.

Maybe the most important task an individual is faced with is the task of work (Dreikurs, 1953). We have to find ways of providing for ourselves and our community in order to ensure our survival. In our culture, many people feel that their occupation defines who they are. Finding the right occupation and succeeding at it presents numerous problems. For some Christians, work needs to be compatible with their Christian values, which presents another set of challenges. There are those who feel that for life to require them to work or provide for themselves is unfair. They would prefer to contribute minimally and yet receive as much as possible. In these and other, less extreme, cases, where the task of work becomes overwhelming, people resort to distancing tactics and other neurotic solutions.

In addition to inquiring about a client's line of work, household chores, and responsibilities, pastoral counselors should ask about the client's satisfaction with work, his or her relationship with coworkers, leisure activities, and retirement plans. Does the client find satisfaction and meaning in his work? What are the client's hopes and future goals in terms of work? How does she get along with her coworkers? Is he worried about retirement, or looking forward to it? Is she enjoying her leisure time, or is she too busy working to allow time for friends and family? Exploring these and other challenges in the area of work is the first step in determining what, if any, problems in terms of work and leisure need to be addressed in counseling.

Next is the task of friendship (Dreikurs, 1953). According to Dreikurs, "each individual is connected with only a few people, but in his relations with them he expresses his attitude to the whole community" (p. 106). Because people are in relationship with God, one may also observe the expression of this attitude toward Christ. The area of friendship is one in which the pastoral counselor is likely to have some existing information. The pastor may know the parishioner, or he or she may have learned about the client through other parishioners and thus have some sense of how the person gets along with the people in his or her community. Assessing the client's relationship with others, including God, allows the pastoral counselor to set the stage for reconciliation, for helping the client reestablish broken relationships (Clebsch & Jaekle, 1964).

Love and marriage play a central role in Christian life. They comprise the most intimate devotion toward another person, an area of such closeness that our vulnerabilities are easily exposed. Therefore, the task of love and marriage requires great courage and cooperation. It involves how we approach members of the opposite sex and how we go about cooperating with partners of the opposite sex. According to Adler (1956)

> Our first finding in the problem of love is that it is a task for two individuals. For many people this is bound to be a new task. . . . We may say that for a full solution of this cooperation of two, each partner must be more interested in the other than in himself. This is the only basis on which love and marriage can be successful. (p. 432)

Issues of marital conflict are common in pastoral care, and clients seeking pastoral counseling often present with concerns regarding love, intimacy, and marriage. Regardless of whether love and marriage are part of the client's presenting problem, the counselor must evaluate this aspect of life with his or her clients. In an effort to structure the counseling process through the life tasks, pastoral counselors want to assess the client's functioning in the task of love. Questions about dating, marriage, intimacy, divorce, feelings of loneliness, and other marital issues should be asked when appropriate. If and when problems are reported, the counselors and the counselee can discuss whether or not those issues should be addressed in the process.

Some Adlerian theorists consider spiritual and religious challenges as a separate task (i.e., Mosak & Dreikurs, 1967). However, most pastors would agree that questions of spirituality, religion, and meaning transcend each of the three tasks of life and are an important aspect of each. Thus, narrowing the questions of spirituality and faith to a separate task minimizes the importance of these challenges. Nevertheless, questions of spirituality and faith comprise a fourth subject that is of particular interest to the pastoral counselor. Questions of faith, God, religion, life after death, salvation, damnation, and the meaning of life all represent a vital issue, important to both the pastoral counselor and the parishioner seeking pastoral counseling.

The Four Phases of Adlerian Psychotherapy

Ecrement and Zarski (1987) compared the ministry of Jesus with the four phases of Adlerian counseling. They argued that the Adlerian model can be integrated with the model of relating that Jesus modeled for us, providing pastors with a solid, structured, and easily adaptable counseling process. Other authors (i.e., Huber, 1987; Oden, 1971) have also compared the various phases of Adlerian counseling to Christian theology and pastoral counseling with the purpose of illustrating the applicability of the clinical approaches offered by Adler.

Relationship

The importance of developing a safe, trusting, empathetic, and egalitarian relationship is shared by both Adlerians and pastoral counselors. Ecrement and Zarski (1987) pointed out that the establishment of an empathetic relationship characterized by unconditional positive regard was modeled to us by Jesus in his interactions with others. Jesus demonstrated compassion (Mark 6:34) and acceptance (John 4), and He showed people their value in God's eyes, thereby giving them a feeling of worth (Matthew 10:29).

Furthermore, in an effort to clarify the relationship between psychotherapy and Christian theology, Oden (1971) illustrated how the four phases of Adlerian counseling are analogous to four aspects of the activity of God. According to Oden, the therapeutic process begins with the establishment of a healing relationship in which the client is understood and accepted by the therapist. In a similar fashion, as we enter into a relationship with God and allow Him to share our human frame of reference, we develop the awareness that we are known and understood by God.

What Rogers (1951) called unconditional positive regard, Adlerians refer to as the unconditional expression of social interest. Whatever term we may choose to use, the empathetic stance of the therapist is seen as essential. It is a gift given to the client, no matter who the client is or what the client does. Huber (1987) discussed the graceful aspects of psychotherapy and talked about the role of grace, or freely given love, in the therapeutic encounter. Similarly to the way God showed grace toward the Jews, a therapist shows grace toward the client.

Part of any therapeutic agreement is that the therapist agrees to work with the client through his or her challenges. In a similar fashion, from a theological perspective, God will not desert his people even in the worst of times. Huber argued that this grace allows the client to attempt things he or she has never done before, thus setting the stage for healing. Huber explained

> grace, implies that one's actions are received favorably by others. Similarly, one who behaves with social interest feels at home with self and others and, therefore, can accept this earth and its people with their limitations. This person, therefore, is viewed as grace-full by others. Indeed, social interest and grace are the ties that keep the social fabric from unraveling. Many social relations embrace rituals that remind humanity that cooperation, empathy, and forbearance, thus graces, are the keys to survival. (pp. 440–441)

For Huber, Adlerian therapy is consistent with various aspects of grace, specifically its unconditional, actualizing, and nonauthoritarian nature.

Understanding

The second phase of Adlerian counseling is often referred to as the lifestyle assessment phase. It is an ongoing phase in which the therapist attempts to fully understand the client. The therapist assesses the client's functioning in the life tasks, including the client's spirituality and beliefs about God. He or she tries to learn about the client's unique way of understanding himself or herself, other people, and his or her place in the world. The therapist also seeks to understand the client's symptoms, how these symptoms are in the service of avoiding responsibility for the life tasks, and how they assist the client in striving for his or her goal.

The client can be understood only as a whole, self-consistent unity that strives from a perceived minus situation to a perceived plus situation. This striving occurs within the client's social context, which must also be understood. The holistic perspective with an emphasis on understanding and appreciating the individual's social context is consistent with Christian theology. The goal of the assessment phase is to fully understand the person and comprehend his or her real needs.

In an effort to make the assessment phase more efficient, Adlerians frequently use guessing as part of the diagnostic process. While listening to the client's story, the therapist formulates various hypotheses about the client's lifestyle and immediately seeks to validate his or her intuitions by guessing (Adler, 1956; Anderson, 1971). This approach allows the therapist to access the motivations that lie behind the client's movement, and, because the therapist is bound to make erroneous guesses, model the courage to be imperfect.

Interpretation and Feedback

Pastoral counselors have traditionally favored empathetic listening over interpretation and feedback. Yet, feedback constitutes an important aspect of the counseling process. Behavioral changes can and do occur without psychological insight, but self-understanding is important to stimulate the individual to change: "ye shall know the truth, and the truth shall make you free" (John 8:32). Jesus both interpreted and confronted those around Him in an effort to help them develop insight. Jesus spoke to people directly and indirectly through parables (Luke 24:25–26; Luke 18:9–14).

Similar to other schools of psychotherapy, Adlerians view change as being the responsibility of the client. Adlerians share their insights with the client by holding up for the client what he or she is doing. They avoid telling the client what to do and instead work to help the client see his or her options. Adlerians use a wide range of therapeutic tactics, including illustrative tactics such as fables, myths, and Bible stories (Mosak & Maniacci, 1998) to provide feedback and interpretation, and to encourage psychological insight.

Having received feedback from the therapist, the client can begin to accept the way he or she is and to test out alternative ways of acting and thinking. Huber (1987) compared grace, God's unmerited favor and empowering presence, to the enlightening experiences clients often have in therapy, calling interpretations manifestations of grace. Grace, as with unconditional regard, is nonauthoritarian. As the client is given interpretations and feedback it is presented without judgment and with unconditional encouragement on part of the counselor. As with grace, psychological interpretations constitute a gift that can be either accepted or refused. Thus, change is entirely up to the client. Just as people can choose to sin in the presence of God's grace, clients are free to choose not to change. Adler (1956) pointed out that under no circumstances should a client feel that he or she is forced to change.

Reorientation

In the final stage of treatment, insight is put into action, and the client's social interest is strengthened. The healing process is not complete until the client begins to move toward others with sincere social interest. Such movement is gradually increased as the therapist continues to encourage the client. Thus, encouragement is the main factor in stimulating change. The outgoing concern of the therapist expressed in his or her faith in and hope and love (Mosak, 1995) for the client provides the client with the self-esteem and confidence needed to move forward. Both Adlerian therapists and pastoral counselors can agree that encouragement is a crucial aspect of counseling. Pastoral counselors stress the importance of encouragement, although the wording may be different (e.g., "lift up," "strengthen," "affirm").

Ecrement and Zarski (1987) pointed to several instances in which Jesus encouraged people to accept responsibility for changing (John 5:6 and Mark 10:51), cautioned and confronted people (Matthew 8:26 and 18:15), gave hope (Mark 10:26–27), taught as a part of counseling (Luke 14:1–6 and 6:39), and helped change people's thinking (Luke 2:22–25 and 12:22–27), all of which are consistent with Adlerian counseling and psychotherapy.

The encouragement given to the client through the therapist's love and unconditional social interest, faith in his or her ability to change, and hope for a better future, encourages the client to move in the direction of social interest. This response parallels the response of faith in a loving God, namely an increased capacity to love, serve, and care for others (Oden, 1971).

In terms of therapeutic techniques and tactics, Adlerian therapists use a variety of cognitive and behavioral techniques. The techniques used by Adlerians (see Mosak & Maniacci, 1998) are in line with the variety of techniques Jesus used to counsel people. Thus, pastoral counselors can adopt Adlerian techniques, knowing they are consistent with their theological outlook.

> Jesus used a variety of counseling techniques, depending on the situation, the nature of the counselee, and the specific problem. At times he listened to people carefully, without giving much overt direction, but on other occasions he taught decisively. He encouraged and supported, but he also confronted and challenged. (Collins, 1988, p. 19)

The four phases of Adlerian therapy can be easily integrated into pastoral counseling. The model is theoretically consistent, and the conceptualization of the counseling process is consistent with what Jesus modeled in his approach to helping individuals heal. The Adlerian approach of relating to and connecting with clients, understanding their motivations and needs, providing insight, and promoting change through the use of encouragement are all analogous to pastoral psychology.

The Four Functions of Pastoral Care

Reviewing the history of pastoral counseling, Clebsch and Jaekle (1964) identified four pastoral functions: sustaining, healing, guiding, and reconciling. These functions have helped structure the pastoral counselor's role, and they help clarify ways in which the counselor may go about helping those in need. The four functions are only descriptors of what and how pastoral counselors help. They are not executed in any order, and counseling may not even include all four in order to be successful and complete. The role of sustaining, healing, guiding, and reconciling is discussed and placed into the framework of the four phases of Adlerian psychotherapy.

Sustaining

The pastoral function of sustaining can be viewed as a part of the relationship phase in Adlerian counseling. It involves helping a person endure and transcend difficult life circumstances. Such endurance and transcendence can occur only in light of an empathetic and encouraging relationship. When a person is faced with such adversity that recuperation or restoration seems either impossible or very remote, the pastoral counselor offers compassionate care. Sustaining may be the main function of pastoral counselors when working with individuals who grieve the loss of a loved one or who face other life challenges such as illness or trauma.

This function involves the maintenance of an empathetic and egalitarian relationship. The therapist promises to stay with the client on his or her journey, thereby enabling the client to endure the adversity he or she is facing. Thus, the counselor provides a stable place for the client to voice his or her thoughts and feelings without worrying about being disapproved of or criticized. For instance, Ingrid, a college graduate who was physically and sexually assaulted during her Freshman year, presented with symptoms of posttraumatic stress disorder (APA, 2000). She had also sustained several physical injuries as a result of the assault, including a shattered knee that caused her to walk with a slight limp. Since the assault, she had completed college, but had difficulty maintaining employment and expressed significant distrust of people. She had lost most of her friends and had little contact with the members of her family. For Ingrid, counseling provided a safe place for her to voice her opinions, share her fears, and express her anger and distrust of people.

Healing

Pastoral healing involves the recovery from a specific challenge or illness. It involves helping an individual move beyond his or her previous condition, thereby helping the person become integrated on a higher spiritual level. Healing does not necessarily mean that the individual is physically cured, but rather that he or she has moved toward emotional and spiritual healing. When clients are suffering from physical ailments for which there is no cure, the counselor can encourage emotional healing in the midst of that physical suffering. The healing function involves the offering of hope and encouragement in an effort to promote spiritual wellness. As such, the pastoral function of healing can be considered an aspect of the reorientation phase of Adlerian therapy. Through her therapist's maintaining a positive and optimistic view of the future and by offering hope and caring, Ingrid was able to find faith and hope in herself, in God, and in life. In Ingrid's care, healing was an ongoing process that dealt with emotional and spiritual healing, as well as with physical recovery. In contemporary practice, pastoral healing may also include various rituals or prayers intended to heal.

Guiding

The third pastoral function is guidance. When an individual is faced with difficult life decisions, the pastoral counselor may offer guidance in various ways. Similarly, Adlerian therapists frequently teach, advise, and offer guidance as part of the therapeutic process. However, guidance does not mean telling clients how they should live their lives. When people turn to pastoral counseling for help and guidance in times of crisis, guidance given to them may be based on the counselor's experience and knowledge, mutually shared cultural values, or a body of truth or knowledge independent of the two parties (Clebsch & Jaekle, 1964). The therapist or pastor may attempt to extract knowledge directly from the client, or he or she may provide direct advice. The pastoral function of guidance is also consistent with the reorientation phase of Adlerian therapy, where the therapist may offer guidance, depending on the client's needs. Guidance is often given as a series of options available, given the client's unique situation and style of life. It also involves helping clients evaluate the consequences of the various options available to them. Having a clearer understanding of available choices and of the consequences involved in each choice, the client is free to make a decision, while knowing that he or she does not have to worry about losing the counselor's acceptance no matter what the choice might be. In the case of Ingrid, guidance meant encouraging her to think about issues of trust and safety in personal relationships. Helping her carefully consider the many issues she faced as she moved forward allowed her to make better decisions. Questions about whether or not she could trust men and engage in a sexual relationship were an important part of the counseling process.

Reconciling

Finally, the reconciling function attempts to heal the relationship between the client and his fellow human beings or between himself or herself and God. This function "means helping alienated persons to establish or renew proper and fruitful relationships with God and neighbor" (Clebsch & Jaekle, 1964, p.56). It may involve the client's offering forgiveness for past sins or transgressions of others, or attempting to place the client in situations in which good relationships may be re-established (Clebsch & Jaekle, 1964). The healing power of the therapeutic relationship comes from its empathetic and unconditional nature. The therapist's modeling of unconditional social interest allows the client to begin reestablishing good relationships, both inside and outside the therapist's office. For Adler, neurotic individuals are alienated from the group. Thus, the function of reconciliation is viewed as an essential path to healing. Reconciliation is the function that moves the individual toward social interest.

From an Adlerian standpoint, the function of reconciliation is maybe the most important function in the treatment process. Every school of psychotherapy maintains certain theoretical goals for treatment. For Adlerians, the main goal of counseling is the development of social interest. Although Adlerians emphasize the many practical goals of therapy—symptomatic reduction, changes in behavior, and increase in self-esteem—they consider the development of a feeling of belongingness to be essential. Helping the client improve his or her relationships with others, including God, allows him or her to find a sense of importance and social connectedness—something the Adlerian therapist correlates with mental health.

In Ingrid's case, reconciliation meant being there for her and offering support and encouragement as she began exploring her fears of relationships with men. Having established a safe and proper relationship with her therapist, she was eventually able to reestablish her relationship with God. She learned to accept that God had allowed this terrible thing to happen to her. She was unwilling to forgive the man who assaulted her, but her reconciliation with God led her to be more open to engaging in relationships with family and past friends. She was able to move beyond her conviction that people could not be trusted, which permitted her to move toward the people in her life.

SUMMARY

Several authors have addressed the integration of various schools of psychotherapy into traditional pastoral counseling, including Cognitive Therapy, Family Therapy, Gestalt Therapy, Jungian psychology, Rational Emotive Behavior Therapy, Solution-Focused Therapy, and Adlerian

Therapy. The contributions of Adlerian Therapy to pastoral counseling involve the personal integrity of the counselor, the concept of the life-tasks as a way to structure the assessment process, and the four phases of psychotherapy to structure the process of pastoral care.

Considering the universal challenges of people—work, social relationships, and love, and the role of religion and spirituality in each of these—the pastoral counselor has a framework from which he or she can determine the client's needs and therapeutic goals. The four phases of Adlerian therapy can also help structure and organize the pastoral counseling process. Considering the phases of treatment and their correlation to the pastoral functions of sustaining, healing, guiding, and reconciling, pastoral counselors will find a user-friendly framework in Adlerian psychotherapy.

6 | Individual Psychology and Judaism: Common Themes

If I am not for myself, who will be for me? If I am only for myself, what am I?
And if not now, when?   — *Hillel the Elder*

Judaism, Christianity, and Individual Psychology have much in common in terms of how they understand human nature. Because Christianity grew out of Judaism, the two religions share a rich tradition documented in the Hebrew Bible (the Old Testament), and philosophical principles such as holism, freedom and responsibility, teleology, equality, and democracy are emphasized in both religions (Manaster, 2004). However, Adlerians have written little on the issue of the Jewish faith and Adler's theories. This may be because of the significant agreement between Christianity and Judaism, and that most authors have chosen to focus on Christianity.

Another factor is that much of the Adlerian literature that has considered Christian theology, and particularly the Old Testament, can arguably be said to be true for Judaism as well. Jews and Christians share several important beliefs and convictions. Both believe that people are created by one all-powerful God and that we are created in the image of God. Unlike Individual Psychology, both Christians and Jews believe that life has a purpose. They believe people were placed on earth to take care of it. Both religions also share the story of creation outlined in the book of Genesis. And Christians and Jews alike view the Ten Command-ments as sacred rules from which they model their lives.

Despite these similarities, there are many important differences as well. According to Weiss-Rosmarin (1997), the most significant difference is that Judaism is committed to "pure and uncompromising monotheism," (p. 15) whereas Christians subscribe to the belief in the Trinity—God, the Son, and the Holy Spirit. This leads us to the question of who Jesus of Nazareth is. Christians believe that Jesus of Nazareth is the literal Son of God. Jews, however, do not view Jesus as divine in any way. They do not accept Jesus as the Messiah promised in scripture. Jews also believe that the Messiah will be a nondivine person—someone who will restore the kingdom of Israel and bring about peace for all nations. Because Jesus is not believed to be the son of God, the Jewish people do not use him as a model for how they live their lives. Instead, they focus their spirituality on the study of the Torah (Kertzer, 1996). An in-depth discussion of differences between the two faiths are beyond the scope of this book (see Weiss-Rosmarin, 1997, for an in-depth discussion).

Judaism is the religion of the Jewish people. Their history can be traced back to Abram's exodus from Ur of the Chaldees in search of the land of Canaan, a significant event that signifies the beginning of Jewish history. The Jewish people trace their origin to Abraham, who established monotheism, not only for the Jews, but also for Christians and Muslims. Abraham, his son Isaac, and his grandson Jacob (Israel) are referred to as the patriarchs of the Jewish people. Judaism is arguably the oldest monotheistic religion and is based on the teachings of the Hebrew Bible, a collection of books divided into the Torah, the Prophets, and the Writings. Jews believe in one universal and eternal God, who is understood as the creator of the world and of everything in it. The Jewish people also believe they have entered into a special relationship with God, a covenant, and that their task is to be a "light to the nations" (Isaiah, 49:6).

The number of Jews in America is estimated to be between 5.2 million (American Jewish Committee, 2005) and 6 million (Barrett & Johnson, 1998), compared to approximately 4 million Jews living in the State of Israel. However, the Jewish people are spread worldwide, and it is estimated that the entire world's Jewish population is close to 15 million (Barrett & Johnson, 1998).

Along with Christianity, the Jewish faith shares a significant amount of common ground with Individual Psychology (Kaplan, 1984; Manaster, 2004; Rietveld, 2004; Weiss-Rosmarin, 1990). Adlerian principles are consistent with Jewish Scripture and Jewish philosophical literature. The purpose of this chapter is to outline and discuss the principles of Individual Psychology in the context of Judaism.

HISTORY AND TEACHINGS OF JUDAISM

Judaism has its roots in the Hebrew Bible, a collection of books written over a period of nearly 1000 years. The Hebrew Bible, also known as the Tanakh, is the collection of books that Christians refer to as the Old Testament. However, the Tanakh is different from the Old Testament in both organization and composition. The Hebrew Bible is divided into three sections: the first is the Torah, also known as the Five Books of Moses—Genesis, Exodus, Leviticus, Numbers, and Deuteronomy. These books are believed to have been written by Moses from divine instruction on Mount Sinai (Parrinder, 1985). The second and third sections of the Hebrew Bible are the Prophets and the Writings.

The book of Genesis tells the story of one all-powerful God creating the world in six days, with human beings created on the sixth day. The book tells the story of how human beings repeatedly turned away from God, which eventually resulted in God destroying the earth with a flood. Jewish history begins after the Flood, around 1800 BCE, when God commands a man named Abram to take his wife Sarai and leave his father's land for the land of Canaan. God promised Abram that his family would become a great nation, a blessing for mankind. Obeying God's commands and traveling to Canaan establishes Abram as the patriarch of monotheism and the first member of what would become the Jewish people.

After traveling to Canaan, Abram and Sarai are given new names by God: Abraham and Sarah. The names signify their new identity. In Hebrew "Abraham" means "father of a multitude." Abraham and Sarah had not been able to conceive a child of their own. But when Abraham had reached old age, God came to him with another covenant. He told Abraham that he would grant him a child with Sarah and that this child would become the ancestor of a great nation. But first, Abraham had to show his commitment to God by circumcising himself and all his male descendents. Again, Abraham obeyed God and entered into a covenant with Him. God upheld his promise, and Abraham and Sarah conceived a child they named Isaac.

The rite of circumcision in Judaism signifies the covenant with God that began with Abraham and continues with each new generation. Every male child is circumcised on the eighth day of his life, marking the step toward social living (Huber, 2006). This ritual binds the child to his faith and confirms his status as a Jewish individual (Kertzer, 1996).

A story that occupies a central position in the collective Jewish consciousness is the binding of Isaac as Abraham prepares to sacrifice him to God (Rabinowitz, 2006). In an effort to test Abraham's faith, God commanded him to sacrifice his beloved son. Once more, Abraham obeys God's commands and prepares for Isaac's sacrifice. Abraham raised his knife in preparation to kill his son. Convinced of Abraham's faith and trust, God sent an angel, who approached Abraham and told him to stop. The story, often referred to as "the binding," emphasizes the importance of trusting and obeying God's commands.

Abraham's son Isaac later has two children, Jacob and Esau. The biblical narrative tells the story of how the two brothers fight continually throughout their early lives. But eventually, Jacob is blessed, and his name is changed to Israel (Yisrael), meaning "one who wrestles with God." It is the descendants of Jacob who then become the "children of Israel" and who establish the major "Tribes of Israel." Weiss-Rosmarin (1990) made an interesting observation of how the youngest child is often favored in Jewish Scripture. She pointed out that Scripture repeatedly illustrates, in Jacob's story as well as in many others, how strength springs from weakness and how individuals strive from what Adler referred to as a minus situation to a plus situation.

In the book of Exodus, the Holy Scripture shifts from telling stories of Abraham's family to telling stories of a people. According to the Scriptures, a seven-year long famine caused the Hebrews to migrate to Egypt. They settled in Egypt and were given a fertile area called Goshen as their new home. But when Pharaoh Ramses II came to power, he began a series of major building projects. And as he needed workers, he enslaved various groups, including the Hebrews. This enslavement of the Israelites by the Egyptians set the stage for the founding of a nation. God rescued the Hebrews from slavery by afflicting the Egyptians with a series of plagues and then drowning the Egyptian army in the Red Sea to allow the Hebrews to escape. Under the leadership of Moses, the descendants of Abraham escaped enslavement in Egypt and came together as a nation at about 1300 BCE. Today, Jews celebrate Passover (Pesach) every year in late March or early April to mark the Exodus from Egypt and the Jews' escape from slavery.

On their journey to the land of Canaan (the Promised Land) the Israelites lost faith in God. They doubted God's ability to help them overthrow the tribes that occupied the Promised Land. As a result, God punished them by having them wander in the desert for the next 40 years before finding their way to Canaan. After the Exodus, a series of miracles took place. Maybe the most glorious moment in Jewish history is the revelation of the Ten Commandments at Mt. Sinai (Rabinowitz, 2006). The Ten Commandments and the Torah (Five Books of Moses) along with its 613 mitzvot (commandments) are at the core of the Jewish faith (Rabinowitz, 2006) and established guidance for human conduct.

After the Exodus, the Israelites settled in Canaan (later called Palestine). A kingdom referred to as the First Commonwealth (or First Temple) was established. Palestine was later divided into two states, Israel and Judah. By 722 BCE, Israel was destroyed by Assyria, and the only Hebrews left were the Judeans. The word Judean has been abbreviated to the word Jew (Kertzer, 1996).

The land of Judah continued to exist for another 130 years before it was captured by the Babylonians around 587 BCE. The capital of Judah, Jerusalem, was completely destroyed, along with the Temple, and the Jewish people were exiled in Babylonia.

Around 536 BCE, the Second Jewish Commonwealth (Second Temple) was established, and Jerusalem and its temple were rebuilt (Kertzer, 1996). It was at this time when the Five Books of Moses, the Torah, were edited and used as a type of constitution. For Jews, the Torah still serves as the main document for history and guidance from the past.

The Second Commonwealth (Second Temple) lasted for about 420 years before it was destroyed, this time by the Romans. Both temples were destroyed on the same day, the ninth day of the month of Av, Tisha B'av. This is considered the saddest day of the Jewish calendar year, which Jews mark by fasting (Rabinowitz, 2006). Over the next several centuries, Jews were dispersed throughout the world, including to Asia, North Africa, Italy, and Spain. The most influential Jewish communities, however, were established in Babylonia (Kertzer, 1996). Babylonian Jews contributed a large body of literary heritage, including the Talmud—a collection of sixty-three books of theological, spiritual, legal, and historical discussions (Kertzer, 1996). The Talmud was created to interpret the Torah as life became more complex. It is the written record of discussions pertaining to Jewish life that Jews are urged to study daily.

As the Jewish people continued to settle in every corner of the world, they have endured extreme hardship throughout history. From anti-Jewish regulations throughout Europe in the thirteenth century to the most horrific atrocities in modern history, the Holocaust, the Jewish people have prevailed and grown into a well-established and very influential religion worldwide.

The Scriptures tell us that the coming of the Messiah will accompany a time of world peace and the building of the Third Temple (Ezekiel 37:26–28). The Messiah will gather the Jewish people in the Land of Israel (Isaiah 43:5–6) and unite all of humanity in an ideal community. Unlike Christian theology, Jewish faith teaches that the Messiah will be an ordinary human being, unlike Jesus. The Messiah will help bring about a perfect community of peace and justice, a community marked by social interest similar to what Adler seemed to articulate (Rietveld, 2004).

What Does It Mean to Be a Jew?

Judaism is often thought to be an ethnic identity rather than a religious one. Although there is a very close connection between peoplehood and religion, Judaism is a distinct religion and not necessarily an ethnic identity. In discussing what it means to be Jewish, Kertzer (1996) outlined four different definitions of what it means to be a Jew: a religious definition, a spiritual definition, a cultural definition, and an ethnic definition.

According to Kertzer (1996), the religious definition of a Jew is anyone who accepts the faith of Judaism. Conversion to Judaism is a process of religious study, contemplation, and ritual ceremonies. The process differs among the various branches of the religion, but all accept converts. The spiritual definition of a Jew is someone who seeks a spiritual base by study, prayer, and devotion to Jewish wisdom and customs. Next, the cultural definition of a Jew is someone who regards the teachings of Judaism as his or her own. The individual may or may not have had much Jewish education and may not have a formal religious affiliation. Yet he or she may still consider himself or herself to be Jewish.

Of all four definitions of Judaism, the ethnic definition is becoming less prevalent in modern society. The ethnic definition includes only those individuals who were born as Jews. Today, however, the Jewish community includes individuals who have converted to Judaism. Kertzer (1996) stated that all Jews are Jewish by choice. He gave the following definition:

> A Jew is therefore a member of a people, by birth or by conversion, who chooses to share a common cultural heritage, a religious perspective, and a spiritual horizon derived uniquely from Jewish experience and Jewish wisdom. (p. 8)

In addition to various definitions, Judaism has four main subgroups or denominations: Orthodox, Reform, Conservative, and Reconstructionist. And even within each of these subgroups, there is great variation in terms of religious practices and philosophy. However, in general, Orthodox Jews accept the Torah as the word of God, literally given to Moses at Sinai. Consequently, they do not allow any room for tampering with Scripture, even when faced with changes in modern culture. Thus, Orthodox Jews are very resistant to changes in old traditions and practices.

Reform Jews believe that individuals are responsible to educate themselves and interpret Scripture based on their own conscience. They make their own decisions about their spiritual practices and are encouraged to interpret Scripture to help them adapt to modern life. For Reform Jews, the Torah is open to significant interpretation, based on the demands of modern society and personal ethics. Reform Jews make up the largest Jewish movement in the United States.

From a philosophical and theological standpoint, Conservative Judaism falls between Orthodox and Reform Judaism. Conservative Jews accept Jewish law and ethnicity, but view both in light of contemporary historical scholarship (Kertzer, 1996). In Europe, Conservative Judaism is known as Historical Judaism. Consequently, personal decisions regarding worship and other religious and personal practices are based on the consensus of learned scholars and the community rather than on personal values.

Finally, the Reconstructionist Jews are considered to be the radical subgroup of Judaism. Reconstructionist Judaism originated with the philosophy of the American Rabbi Mordecai Kaplan, who believed that Judaism was an evolving religious civilization (Kertzer, 1996). He believed that each generation is obligated to reconstruct its religion by reinterpreting Scripture and finding meaning that is relevant for the time. Kaplan did not believe in a personal God, but stated that God is a force of nature. Reconstructionist Jews maintain a variety of nontraditional views, such as ordination of women (similar to Reform Jews). It is the smallest of the Jewish movements and continues to evolve and encourage continued reworking of rituals and other religious practices.

PHILOSOPHY OF HUMAN NATURE

Judaism views human beings as social, unified, goal-oriented, creative, and responsible beings who possess the freedom to act in accordance to their interpretation of their environment (Manaster, 2004;

Weiss-Rosmarin, 1990). Kaplan (1984) examined the maxim of Hillel the Elder that begins this chapter from an Adlerian perspective and concluded that the Jewish philosopher understood the social and psychological aspects of the Jewish faith. He argued that Hillel's writings underscored the social embeddedness of the individual promulgated by Adler. Additionally, Rietveld (2004) discussed Adler's concept of social interest in the context of Jewish Messianic philosophy and its expectation of the kingdom of peace.

Adler's Individual Psychology parallels the teachings of Jewish philosophy, its morals and its ethics. Let's begin by examining responsibility and the freedom to choose.

Soft Determinism

Adler rejected the deterministic view set forth by Freud and replaced it with a soft deterministic philosophy. The soft deterministic principle suggests that individuals have freedom to make their own choices. Although our choices may be limited, given the constraints of our environment and our heredity, we still have the option to choose how to respond and how to use the things life has provided us with. However, many, if not most, of our decisions are made unconsciously. Safeguarding mechanisms, fictional goals, and life style convictions are created out of awareness. In this way many of our behaviors may appear determined, but from the Adlerian standpoint we are responsible for our own choices. Christians certainly believe in freedom to choose and personal responsibility. Similarly, Muslims frequently embrace soft determinism, although there are some conflicting beliefs within the Islamic faith on this issue.

As with Christians, Jews believe in sin, atonement, and forgiveness. Jews do not, however, believe in the Christian doctrine of "original sin." Adler (1956) emphasized that the individual is neither good nor bad, but that he or she has the potential for either. Similarly, Jews talk about peoples' good inclination (yetzer tov) and bad inclination (yetzer rah), stating that people have the freedom to choose to either do good or evil. According to Kaplan and Schoeneberg (1987)

> The term *yetzer* or inclination (also variously translated as instinct or impulse), was not meant to indicate a biological entity beyond one's control. Neither the *yetzer rah*, more frequently found in the literature, nor the *yetzer tov* has a nature by itself. Judaism holds that people are born with

free will (despite God's foreknowledge of things to come). If the yetzer rah, for example, were an instinct in the biological sense, people would no longer have the free will given them, nor could God be just in judging preprogrammed persons for following their script. (p. 315)

Kertzer (1996) quoted an ancient story of Cain on trial before God for having killed his brother. In the story, Cain pleads with God not to punish him, telling God that "it's your fault that I committed the murder. After all, you made me this way." God rejects his argument, maintaining that Cain had the free will to follow his "good inclination" had he decided to do so.

Judaism teaches that people are born with a clean slate. Therefore the individual cannot blame his or her actions on parents, environment, or biology. When comparing and contrasting Individual Psychology and Judaism, Weiss-Rosmarin (1990) agreed, stating that the Prophets

Disowned the compulsion of the phylogenetic experience and memory by proclaiming that the proverb, "The fathers have eaten sour grapes and the children's teeth are set on edge," shall no longer be used in Israel, for the actions of the fathers do not oblige the children, just as the actions of the children cannot be blamed on or credited to the fathers. The watchword of Judaism is freedom of choice in all action-situations, and its attitude to "caring or not acting" is identical with that of Individual Psychology. (pp. 115–116)

Rabbi Kertzer (1996) also suggested that Judaism is a soft deterministic religion when he declared that:

Generally speaking, Judaism is not a fatalistic religion. Jewish teaching stresses repeatedly that we are, to a large degree, masters of our own destiny. Much of life is, of course, beyond our control. We cannot choose the family into which we are born, or our gender, race, color, or native nationality. But the quality of our life—our human relationships, our character, and our spiritual destiny—is, the Rabbis teach us, our own to fashion. (p. 121)

Biblical stories repeatedly illustrate our potential to choose our own course. Maybe the most obvious story appears in the book of Genesis, where Adam and Eve choose to eat from the Tree of Knowledge of Good and Evil. Christians, Jews, and Muslims all point to this story to illustrate our freedom to make our own choices.

Teleology and Striving for Superiority

One of the fundamental principles of the human psyche is that motivation springs from the universal feeling of inferiority. This inferiority feeling, developed in early childhood, sets the stage for compensation and motivates us to improve our circumstances. Thus all human behavior is characteristic of movement from a subjective minus situation to a subjective plus situation. Judaism, along with Christianity and Islam, teach that we can expect a better life in the future. So our striving in life here on earth is thought to lead to a better future, either in this life or the next.

Jews are concerned mostly with improving the world in which they live. And life is therefore considered a challenge to move from the minus position of imperfection to a plus position of peace, justice, and brotherhood (Weiss-Rosmarin, 1990). Although they believe in life after death, Jews, in contrast to Christians, are typically more concerned with our life here on earth than with the Afterlife. Jews also focus more on deeds and the work we do instead of on faith. Thus the goal of superiority for Jews is to be "holy" in their relationship to others, rather than salvation in the Christian sense. Jews view God as the ideal goal for human ethical behavior, so modeling themselves after God and focusing on human relationships becomes their main focus.

Weiss-Rosmarin (1990) discussed the role of the youngest child in Jewish Scriptures and argued that Biblical stories time and again illustrate how strength springs from weakness. In the story of Cain and Abel in the book of Genesis, Abel was God's favorite. In the story, God takes favor with Abel after he sacrifices the youngest animal in his herd. Feeling angry and jealous, Cain decides to murder his younger brother. Weiss-Rosmarin also points to the youngest of Isaac's twins, who was chosen to receive the patriarchal blessing. She also points out that the Torah was given to the Jewish people on the smallest of all mountains, Mount Sinai, and the weakest nation was the one who became God's chosen people. According to Weiss-Rosmarin, these stories illustrate how achievement develops from a feeling of inferiority and a desire to achieve a more positive state. This theme of moving from a felt minus situation toward a felt plus situation is evident in the Jewish tradition, where adversity and suffering are also thought to be filled with blessings.

The teleological concept is evident, not only in Christian theology, but also in the Jewish tradition. Judaism conceives of God as the goal individuals must aspire to: God is the final goal for human striving and perfection. Compared with Christians, Jews aspire to be like God, "You shall be holy, for I am holy" (Leviticus 19, 2), whereas Christians aspire to model their lives after Jesus of Nazareth. Both believe that history will end with the coming of a perfect messianic reign of God (Kertzer, 1996).

Holism

A Jewish idea that is echoed in Adler's psychology is the holistic perspective that teaches us that the personality is a unified whole. Smuts (1926/1973) discussed holism and that argued that we cannot and should not attempt to understand people through reductive analysis. According to Smuts

> each human individual is a unique personality; not only is personality in general a unique phenomenon in the world, but each human personality is unique in itself, and the attempt at "averaging" and generalizing and reaching the common type on the approved scientific lines eliminates what is the very essence of personality, namely, its unique individual character in each case. (p. 279)

Both Judaism and Individual Psychology acknowledge that the whole is greater than the sum of its parts. Weiss-Rosmarin (1990) wrote that

> Individual Psychology, like Judaism, sees man as a whole. . . . both the Jewish tradition and Adler are aware that the whole consists of parts which must be understood. But the atomistic approach of psychoanalysis is alien to their integrating tendency. Religion is predicated on the axiomatic assumption that the whole is greater than the sum total of its parts. (p. 115)

Social Interest and Human Equality

The strongest area of common ground between Individual Psychology and Judaism is their shared focus on social connectedness and social responsibility, or in other words, social interest. Weiss-Rosmarin (1990) alleged that

> Adler's identification of a normally developed social interest with health, and of its opposite with neurotic affliction has a precise parallel in the role Judaism assigns to the community as the focal point of all healthy human endeavor. Jewish religion is community-centered first, and only then God-centered. Thus, the commandments enjoining neighborly love and charity have unqualified precedence over the ritual commandments. (pp. 110–111)

Kertzer (1996) also mentioned the relational perspective of Judaism:

> being a Jew does mean having a profound love and respect for the ideal of community. It means seeing yourself as a sacred link between past and future, a link that is shared with all other Jews of your generation, forming a sort of mystical continuity. (p. 3)

The relational perspective and importance of social interest are readily apparent in the Ten Commandments, shared by both Christianity and Judaism. The sociopolitical nature of the Ten Commandments and their focus on social relationships were discussed in the chapter on Christianity. But in addition to the Ten Commandments, social interest is, according to Rietveld (2004), similar to the Jewish Messianic philosophy's expectation of the kingdom of peace. By fulfilling the requirements of the Torah, Jews believe they can anticipate the coming of a perfect world. According to Rietveld, Adler placed social interest into a future perspective within the context of an ideal community. As Adler (1933/1964) put it

> Our idea of social feeling as the final form of humanity—of an imagined state in which all the problems of life are solved and all our relations to the external world rightly adjusted—is a regulative ideal, a goal that gives us our direction. This goal of perfection must bear within it the goal of an ideal community because all that we value in life, all that endures and continues to endure, is eternally the product of this social feeling. (p. 276)

Given this future perspective, Rietveld questioned whether Adler's philosophy is instilled with an expectation of salvation. Rietveld also asked, "Is his orientation toward utopia a belief in a perfect community that also anticipates a savior who brings this ideal about?" (p. 212). According to Rietveld, Adler seemed to anticipate a Messianic time, a future in which peace, justice, and social interest would dominate. This ideal future can be brought forth by humans putting social interest into practice by taking responsibility for themselves and others in the here and now. Similarly, Scripture appeals to humans to be holy and just. It is by following God's way and realizing that we all have equal importance that humans can achieve the ideal community and coexist in perfect harmony. The significance of human equality is exemplified in the following quote:

> At school I read in the Torah: Why did God create only one man? The answer: All men have the same ancestor, so that no man, later, could claim superiority over another. (Wiesel, 1978, p. 7)

Rietveld went on to compare Individual Psychology with the writings of the philosopher and Talmudic commentator Emmanuel Levinas. According to Levinas (1993), the Messiah will come when the Israelites have fulfilled the requirements of the Divine Law and are ready to receive Him. As humans strive to perfect society, peace becomes a reality (Rietveld). Levinas emphasized that religion and ethics are strongly connected and suggested that this is true of the Jewish faith as well. He stated that though the Jewish faith acknowledges God's holiness, that holiness is not necessarily glorified. The statement that God is holy, just, and merciful is a command that humans be holy, just, and merciful. Thus, to follow the teachings of the Torah, we make God tangible in this world as we take responsibility for each other. Levinas (1993, as quoted in Rietveld, 2004) comments on the importance of Jewish ethics and its parallels to Adler's theory are obvious:

> The Jewish religion knows the primacy of ethics, of the path of life, the lifestyle. Ethics calls upon me to be there for the benefit of my fellow man and when I answer this request, I make God visible in this world . . . That ethical praxis can be translated as charity, sanctification of life, service to the community, as the hope and the expectation that we are on the way to a perfect society, of which God is the ultimate symbol. . . . This perfect society is a supra-national, worldwide community, where the Messianic peace reigns. (p. 216)

Our social roots and the value of social contribution are also to be found in the writings of one of the greatest Jewish philosophers, Hillel the Elder. Hillel was born in Babylonia during the first century BCE and wrote extensively on religious, ethical, legal, and philosophical issues. The quote that begins this chapter ("If I am not for myself, who will be for me? If I am only for myself, what am I? And if not now, when?") was recorded in the Pirkei Avot (Ethics of the Fathers, a tractate of the Mishnah) and reflects the values and beliefs of Judaism, as well as that of Individual Psychology. Kaplan (1984) examined Hillel's maxim from an Adlerian perspective and made several important observations.

First, the question, "If I am not for myself, who will be for me?" may appear to imply a level of selfishness. Kaplan argued, however, that Hillel was speaking of self-respect and concern for one's well-being. He went on to argue that a genuine care for one's physical safety is a legitimate concern that also benefits those around us.

The second part of Hillel's maxim asks: "If I am only for myself, what am I?" To Kaplan, this question suggests that Hillel understood that the individual must exist for his or her fellow human beings. In other words, people cannot and should not separate themselves from the community. The third part of the adage asks: "And if not now, when?" This last question certainly reflects the reality of the day, that the lifespan was short. Consequently, we should not put off our purposes, but rather seek to work, contribute, study the Torah, and enjoy our time here in this life. The question also reflects Hillel's observation, according to Kaplan, that there is a correlation between low social interest and inactivity. Adler also made this observation and believed that these are consistent with a discouraged lifestyle, indicative of psychopathology. In counseling and psychotherapy, Adlerians emphasize movement rather than intentions. Thus confronting clients with "when" they are going to change is a technique they use frequently (Mosak & Maniacci, 1998). For example, a twenty-nine year-old Jewish man was gently confronted with a "when" after telling his therapist that he "should" (read: "but I don't intend to") go back to school and finish his degree. His failure to complete his degree had kept him from getting a job, and he used his depression along with other symptoms to avoid working and taking responsibility for himself. At the time he entered therapy, he lived with his parents, who cared for him. Focusing on actions rather than feelings and intentions, and placing these within his religious context encouraged him to take the necessary steps toward completing his degree and finding work. Kaplan concluded that Hillel's maxim, examined from an Individual Psychology perspective, allows us to better understand its "social-psychological importance" (p. 95), and in relying on the teachings of Judaism when formulating his concepts, Hillel anticipated accepted theories of modern psychology.

In conclusion, both the Jewish faith and Individual Psychology emphasize the importance of respecting, caring for, and cooperating with our fellow human beings. Both subscribe to the idea that a perfect peaceful community is possible, as long as we are willing to accept and take responsibility for each other. Moreover, both are also optimistic in their expectation that such a community is possible and to be expected in the future.

The Life Tasks

The work task is of great importance in the Jewish tradition. Jews admire those who work hard and diligently, and Scripture consistently honors those who take responsibility in the task of work. In the book of Proverbs we read that: "One who works his land will be sated with bread, but one who runs after empty things lacks understanding" (12:11). In view of this, a lack of responsibility in the work task is discouraged: "The slothful person desires but has nothing; but the soul of the diligent will be sated" (Proverbs 13:4).

Despite the fact that work is considered as an essential part of communal living, it is not considered the only thing of importance. Consequently, total devotion to work is also discouraged. In addition, work should not become a primary source of meaning for the individual. There must be room for both work and worship, and a person's deeds speak directly to his or her spiritual and religious devotion. Thus, Jews express their religious devotion through their work and contribution to society.

> Judaism is concerned with right living in which deed and thought are bound into one. Religion of ethics comes to grief when it emphasizes motive alone and stresses purity of heart to the exclusion of the purpose and substance of the good action. What man does in his concrete, physical existence is directly relevant to the divine. (Friedman, 1987, p. 40)

Work should not be emphasized to the exclusion of worship and the study of the Torah. Nor is it primary to the other tasks of life. Family, love, and community contribution are all thought to be equally important.

Marriage is particularly important and strongly encouraged in Judaism. The high value placed on marriage in Judaism stems from the fact that family is considered the center of religious life. Traditionally, husbands are the leaders of the family, but wives usually run the family. Although the traditional male and female roles have changed throughout history, both hold a central position in family functioning (Miller & Lovinger, 2006), thus emphasizing the importance of equality among men and women. As for sexual relations, Jews view sexuality as a gift to be enjoyed. Premarital sex is discouraged, particularly among Orthodox Jews; however Conservative and Reform Jews mostly consider premarital sex to be a matter of personal choice (Miller & Lovinger, 2006). Homosexuality is prohibited and dates back to the writings in Leviticus, which describe homosexual acts as a capital offence. Modern views of homosexuality differ between Orthodox and Conservative Jews, with some conservative groups being much more open to homosexuals. However, homosexuality has generally been considered sinful as described by the Torah. Given these Jewish teachings, homosexuals presenting for therapy may present with pronounced feelings of guilt or fears of being excluded from the Jewish community. Others may seek therapy to help them abstain from homosexual activities. Another issue that may bring Jewish families to seek therapy is male masturbation. Male masturbation is not permissible, and its practice by adolescent males frequently results in families seeking therapy (Rabinowitz, 2006).

As divorce is becoming more common in our culture, it is also becoming more common among Jews. Though Judaism prefers that marriages last, divorce is encouraged when differences between a husband and his wife become intolerable (Kertzer, 1996). Judaism has always accepted divorce as part of life. And Jews generally believe that it is better for couples to divorce than to stay together in a relationship marked by conflict. Divorce is even required in cases in which the wife commits a sexual transgression.

According to Jewish law, a divorce can be issued only by men, but women may sue in rabbinic court and urge their husband to issue a divorce (Miller & Lovinger, 2006). According to the Torah, divorce is accomplished by writing a bill of divorce and presenting it to the wife. The document is referred to in the Talmud as a "scroll of cutting off," but it is more commonly referred to as a get. In order for a Jewish marriage to be dissolved, the woman must be presented with the get. A civil divorce is not sufficient to end a Jewish marriage. Problems relating to love, marriage, divorce, and homosexuality are often the kinds of struggles that lead Jews to seek psychotherapy. (See Seltzer [2000] and Sperber [2008] for discussions on marriage and divorce in the Jewish faith.)

The individual's responsibility to the life tasks is critical in Judaism. These responsibilities are put forth in the Torah and in Jewish law, and people are believed to have a religious responsibility to meet them.

APPLYING INDIVIDUAL PSYCHOLOGY TO PSYCHOTHERAPY WITH JEWISH CLIENTS

The therapist's respect and understanding of religious values and beliefs constitute the most important component in successful psychotherapy with Jewish clients. Many religious clients, Jewish or otherwise, may tolerate a therapist's lack of understanding of their religion, but they are less likely to engage in a relationship with therapists who do not respect and appreciate their religious values and traditions. So not only is it important for a therapist to have a basic understanding of Jewish philosophy, but the therapist must also respect the client's worldview. This approach to counseling fits the Adlerian emphasis on developing an egalitarian and respectful therapeutic relationship. The idea of equality is similar to both Christian and Jewish theology which teaches that people are all created in the image of God.

When working with Jewish clients, it is helpful for therapists to be familiar with the Jewish holidays and religious observances. For example, the Sabbath (Shabbat) is the holiest day of the week. It begins at sunset on Friday, and ends at sunset on Saturday. It is a weekly celebration in which Jews remember God's completion of the creation of the universe and his rest after his labor. It is a day of rest because God blessed the seventh day and sanctified it.

Two other important Jewish holidays are the high holy Days of Judaism of Rosh Hashanah (the Jewish New Year) and Yom Kippur (Day of Atonement). Rosh Hashanah usually occurs in September or October. It is a period of self-examination and repentance. The celebration lasts two days, and is followed by Yom Kippur eight days later. This ten-day period between the two holy days is known as the Ten Days of Repentance. Jews are urged to examine themselves and their behavior during the past year. Celebrations vary among the various denominations. For example, prayer services in Orthodox and Conservative synagogues may last five to six hours, whereas Reform services tend to be much briefer (Mosak, 1993).

The fact that an entire ten-day period is set aside annually for self-examination and repentance speaks to the significance Jews place on examining their actions and beliefs. In a similar fashion, the second and third phase of Adlerian psychotherapy focus on assessment and insight and therefore represent another point of philosophical overlap.

For child and adolescent therapists, an important Jewish tradition they should be mindful of is the Bar Mitzvah. When a boy turns thirteen years of age, he becomes a bar mitzvah or responsible man, at which point he is responsible for the same religious duties as adults. In many synagogues, girls go through a similar ceremony at the age of 12 (Bat Mitzvah). Many modern Jews do not require the young teenager to be completely responsible for his religious duties at this young age. Nevertheless, the Bar Mitzvah is an important celebration in the Jewish life-cycle that can be a source of great pride as well as great stress as families gather for the important occasion.

As with Christian patients, the Adlerian conceptualization of psychopathology as discouragement may offer Jewish patients a more positive view of the problems that bring them to therapy. Similarly, the emphasis on encouragement and the communication of faith, confidence, and support in Adlerian therapy are consistent with Jewish Scripture

(Jeremiah 29:11). Finally, the ultimate goal in Adlerian psychotherapy is the development of a feeling of belonging, a sense of respect and caring for others, and the willingness to cooperate with and contribute to the community—in other words, social interest. This goal is certainly congruent with the goals of the Jewish religion, which repeatedly emphasizes the importance of a commitment to God and the life tasks.

The vast overlap between Judaism and Individual Psychology allows Adlerian therapists to work effectively and respectfully with Jewish clients. However, therapists must pay particular attention to various moral and ethical issues that differ among denominations. Issues such as sexuality and sexual orientation, abortion, marital conflict, alcohol and drug abuse, and suicide do vary among denominations and generations. Therapists should also note that Jews may have very different ideas of what it means to be a Jew. For some, being Jewish is more of an ethnic or cultural identity rather than a religious one. Yet others maintain a more spiritual definition of Judaism. Those who maintain a spiritual or religious identity, however, may be more likely to adhere to religious values and beliefs. Another aspect for therapists to consider includes clients who have converted to Judaism. These individuals may present for therapy because of difficulties arising from their attempts at adapting to their new faith and feeling part of their new religious community.

The Adlerian therapist working with Jewish clients should feel comfortable asking about religious values, beliefs, and practices. He or she should also be comfortable incorporating the Hebrew Bible in therapy, and openly discuss issues of religious identity and practice.

Case Example

Twelve year-old Daniel was brought in for counseling by his parents. They were concerned about his performance in school, and particularly his difficulty reading Hebrew. Daniel had been diagnosed with attention deficit hyperactivity disorder (APA, 2000) when he was nine. He appeared to be very intelligent, which cognitive testing, completed a few years earlier, had confirmed. However, he had significant problems paying attention in school. Daniel had been in religious school since he was in first grade. His parents told me that he liked reading, but he hated studying the Torah and reciting prayers. Daniel's parents expressed deep concerns, particularly as his Bar Mitzvah was less than one year away.

When a boy turns thirteen years of age, he becomes responsible for the same religious duties as adults. The Bar Mitzvah is an important celebration, but it also requires extensive study on part of the child. Upon getting to know Daniel's family I learned that he had been studying for his Bar Mitzvah ever since he was diagnosed with ADHD. His parents were extremely anxious about his ability to learn the material, particularly Hebrew, and had begun to place a lot of pressure on him. Despite his difficulties with attention and concentration, he had managed to maintain a B average in school. But his performance in Torah study was poor.

Daniel was the oldest of three boys in a Conservative Jewish family. He had two younger brothers, ages six and nine. His parents were very invested in their children's education and had worked tirelessly to afford private education for the children. They felt tired and angry with Daniel's poor performance. Although they acknowledged his diagnosis of ADHD, they simultaneously referred to him as lazy and unmotivated. Father also expressed concerns that Daniel's grades were poor. In their efforts to motivate him to study, they threatened to take away TV and computer privileges.

My initial impression was that Daniel's mother and father wanted him, as opposed to the family, to receive treatment. The problem, they believed, had to do with Daniel and his attention deficit disorder. But after working with Daniel for a few sessions, it became increasingly clear that he was objecting to his parent's pressure. He felt he had worked hard to maintain good grades in school, and their insistence that he study Hebrew at school, at home, and with a tutor was too much. Daniel was showing his parents that he could not be forced to study. With the help of medication and tutoring at school, he had managed to maintain excellent grades. But he was responding to his parent's pressure to study the Torah by exhibiting his power.

Over the next few weeks I encouraged his parents to visit with me separately from Daniel. We discussed their ambitions for him and for his two younger brothers. We also discussed their fear of their children failing academically, and the implications of ADHD. I soon learned that the Bar Mitzvah was a very important ritual, particularly for Daniel's father. He shared his experience of fear and dismay when he first learned of Daniel's disability and how this spurred him into action to help. Unfortunately, his helping had been perceived by Daniel as an attempt to overpower him and take away his independence. As he was approaching "manhood," Daniel wanted to study and face the challenges involved in his Bar Mitzvah by himself.

Daniel's treatment involved individual sessions with him and regular consultations with his parents. In working with the family it was important to acknowledge the meaning and the value placed on Daniel's coming of age. His reluctance to study the Torah and take an active part in preparing for his Bar Mitzvah created anxiety and anger with his parents. We discussed how Daniel was at a point in his life where he, not his parents, was responsible for his behavior and his religious obligations. We talked about how children develop their own moral awareness and maturity and about their doubts concerning Daniel's ability to meet those responsibilities. The more they stepped in to rescue him and pushed him to perform, the less responsibility he learned, and the more oppositional he became.

Through treatment, his parents came to acknowledge his impressive academic performance in face of a significant disability. Over the course of a few months, Daniel's parents struggled to step back and let Daniel take responsibility for studying the Torah. We discussed various parenting strategies, including the use of natural and logical consequences, the four goals of misbehavior, and the importance of encouragement (Dreikurs & Soltz, 1964). Daniel gradually came to accept responsibility and, when he was left to work on his own with his Rabbi and his tutor, his Hebrew skills began to improve.

SUMMARY

Judaism is the religion of the Jewish people. People often mistakenly believe that the Jewish religion is an ethnic identity. And although Judaism is closely tied to Jewish ethnicity, many people of various backgrounds are converting to Judaism. In his discussion of what it means to be Jewish, Kertzer (1996) discussed four different definitions: religious, spiritual, cultural, and ethnic. There are also four main denominations of Judaism that all represent varying beliefs, values, and practices: Orthodox Jews, Reform Jews, Conservative Jews, and Reconstructionist Jews.

Rietveld (2004) argued that Adler placed social interest into a future perspective within the context of an ideal community. Thus, the ideal future characterized by social interest is anticipated by both Adler and the Jewish people. The Jewish philosopher Hillel the Elder's maxim captures the essence of Adler's psychological and sociological perspective. Consequently, as with Christianity and Islam, Jewish philosophy fits well with the principles of Adler's Individual Psychology. The concepts of holism, soft determinism, striving for superiority, social interest, equality, personal responsibility, and teleology are all analogous to Jewish teachings. The emphasis Adler placed on social responsibility and the life tasks are also found in Jewish philosophy.

SUGGESTED READINGS

Hoffman, S. (Ed.) (2007). *Issues in psychology, psychotherapy, and Judaism.* Lanham, MD: University Press of America.

Kertzer, M. (1996). *What is a Jew?* NY: Simon & Schuster.

Robinson, G. (2001). *Essential Judaism: A complete guide to beliefs, customs, and rituals.* New York: Pocket Books.

Smith, H. (1991). *The world religions.* NY: Harper Collins.

7

Theories of Adler and the Islamic Faith

There is no God but God, and Muhammad is His Apostle.
— *The Shahada, the Muslim profession of faith*

With over one billion followers worldwide, Islam is the world's fastest-growing religion. Islam is a monotheistic religion that originated in what is now Saudi Arabia and later expanded along trade routes to Asia and Africa. Today, Indonesia is the country with the most Muslims, with over 196 million (Lippman, 2002). Countries such as Pakistan, Bangladesh, Mali, Afghanistan, Malaysia, Albania, Iran, Iraq, and Syria have a Muslim majority. But Islam is also a growing religion in North America. The number of Muslims in the United States and Canada is somewhat uncertain, but it appears to range between 4 million (Barrett & Johnson, 1998) and 6 million (Power, 1998).

However, according to the U.S. Religious Landscape Survey (Pew, 2008), Muslims in the United States make up about 0.6 percent of the entire population (about 1.8 million people). According to Power (1998), about 12.4% of Muslims in North America are Arab, 42% are African American, 24.4% are Asian, and 21% are "other." So Muslims vary to a great extent in terms of their ethnic and national background. They also differ significantly in terms of economic status and level of educational. Islam is likely to continue to grow, and there is a need for psychotherapists to develop an understanding of the Islamic faith. Therapists

121

working with this population should familiarize themselves with cultural factors as well as with the religious ones.

Most of the literature focusing on Individual Psychology and religion has examined Christianity (Baruth & Manning, 1987; Ecrement & Zarski, 1987; Kanz, 2001; & Watts, 2000). But Adler's theories have been applied to the teachings of the Islamic faith, and there is a significant overlap between the two philosophies. Individual Psychology and Islam share similar ideas in terms of behavior being goal directed, as well as the concepts of soft determinism, goal directed behavior, and social interest. A point of major disagreement, however, is the lack of equality between men and women in Islam and the apparent lack of democracy in the Islamic faith. Despite these differences, Individual Psychology is applicable to psychotherapy with clients of the Islamic faith (Johansen, 2005).

This chapter reviews the historical background of Islam, its basic doctrines, and its philosophy of human nature. Its teachings are compared to the principles of Individual Psychology, and issues relevant to therapists are discussed.

HISTORICAL BACKGROUND

The prophet Muhammad was born in Mecca in 570 CE. At the time there was no Arabian nation, and the area belonged to various tribes who worshiped a variety of different deities. Experiencing a childhood fraught by death and loss, and raised by his uncle, Muhammad would come to experience a series of revelations that would lead to the birth of Islam. Over the course of his life, Muhammad strengthened his position as God's prophet. He united local tribes and created a vast army whose purpose was to conquer the world for God. Muhammad would eventually conquer Mecca and rid the city of lesser gods and idols. By the time of his death in 632 CE, most of the Arabian Peninsula had converted to Islam.

Muhammad lost both his parents at an early age. His uncle looked after him and raised him in the commercial town of Mecca. By the time Muhammad reached his 20s, he would work as a merchant for a wealthy widow named Khadija, whom he later married (Hedayat-Diba, 2006). Khadija proved to be a strong supporter of his convictions and was the first to become a Muslim. Together they had seven children, three girls and four boys. All his boys eventually died, but his daughters survived.

After being married, Muhammad spent much of the next 15 years in solitary meditation. He received his first revelation at the age of 40 while meditating in a cave on Mount Hira near Mecca. Molla (as cited in Hedayat-Diba, 2006) describes Muhammad's experience when he was first called upon by the Archangel Gabriel:

> Muhammad tells us: I had fallen asleep in the cave of Hira, when the Angel Gabriel appeared to me. He was waving a long silk cloth embroiled with writings. "Read," he told me. "I am not of those who read" I answered [Muhammad was illiterate]. He seized me at once and crushed my limbs and mouth in the silk cloth with such force that I could no longer breathe and believed I was dying. Then, when I released myself, He repeated: "Read!" "I am not of those who read" I answered again. He crushed me once more, and I felt a last breath escaping from my chest. Finally he released me and for the third time repeated "Read!" "What should I read?" I asked in despair. He then told me: "Read in the name of your Lord Who created; Who created man from congealed blood. Read, for your Lord is most generous Who taught the Word to him who did not know it." I repeated these words; he disappeared. Then I woke up with the impression that an entire book had been carved in my heart. (pp. 290–291, my emphasis)

This marked the beginning of a series of revelations that would be given to Muhammad. His reciting of God's message would become the Koran, the Holy Scripture of Islam. In the years following this revelation Muhammad was concerned that he might be possessed by supernatural beings. He shared his experience with his wife, who was confident that he was telling the truth and who encouraged his beliefs. With the support of his wife, Muhammad eventually began to preach the words given to him by the Archangel Gabriel in the streets of Mecca. He slowly began to develop a flock of followers, while enjoying the protection of his wife and his uncle.

Although his followers were beginning to grow in numbers, Muhammad was met with hostility from the various tribes of Mecca. He enjoyed the protection of his wife as well as his uncle, but after their passing in 620 CE, Muhammad's enemies set out to kill him. On June 16, 622 CE, he was forced to flee to the city of Yathrib. The flight to Yathrib is called the hegira and marks the beginning of the Islamic calendar. To honor Muhammad, Yathrib was later renamed Madinat an Nabi (City of the Prophet), also known as Medina.

Having fled to Medina, Muhammad managed to unite the tribes of that area and developed an army to protect him from the Meccan military who had set out to kill him. The fighting finally ended eight years later in 630 CE when Muhammad and his followers conquered

Mecca. Muhammad set out to destroy every idol in the main temple of the city, the Kaaba. But Muhammad spared the Black Stone (a sacred meteorite enshrined in the Kaaba) and declared it to be the holy shrine of Islam. The Kaaba in the city of Mecca has since been the holiest shrine in Islam, a site which is visited by millions of Muslims each year during the annual pilgrimage.

Beliefs and Practices of the Islamic Faith

Muslims believe in the same God as Christians and Jews. They see their religion as a "continuation and rectification of the Judeo-Christian tradition" (Lippman, 2002, p. 5). They believe that God is one, as opposed to triune according to Christians. God is all powerful and all knowing. Lippman (2002) described how Muslims perceive God:

> Allah has no physical attributes. He has no age, no shape, no mother, no appetites; but neither is He an abstraction. He is an immediate and constant presence, cognizant of every person's deeds and thoughts, aware of who follows His commands and who does not. Those commands require acceptance of Muhammad's message, social justice, personal honesty, respect of others, and restraint of earthly desires, as well as the performance of devotional duties such as prayer and fasting. (p. 1)

Muhammad used the word Allah to refer to God. Although the word was originally used to describe an Arabian pagan deity, the Koran identifies Allah as the same god worshiped by Jews and Christians. According to Lippman (2002), many Muslims disapprove of the name Allah in the English language, stating that it incorrectly suggests that Allah is a different god from the one Christians and Jews worship.

As opposed to Christianity and Judaism, Islam is a faith without clergy, saints, hierarchy, or sacraments (Lippman, 2002). Muslims strongly believe that nobody stands between the individual and God. Although there are Muslims who study theology, lead congregational prayers, and interpret the Koran, there is no central doctrinal authority in Islam.

There are, however, a number of various subgroups within Islam. The main branches include the Shia, the Sunni, and the Sufi. In the United States, the African American Muslims represent yet another branch. The Sunni are the largest denomination of Islam, comprising about 85 percent of all Muslims (Lippman, 2002). The Sunni follow the teachings of the Sunnah, the recordings of the actions and statements of

Muhammad. They believe that Muhammad never appointed a successor before he died. So unlike the Shiites, they do not recognize a divine heir to Muhammad's spiritual authority (Lippman, 2002).

The Shia is the second largest denomination in Islam. The Shiites believe that Imams have been appointment by God after Muhammad. They believe that Ali, Muhammad's cousin and son-in-law, was chosen by God to be the direct successor of the Prophet. A somewhat distinct group of Islam is Sufism. These are considered to be the mystics of Islam. Sufi followers strive to achieve a direct experience of God. They tend to be much more spiritually inclined than the other groups.

Finally, in the United States an African American Muslim movement began to grow over the past century. African American Muslims tend to concern themselves with issues of freedom and justice. The movement has its roots in the history of slavery, as many Africans who were brought to the United States were Muslim. A more recent event that turned many African Americans toward the religion was Malcolm X's conversion to Sunni Islam in 1964. African Americans consist of about 42% of the Muslim population in the United States, most of whom are Sunni Muslims (Turner, 2004).

Islamic beliefs and practices are clearly provided in two sacred texts, the Koran and the Sunnah (path). The Koran is the Holy Book of God's revelations to mankind. It is believed to be the literal word of God, handed down to us through the prophet Muhammad. It is thought to be the continuation of the Jewish and Christian scriptures (Lippman, 2002). But instead of being written by various authors over the course of centuries, the Koran, according to Muslims, is the actual word of God, dictated to Muhammad.

The Sunnah provides a second source of Islamic doctrine and practice. It became a base for traditions developed from Muhammad's teachings, Koranic interpretations, and conduct. The Sunnah was gathered into a body of work called the Hadith (Ridenour, 2001). According to Lippman (2002) Muslims accept the authority of the Hadith, but there are different ones, and not all Muslims accept the same Hadith as authentic. Together, the Koran and the Hadith instruct Muslims in what to believe and how to behave in order to win favor with Allah. According to Lippman (2002)

> The basic principle of Islam that emerges from the Koran and from Muhammad's life is that the religion is based upon behavior as well as belief. To be a Muslim is to believe in God, the prophecy of Muhammad, and the Last Judgment; but it is also to live in a prescribed way. The soul's

submission to God's supremacy has its indispensable earthly counterpart in the individual's submission to God's code of conduct. (p. 69)

Thus, the Holy Scripture of Islam provides specific guidelines in how people should behave and worship. It provides guidelines for how to address the various life tasks of work, sex and marriage, and social relationships.

The Six Basic Doctrines of Islam

The six basic doctrines of Islam are faith, belief in angels, recognition of prophets and scripture, the Day of Judgment, predestination, and life after death.

Faith

The first and most basic doctrine in Islam is faith. Having faith and maintaining faith in the oneness of God is a fundamental requirement of Muslims. Faith means "acknowledgment of God, his Messengers, his Books, his Angels, and the Last Day" (Haddad & Lummis, 1987, p. 17).

Belief in Angels

The second basic doctrine is the belief in angels. The chief angel is Gabriel, who appeared to Muhammad and inspired him to write the Koran. But angels are believed to be important helpers of God. Although most of them are good, Satan is the angel who was cast out of heaven after refusing God's command to bow down to Adam (Denny, 1985).

Prophets and Scriptures

The belief in the oneness and uniqueness of God and his prophet Muhammad form the basis for the various moral values, attitudes, and guidelines for behavior in Islam. Muhammad is believed to be the last and the greatest of the prophets. Accordingly, Islam has been referred to as "Mohammedanism." This word, however, incorrectly suggests that Muslims worship Muhammad in the same way Christians worship Jesus Christ (Parrinder, 1985). Muslims view Muhammad as an ordinary man. He is by no means thought to be a divine figure.

In addition to Muhammad, Muslims recognize twenty-four prophets who came before him. Biblical characters such as Adam, Abraham, Moses, and Jesus of Nazareth are mentioned in the Koran as prophets. All the prophets are thought to have received their revelations directly from God; thus Scripture is considered to be God's work (Hedayat-Diba, 2006). Muslims believe in four books they view as being inspired by God: the Torah of Moses, the Zabur (Psalms of David), the Injil (Gospel) of Jesus, and the Koran. However, they believe that Christians and Jews corrupted their Scriptures, thus leaving the Koran as the final word of God (Ridenour, 2001). The Koran supersedes all the other Scriptures.

The Day of Judgment

The Day of Judgment is a basic doctrine of Islam. Denny (1985) described the doctrine as a test of faith in that every individual can expect to be judged by God. Hedayat-Diba (2006) explained that the Day of Judgment is described as the end of the world as we know it, a time when the natural order of things will be thrown into chaos. On the Day of Judgment, the world will be destroyed, and every soul will stand before God. The righteous, those who have stood by their religious beliefs and obeyed God, will be conveyed to eternal paradise. The unrighteous, however, those who have betrayed their faith, will be conveyed to hell. The fear of hell and hope of eternal paradise become the basic motivating factor for many Muslims. It is comparable to what Individual Psychology refers to as the final goal.

Predestination

The fifth doctrine of Islam is that of predestination, which has been a controversial topic among Muslims. The Koran is often unclear and sometimes contradictory in matters of destiny, fate, and free will. This concept is particularly important to Adlerian psychotherapists, who strongly believe in soft determinism. According to Haddad and Lummis (1987), modern Muslims view individuals as responsible agents of God. Thus, people are thought to have the ability to choose and make their own decisions. The issue of predestination will be discussed in more detail in the section on soft determinism.

Life Hereafter

The last doctrine addresses life in the Hereafter. Muslims strongly believe in life after death. The Koran emphases repeatedly that there is a life after death, even stating that life as we know it is hardly worthwhile compared with life in the Hereafter. Again, Muslims believe that those who have stood by their faith will be rewarded with eternal paradise.

The Five Pillars

In addition to the basic doctrines of Islam, the Five Pillars form the principle elements that make up the worship of Muslims. These are the duties expected of Muslims as part of their religious obligations. Failure to meet these obligations may be a source of depression or anxiety and may lead some Muslims to seek the services of a psychotherapist. The Five Pillars include the profession of one's faith, ritual prayer, giving to charity (giving alms), fasting, and going on pilgrimage to the city of Mecca in Saudi Arabia—the holiest city in Islam.

Profession of Faith

The profession of faith, or Shahada, is the first and most significant pillar. The profession of faith is a declaration that Allah is the true God and that all other deities are false. The Shahada, "La ilaha ill Allah, Muhamadan rasul Allah," which translates to, "There is no God but God, and Muhammad is His Apostle," is repeated several times daily through prayer and/or meditation. Anyone who chooses to become a Muslim must publicly profess and act upon this declaration. The expression of the profession of faith is evidence of membership in the Muslim community. Although other Muslims may scrutinize an individual's behavior, they may not challenge a person's belief and faith as expressed in the Shahada. Professing one's faith is not sufficient to remain a devout Muslim, however. This is only one of the individual's religious obligations, and the remaining four pillars are important parts of the worship of Muslims.

Ritual Prayer

Ritual Prayer—salat—is the second pillar of Islam. Islam requires five prayers daily, and these prayers are conducted at dawn, noon, midafternoon, sunset, and in the evening. The salat is the most visible of the Five Pillars. It begins with a ritual cleansing of the body and ends with the purification of the soul. These prayers can take place anywhere. The only requirement is that the individual face in the direction of Mecca. Despite being allowed to pray at any place, Muslims hold congregational prayers in the mosques every Friday at midday. The Friday prayer is comparable to Sunday worship for Christians and Saturday worship for Jews. The prayers are led by an imam, who also performs sermons after the prayers. Any Muslim with sincere faith may serve as an imam. Imams are nonordained religious leaders, as the religion has no ordained clergy (Hedayat-Diba, 2006). In addition to the five daily prayers, Muslims are urged to pray at any occasion throughout the day (Lippman, 2002).

Giving Alms

The third pillar of Islam is giving alms—zakat. The zakat involves giving a portion of one's income to the poor and the needy. The Koran does not specify how much Muslims should give. However, in practice Muslims are required to give 2.5 % of their income away to the poor (Hedayat-Diba, 2006). Individuals who do not have much are not required to pay zakat. Thus the duty to give alms is incumbent upon one's means. The purpose of this pillar is to purify the donor of selfishness and to remind the individual that he or she should be grateful for the things given to him or her by God. In this way it attempts to influence the individual to focus on his or her fellow human beings. Individual Psychology asserts that acting for the good of one's community promotes mental health in the individual.

Fasting

As-siyam, in the month of Ramadan, is the next pillar of Islam. Ramadan is the ninth month of the Islamic lunar year, and thus it occurs on different dates in each year of the Gregorian calendar (Lippman, 2002). Ramadan is the most important holy season, and Muslims spend the month fasting, during which they must abstain from eating, drinking, smoking, and having sexual relations from dawn until sunset (Parrinder, 1985). Through this practice of fasting, Muslims commemorate the revelation of the Koran. It is the month in which the first verses of the Koran were revealed to the Prophet. Every individual who is in good health is required to participate. The elderly and travelers can be exempted, as well as nursing and menstruating women. Travelers have to make up the fast days they miss. And children as young as age 7 are encouraged to take part in this joyous month (Hedayat-Diba, 2006). The end of the month of Ramadan is celebrated by the Eid-fitr, one of the two main holidays in Islam.

Pilgrimage

The fifth and final pillar involves a pilgrimage to the Kaaba in Mecca—the Haji. Every Muslim over the age of 16, and possessing the means to travel, is expected to go on pilgrimage at least once in his or her lifetime. Those who cannot travel due to illness or lack of money are excused from this final obligation. The Haji consists of various ceremonies meant to symbolize and honor the trials of the prophet Abraham and his willingness to sacrifice his son. It is a form of worship that involves the entire body and soul. It also demonstrates the commonality of the Muslim people, as people from all over the world, representing different cultures, languages, and nationalities, come together to worship God. The basic Islamic doctrines along with the Five Pillars provide a foundation for what Muslims believe and how they practice their faith.

PHILOSOPHY OF HUMAN NATURE

The Islamic philosophy of human nature is consistent with the Adlerian assumptions of soft determinism, striving for superiority, teleology, holism, and social interest. The life tasks as discussed by Adler are also discussed in great detail in the Koran. In fact, the Koran provides detailed guidelines for how the individual should act in regard to his or her community and family (Johansen, 2005). Islam is an all-encompassing ethical, spiritual, and social system that lays out in detail how the individual should live his or her life. According to Lippman (2002)

> These obligations are of two kinds. One kind is spiritual and mental, involving the attitudes and states of belief that God demands of those who believe in Him. The other is legal and social, involving the rules of conduct and codes of law that exemplify the proper spiritual attitudes and put them into practice in daily life. (p. 29)

Soft Determinism

Soft determinism is an important concept in Individual Psychology. Adlerians strongly believe that people have the power to change their thoughts, feelings, and behaviors. Consequently, they have the ability to make the necessary changes to get better. This idea is consistent with Islamic beliefs. Islam emphasizes the importance of action. It encourages people to strive, to do their best, and to make an effort. Despite contradictory teachings in the Koran, most Muslims believe that people are free to choose their course of action and to make their own decisions. However, they also believe that making a decision does not guarantee the desired results. The outcome of our choices is believed to be determined by God and his controlling will. This belief fits with the Adlerian view of freedom to choose:

Man, as a chooser, can shape both his internal and external environment. Although he is not complete master of his fate and cannot always choose what will happen to him, he can always choose the posture he will adopt toward life's stimuli. (Mosak, 1979, p. 49)

The concept of soft determinism remains controversial to many Muslims. The Koran is often unclear and even contradictory on the issue of free will. The Holy Book teaches that Allah has complete control of human affairs, including the decisions they make. On the other hand, it also addresses the importance of choosing whether or not to obey God (Parrinder, 1985). Because of such contradictory teachings, some Muslim clients may insist that their fate is completely determined by God, and they therefore refuse to believe that they can experience different results by changing their own behavior.

However, according to Haneef (1996) most Muslims do emphasize the freedom to choose. And several Koranic stories have been interpreted to mean that the individual has freedom to make decisions. For example, the Koran tells the story of Adam and Eve and how they chose to disobey God's command (7:18). Their decision to defy Allah resulted in the loss of their innocence and of a life of peace and harmony.

When working with Muslim clients, psychotherapists would be wise to investigate their client's beliefs about free will and predestination. But for most Muslims, the Adlerian concept of soft determinism is consistent with Islamic teachings. Clients, Muslims and non-Muslims alike, are often quick to point out what others are doing or not doing, while they fail to notice their own behaviors and their own role in relating to others. When this is the case, Adlerians attempt to place responsibility back on the client's shoulders. Questions such as "What have you done to try to solve the problem?" "And then what did you do?" "What have you done about it in the past?" and "What are you going to do about it?" challenge the client to look at his or her own behaviors (Dreikurs, 1967; Mosak & Maniacci, 1998). But these and similar questions also allow the therapist to assess the client's placement of responsibility and whether or not he or she views himself or herself as playing an active role in the process.

Consider the following example. When Azim, a 19-year-old college dropout, was asked what he had done to alleviate his depressive symptoms, he appeared surprised and explained: "Nothing, I've done nothing." "What do you mean?" he asked.

"Well," said his therapist, "When you were feeling hopeless and depressed last week, what did you do?"

After thinking about the question for a little while Azim looked up and said: "I stayed at home and went to bed. If God wants to dishearten me, what am I supposed to do?" As the conversation continued, Azim went on to explain that God was in control of his life, and he had no power to change his situation. Although he questioned whether he had sinned (suggesting he has the freedom to choose), he believed that he was powerless and could do nothing to make himself feel better. Given that Azim assumed God's total control over his behavior, issues of predestination, fate, free will, and personal responsibility had to be addressed before therapy could continue.

Teleology

The teleological premise of Adlerian psychology can also be found in Islam. Adler (1956) stated that an individual's mental life is determined by the goal he or she sets for himself or herself. Thus, all persons strive towards a sense of significance, a self-ideal, which becomes the motivating force behind all human behavior. For many Muslims, this motivating force is evident in their endeavor to fulfill God's purpose and benefit from the rewards in the Hereafter.

Muslims believe that reward in the Hereafter awaits those who fully submit to God and demonstrate faith and devotion throughout their lives. The Koran speaks about rewards in the afterlife:

> Verily, men and women who submit, and men and women who believe, and men and women who are patient, and men and women who are truthful, and men and women who are humble before God, and men and women who give in charity, and men and women who fast, and men and women who guard their chastity, and men and women who remember God much to them, God has promised forgiveness and a great reward. (33:35)

Another motivating factor is fear. In fact, fear of the Last Judgment and eternal damnation is emphasized throughout the Koran. And thus many Muslims are inclined to follow the religious obligations out of fear, rather than in hopes of being rewarded with paradise. Given the strong emphasis on damnation and fear of God, some Muslims who present for psychotherapy may harbor strong feelings, even hopelessness, about their ability to reach paradise and feel that they are doomed to eternal damnation.

Many Muslims conceive of the Day of Judgment as an objective reality. Thus, life after death is a very real concept, and Muslims strive to avoid the harsh judgment of God and gain the rewards of paradise. Hence, many Muslims are likely to accept the idea that our actions are not caused by past events, but rather directed at some future goal, which the individual has set for himself or herself.

Similar teleological strivings can also be found in Christian theology (Kanz, 2001). According to Kanz, conservative Christians perceive the ultimate goal of salvation as an objective reality. Attaining salvation, or escaping damnation, therefore becomes the ultimate goal, the main motivating factor in Islamic theology.

Striving for Superiority

Our striving for superiority is an attempt at overcoming difficulties and gaining a feeling of being complete (Adler, 1956). It is a striving for adaptation in evolutionary terms, an attempt to become as good as one can get. It is not an effort at becoming better than other people. As such, the striving for superiority among Muslims can be found in their effort to submit and surrender themselves to Allah and to show their commitment to God through adherence to His laws (Johansen, 2005). Adler (1958) pointed out that

> The goal of superiority, with each individual, is personal and unique. It depends on the meaning he gives to life; and this meaning is not a matter of words. It is built up in his style of life and runs through it like a strange melody of his own creation. (p. 57)

The concept of striving for superiority is consistent with Islamic teachings. For Muslims, the goal of this striving is not only to follow God's law, but also to experience and possess a deep inner certainty of faith (Haneef, 1996; Johansen, 2005). This striving is consistent with Adler's teleological philosophy as well. Adlerians would consider it psychologically healthy as long as the motivation is aimed at the welfare of others and is not an effort to place the individual above or ahead of others. The main difference between Adler's theory and Islam on this issue is that Adler's concept of the final goal is believed to be largely unknown (e.g., unconscious).

Social Interest, Equality, and the Life Tasks

Islamic theology emphasizes the importance of relationships, encouraging Muslims to cooperate with and care for other people. But this cooperation and care for others is often directed only at other Muslims. And people of other faiths are not perceived as equal to those of Muslim faith. In addition, the religion teaches that men are superior to women. These practices are in stark contrast to Individual Psychology, which recognizes the equal rights and equal value of all individuals.

Ridenour (2001) contrasts the friendly images Islam projects in the West with a rather uncompromising nature of Islam practiced as a political religion in the East. Although this is a very complicated subject matter involving cultural, national, and religious variables, it should be noted that many Muslims, particularly immigrants, are likely to disagree with the Adlerian theory of equality and democracy. Islam in America is very different from the way it is practiced in the East. It is also in transition (Hedayat-Diba, 2006), and the religion is undergoing many different changes, giving rise to even more diversity in terms of practices and beliefs. For example, according to a report by the Gallup Center for Muslim Studies conducted in 2008, American Muslims include some of the world's most liberated Islamic women. According to the report, 59 percent of Muslim-American women work. The survey also concluded that Muslim women in the United States are more likely to attend mosque, attain an education, and maintain employment than they are in other predominantly Muslim countries such as Saudi Arabia and Egypt (Duin, 2009).

As for the life tasks, Islam provides a complete system of how the person should live his or her life. The Koran offers strict guidelines for social relationships and the individual's relations to the community. It also offers guidelines to family life, relations between men and women, and work (Johansen, 2005). The importance of cooperation is of great importance in social relationships.

The life tasks are thoroughly addressed by Islamic teachings. They represent the demands placed on the individual by the human community. According to Individual Psychology, successful fulfillment of the challenges of work, social relationships, and sex, depends on the individual's willingness and ability to cooperate with those around him or her.

Individual Psychology and Islam are both relational philosophies. As with Christianity, Islam places great emphasis on the importance of relating and cooperating with others. According to Haneef (1996):

Cooperation is the rule rather than competition; in fact, competition should consist of trying to excel in being and doing good rather than in outdoing others in acquiring possessions, status or other such aspects of life. Unity of purpose and action, mutual helpfulness and working together are very strongly stressed. (p. 117)

Task of Friendship

The value placed on cooperation versus competition can be found in most religions. It is also something that Adler (1956) stressed when talking about healthy human relationships. A concept that follows this idea of cooperation is the importance of the individual placing his or her attention on others, as opposed to on himself or herself. Focusing on the needs of others and striving to serve the community foster mental health. Muslims also emphasize the importance of avoiding selfishness and greed. In fact, one of the purposes of the zakat (almsgiving) is to avoid selfishness. Muhammad also taught the importance of acting for the sake of God, as opposed to acting for the sake of the self. While discussing the migration from Mecca to Medina, Muhammad is quoted in the Hadith as saying

> Actions are but by intention, and every man shall have but that which he intended. Thus he whose migration was for Allah and His messenger, his migration was for Allah and His messenger, and he whose migration was to achieve some worldly benefit or to take some woman in marriage, his migration was for that for which he migrated." (as cited in Lippman, 2002, p. 30)

This has been interpreted to mean that only those deeds done for the sake of God are righteous. And the individual is encouraged to focus on God, rather than on his or her own needs and desires. The value placed on cooperation with one's fellow human beings is consistent with Adlerian psychology.

Task of Work

The obligation to contribute to society is a religious one. The Koran places great emphasis on the importance of work. The Holy Book teaches that God helps those who are committed to work: "And those who strive hard for Us, We will most certainly guide them in Our paths. For verily God is with those who do right" (29:69).

The task of work is given special importance in that it is considered an act of worship in itself. Thus, the teachings of Islam are not simply to profess one's faith and do nothing for the community. Muslims are expected to demonstrate their faith through sincere deeds and contribution to society. Muslims are expected to contribute in whatever way they can. Thus, children along with adults are expected to use whatever ability and skill they possess, and put these to good use. Islam values both hard work and devotional activities (Johansen, 2005). Therefore, total devotion to praying and meditating is seen as inappropriate if the individual neglects his or her obligation to work and thus his or her responsibilities to the community (Haneef, 1996).

Task of Sex and Marriage

According to Haneef (1996), family life is one of the most important areas of the Islamic system of life. Indeed, the family unit is sacred in Islam (Hedayat-Diba, 2006). And Muslims are often taught to depend on the family for support and assistance. Muslims are also encouraged to marry and have children as early as possible (Hedayat-Diba, 2006). Marriages are often arranged, and Muslims believe that love is something that develops from marriage. It is not customary to fall in love and then marry. In terms of marriage, the Koran allows for polygamy (4:3), but because men cannot maintain equal relationships between their wives (4:129), it recommends that men marry only one woman. Thus, polygamy is discouraged, but not forbidden.

The Koran teaches that "men are superior to women on account of the qualities with which God hath gifted the one above the other" (4:30). Thus, men are seen as the leaders of the family and wives are considered to be companion to their husbands. In terms of family relations, the husband is generally responsible to support the family economically. And although the husband is expected to assist in childrearing, that role belongs primarily to the wife. The responsibilities of women in marital relationships include caring for the household and parenting. These responsibilities are divided, based on what men and women are traditionally thought to handle better than the other (Haneef, 1996).

In view of the fact that Individual Psychology places great emphasis on equality between people, the notion that women are inferior to men creates a major dividing point between the two philosophies (Johansen, 2005). The Adlerian concept of equality—"that people, despite all their individual differences and abilities, have equal claims to dignity and respect" (Dreikurs & Soltz, 1964/1990)—is in direct contradiction to the Koran. Therefore it is likely to pose a major challenge to Adlerian psychotherapists, particularly in couples and family therapy.

To conclude, the various life tasks are clearly addressed in Islam. And Muslims are instructed in how each challenge should be met.

> Adler's tasks of life and the challenges therein are responsibilities that Muslims are faced with directly through their religion. Thus, successful coping in terms of meeting the life tasks is not simply a means of survival but also a religious requirement that is specifically elucidated in the Koran. Therefore, Adler's concept of the life tasks fits well with the views of Muslims. These are challenges that Muslims are well aware of, and their inability to address successfully any of these tasks may lead to social, spiritual, and/or psychological and emotional problems, thereby bringing them into therapy. (Johansen, 2005, p. 181)

ADLERIAN PSYCHOTHERAPY WITH MUSLIMS

In general, Muslims have a negative view of the mental health field. Although these views vary based on education, cultural background, and level of acculturation, mental disorders are often thought to be a result of loss of faith. So Muslims tend to be very fearful of mental illness, given that a loss of faith is believed to result in damnation in the life hereafter. Furthermore, the expression of negative feelings is not well accepted among Muslims. Physical symptoms, however, are more acceptable (Hedayat-Diba, 2006).

The Adlerian conceptualization of mental illness as discouragement rather than as a pathological condition may offer these clients a more positive view of their presenting concerns and encourage them to engage in the therapeutic process. Given its view of mental illness, Adlerian treatment attempts to increase the client's feelings of self-worth and confidence. For Muslims who often perceive their symptoms as resulting from a lack of faith, addressing the purpose of symptoms and learning how they help the client reach his or her goals can be very encouraging (Johansen, 2005). The emphasis placed on personal responsibility and action in Adlerian psychotherapy is also consistent with the Islamic faith.

Muslims who are experiencing emotional and psychological problems are likely to seek help from their spiritual leaders before seeking out a therapist. When Muslims do present for psychotherapeutic services, however, they tend to present with marital problems, immigration problems, spouse abuse, and problems with disciplining children

(Aswad and Gray, 1996). Consider the case of Shafia, a married woman in her mid-thirties with two small children.

Shafia brought her six-year-old son in for treatment, asking specifically for play therapy to help with disruptive and hyperactive behavior. Upon intake she reported that the boy had been disruptive all his life. He refused to listen to directions, he had difficulty sitting quietly, and he would frequently antagonize his father. The therapist recommended that the boy engage in play therapy, but also recommended that Shafia and her husband meet with her on a regular basis to address parenting strategies. Shafia explained that her husband was not supportive of counseling, and that he did not understand how counseling could be helpful. As the discussion turned to her husband and his interactions with the family, Shafia explained that there was no intimacy between the two. She explained that she slept in the children's bed to keep them from being afraid of the dark. She also expressed a concern about the possibility of having more children. She felt overwhelmed with managing the two boys, and sleeping in bed with her sons allowed her to avoid sexual intimacy with her husband, as she feared she would become pregnant again. Shifting the focus off the children and onto the parents' relationship was a slow yet necessary process. Shafia needed help, not only with her children, but also in her relationship with her husband. She felt alone, isolated, and overwhelmed.

Adlerian therapists can work effectively with Muslim clients, as long as they remain knowledgeable about the teachings and guidance provided by the Koran. Issues such as alcohol, sexuality, marriage and divorce, abortion, and birth control are beyond the scope of this chapter, yet they are important issues that the therapist needs to understand and pay attention to.

Psychotherapists who work with Muslim clients should be connected with the mosques and other Islamic institutions in the community. The support these institutions can provide can be a great ancillary service to psychotherapy. In addition to a general understanding of Islam, the therapists should be familiar with the client's cultural, economic, and educational background, as well as his or her level of acculturation. Knowledge of the various subtraditions of Islam, such as Sunnism, Shi'ism, Sufism, and African American Islam will also be helpful to the therapist.

Clinicians also need to remember that Muslims understand the Koran as being the only truth. Thus, therapists should be familiar with the basic teachings of the Holy Book and be open to incorporating them into therapy sessions. Last but not least, Muslims view the Koran as a complete set of guidelines for how to live one's life. Thus, guidance is what they expect from their religion. So guiding the client in a way that is consistent with the teachings of the Koran will set the stage for a trusting and collaborative relationship with the Muslim client.

Case Example

Altan, a 24-year-old Turkish man studying economics in the United States, came for therapy because of intrusive thoughts and excessive anxiety. He could not stop himself from thinking that people were criticizing him whenever he was spending time with friends or fellow students. As a result of this imagined criticism, he found himself feeling nervous almost all the time. Although he considered himself a devout Muslim, he did not attend Mosque, saying he was unsure whether it would be appropriate for him to go. He felt he had broken his promise to be a good Muslim and questioned whether or not any religious community would accept him.

Altan was the middle of three children. He had an older brother who had finished a master's degree in computer programming in England. His younger sister lived at home in Turkey with his parents. Education was highly valued in Altan's family, and both boys were expected to travel abroad to become educated. Altan followed in his brother's footsteps and completed his Bachelor's degree in computer programming. But when he went to graduate school, he decided to pursue a degree in economics, believing he would find it much more rewarding than working with computers. Altan was near the end of his first year in graduate school when he entered therapy.

Altan described himself as a religious man. But the five years he had spent in the United States had made it difficult for him to follow his religious practices. For the first few years in college, he decided to immerse himself in the American college culture. He dated, partied, and drank heavily for some time. He also neglected the celebration of Ramadan one year, which left him feeling very shameful. Toward the end of his college experience, Altan decided to stop using alcohol and made an effort to find a religious community. He connected with the members of a nearby mosque, but lost contact shortly after when he transferred to a new university to pursue his master's degree.

A lifestyle assessment was conducted over the course of the first few sessions. His early recollections revealed that Altan wanted to be a good person. It was important to him to do what others expected and to follow rules. He viewed other people as more knowledgeable, critical, and demanding. As a result, he had concluded that he needed to go along with the demands of others in order to be perceived as a good person and to be accepted.

His desire to go along with others had led Altan to engage in alcohol use and some experimentation with marijuana, while trying to immerse himself in the American culture. Looking back at his experience in college, Altan expressed regret that he had decided to go along with alcohol and marijuana use in order to fit in. "At the time," he said, "I just wanted to make friends. I forgot about my responsibilities as a Muslim." Altan neglected his religious obligations in order to spend time with new friends and explore his host country. Now he found himself feeling guilty and anxious about the consequences of his behavior. He was worried his father might somehow find out about his misdeeds when he returned to Turkey, but he was also afraid that God would punish him. Over the course of therapy, Altan's loss of faith and fears of damnation became increasingly evident.

Altan's symptoms made sense, given his lifestyle convictions. Having violated his own standards, he found himself experiencing guilt feelings and anxiety related to the consequences of his behavior. He also felt that people somehow knew what a bad person he was and that they were secretly criticizing him. This reinforced the idea that he was unacceptable and led him to distance himself from others.

Learning how his lifestyle convictions influenced his feelings was helpful to Altan. He had been secretly questioning whether God was punishing him with relentless anxiety. Little by little he learned that he was responsible for his own feelings and that he had the power to change those emotions as he gradually began to challenge his own thinking.

Altan continued to process his sinful deeds and began to understand how he had so easily let go of his religious practices when he started college. He was alone in a foreign country, he had no religious affiliation, and he felt a need to explore and follow the directions of others. Given his circumstances, it made sense to do what he did. Although he made what he considered to be sinful choices, the possibility of forgiveness was promising.

Altan and his therapist discussed the issue of forgiveness over the course of several weeks. Altan eventually decided that he needed to reconnect with God, and so he found a Mosque where he decided to attend services. This allowed him a place to finally ask God for forgiveness. But Altan also felt he needed his father's forgiveness. And sharing his sins with his father and asking him to forgive him was a scary prospect. Fortunately, over the course of his last year in school, he decided to share his concerns with his older brother, who had already moved back to the homeland. When he learned that his brother had had similar experiences, he felt relieved and decided to tell his father about what he had done. His father, although disappointed, forgave him.

Altan's therapy was successful. He learned to recognize his maladaptive convictions, and he found the courage to reconnect with his religion and other Muslims despite feeling disliked and ostracized. Having received his father's forgiveness, Altan felt he could start over. His worries about what other people thought of him were no longer an issue, and he had found peace with himself.

In an effort to establish a safe and trusting therapeutic relationship with Altan, the therapist spent the first few sessions educating him about psychotherapy and the role of the therapist. He pointed out that, although he (the therapist) might be an expert in psychology, Altan was an expert on himself and his religion. This allowed Altan to feel comfortable educating his therapist about his religion and his religious practices, and they were able to have open discussions about his religious belief. In their discussions phrases such as *mental illness* and *anxiety disorders* were replaced with the terms *loss of faith* and *feelings of discouragement.* This allowed Altan to feel comfortable about sharing his feelings of fearing that there was something wrong with him.

SUMMARY

Muslims strongly believe that nobody stands between the individual and God, so their religion is one without clergy, saints, hierarchy, or sacraments (Lippman, 2002). Islamic beliefs and practices are drawn from two sacred texts, the Koran and the Hadith. The Koran is the Holy Book of God's revelations to humankind. The text is believed to be the literal word of God handed down to man through the prophet Muhammad. The second source of Islamic doctrine is the Hadith. The Hadith is a compilation of Muhammad's statements, practices, and Koranic interpretations.

The Islamic philosophy of human nature is consistent with Adlerian psychology. The principles of soft determinism, striving for superiority, teleology, holism, and social interest fit with the values and beliefs of the Islamic faith. As for the life tasks, the Koran provides detailed guidelines for how people should act in regard to community and family (Johansen, 2005). Islam is an elaborate system of ethical, spiritual, and social values that lay out in detail how people should live their lives.

However, the issue of equality between men and women, and democracy are major dividing points between the two philosophies. Psychotherapists should be mindful of these differences when working with Muslim clients. On the other hand, Adlerian therapists can work effectively with Muslim clients as long as they remain knowledgeable about the teachings and guidance provided by the Koran and are familiar with the client's educational and cultural background and his or her level of acculturation.

SUGGESTED READINGS

Haneef, S. (1996). *What everyone should know about Islam and Muslims.* Chicago: Library of Islam.
Kobeisy, A. N. (2004). *Counseling American Muslims: Understanding the Faith and Helping the People.* Westport, CT: Praeger.
Lippman, T. (2002). *Understanding Islam: An introduction to the Muslim World.* New York: Plume.
Smith, H. (1991). *The World Religions.* NY: Harper Collins.

8

Adler and the Paths to God: Hindu Philosophy and Individual Psychology

Whatever and whichever way men approach Me, even so do I accept them; whatever paths they may choose finally lead to Me — ***Lord Krishna***

Hinduism is an exceptionally diverse religion found primarily in India, where about 80 percent of the population is Hindu. There are hundreds of various divisions of the Hindu religion, depending on language and geography, caste, and community. These vast differences within the tradition make it very difficult to define exactly what Hinduism is. With a four-thousand-year history, Hinduism has no specific creed or teacher that is seen as central to the religion. There is no specific theological system, nor is there a single system of morality. And although there are several holy texts, there is no single holy book similar to the Christian Bible or the Muslim Koran.

Defining Hinduism is no easy task. In fact there is no specific definition that encapsulates the diversity found within the religion. One might say that a Hindu is someone who adheres to or worships the gods Vishnu or Shiva, or the goddess Shakti, or their incarnations, spouses, or offspring. But even this definition is not sufficient to describe a religion as complex as Hinduism. Narayanan (2003) points out that regional traditions and practices are often more important to Hindus than any overarching Hindu concept. Consequently, sometimes it may be appropriate to talk about various Hindu customs and beliefs and at other

143

times to talk of a specific Hindu tradition. Yet despite these variations in practice and worship, there are central tenets that unify Hinduism as a religion. The core belief in Hinduism is the belief in Brahman—the Supreme Being. Brahman is an infinite universal life force that cannot be described. Suffice to say that Hindus view Brahman as encompassing existence. Hindus also believe in the endless cycle of birth, death, and rebirth (samsara), and that the highest goal for any individual is to achieve liberation of the soul from the continuous cycle of life and death. The paths to liberation are also a central tenet of Hinduism.

In addition to these core beliefs, there are four main doctrines that are key to understanding Hinduism and with which psychotherapists working with Hindus should have some familiarity: the four stages of life, the four goals of life, the four paths to God, and karma and reincarnation. In particular, the doctrine of the paths to God is central to Hinduism. This doctrine emphasizes the Hindu religion's tolerance of all sorts of beliefs and practices. For example, one can be a monotheist, a polytheist, or even a nontheist and still practice Hinduism. One of the most basic assumptions of Hinduism is that people are different, and its insistence that people are distinct from one another calls for a variety of paths to God.

Little has been written on Hinduism and Individual Psychology. A review of the literature resulted in only one article that addressed the lifestyles of women of Hindu origin (Reddy & Hanna, 1995). As we begin to examine the basic ideas of Hindu philosophy, many parallels can be found with Adler's Individual Psychology. The teleological approach to Adler's theory appears to be similar to that of the Hindu concept of life's four goals. Both philosophies are based upon a teleological understanding of human life. There is also agreement in terms of the individual's freedom to choose and personal responsibility, although this issue is sometimes contradictory to the concept of karma. Hindu scripture emphasizes the importance of selflessness, social contribution, psychological insight, and various roles or responsibilities throughout the lifespan, all of which are consistent with Individual Psychology. On the other hand, there are major differences between the two philosophies to which Adlerian psychotherapists should pay close attention when working with Hindu clients. Hindus often have very rigid ideas of gender roles, and women are generally seen as inferior beings despite their complementary role in family life. The other aspect of Hinduism that runs contrary to Adler's strong belief in human equality is the caste system.

The purpose of this chapter is to review the basic teachings of Hinduism and compare and contrast those ideas to the philosophy of Alfred Adler. The stages and wants of life, the paths to God, Karma and reincarnation, and the caste system are addressed. Finally, issues that are relevant to psychotherapy are addressed in the context of the life tasks and the four phases of Adlerian psychotherapy.

HISTORY AND TEACHINGS OF HINDUISM

Unlike Christianity, Judaism, Islam, and Buddhism, the Hindu religion has no central figure or founder. The exact year or even century of its beginnings is also uncertain. Most scholars believe that Hinduism originated among the ancient indigenous cultures of India around four thousand years ago (Narayanan, 2003).

The early stage of Hinduism is marked by the composition of orally transmitted sacred texts over the course of several centuries. These texts hold the many key concepts that today are considered Hinduism. Unlike the other world religions discussed in this volume, whose foundations are marked by unusual or exceptional individuals, Hinduism is a result of the composition of these sacred texts.

Hinduism started with men who had perfected themselves through meditation (Rishis) and were said to have heard the eternal truths of God. These revelations were later transmitted to their disciples telepathically (Viswanathan, 1992). For long periods of time there was no Hindu literature, as these truths were passed on orally through the generations. They were eventually written in Sanskrit in the form of the Vedas.

Hinduism is considered a living religion in that it is constantly evolving and changing itself. Hindus do not claim to have a monopoly on wisdom, and they encourage all pursuits of understanding God. They strive to make people strong in their faith, no matter what their religion may be. And because of this there are no Hindu missionaries attempting to preach and convert people to Hinduism (Sharma, 2006). Instead, Hinduism is a religion that is constantly absorbing new ideas and philosophies. It is also constantly adapting to the new developments in science and technology. In the quote from the Bhagavad Gita (4:11) that begins this chapter, Lord Krishna speaks to the freedom of thought within the religion. Hence, Hinduism does not project itself as the only way to God-realization and it accepts all kinds of thoughts, beliefs, and religious faiths.

Although they do not portray themselves as having a monopoly on wisdom, Hindus believe there is only one truth and that people call this truth different things. So from a Hindu perspective, a Christian, a Muslim, a Jew, and a Hindu are all the same. The Bhagavad Gita states that in whatever form a person chooses to worship God, he or she is on the right path toward God-realization. Hinduism adopts a phenomenological perspective, as do Adlerians, in that whatever the truth may be, whenever an individual finds it, he or she simply calls it different things. Given that every path toward God is considered the right one for that individual, nobody can be lost according to Hinduism (Viswanathan, 1992).

Temple worship is an important aspect of Hindu religious life. Worship generally consists of viewing a deity, making an offering, and getting the blessing of the divine being. Hindu temples do not have places to sit, and the worshippers usually stand while they view the deity in its shrine. Worship is usually not congregational, where people gather for communal worship at specific times. However, Hindus may gather in public halls to listen to religious leaders or to sing religious songs (Narayanan, 2003). The Hindu religion also has numerous rituals and religious celebrations, marking an individual's transition from one stage of life to another (Narayanan, 2003). For some, the life-cycle sacraments begin at birth. Others consider marriage to be the actual beginning of a person's life, and so the life-cycle sacraments begin with marriage. Some of these rituals are consistent for all Hindus, but many are local celebrations unique to individual communities.

The Gods of Hinduism

There are a tremendous number of Gods in Hinduism, and their roles and relationships are extremely complicated. However, a brief overview is in order. Although Hindus often acknowledge many deities, they only consider one to be supreme. Some Hindus, however, may consider all gods to be equal, but they usually worship one particular god they consider to be their favorite (Narayanan, 2003).

The main God in Hinduism is Brahman, the indefinable, timeless God. From Brahman came Aum (or Om) who is also a divine being. From Aum emerged Kali (Mother God) and the Godhead. The Godhead then divided into the Trinity: Brahma the creator; Vishnu the Preserver; and Shiva the Destroyer (Narayanan, 2003; Parrinder, 1985; Viswanathan, 1992). Of these gods, Shiva the Destroyer is well known and frequently misunderstood by Westerners. Shiva is often thought to be a wrathful

God that seeks to cause evil. But, to the contrary, Shiva, the Destroyer plays an important role in the cycle of birth, death, and rebirth. Shiva recognizes the completion of one form of existence and aids in the transformation from one form to another (Sharma, 2006). Thus, Shiva is sometimes referred to as Shiva the Completer.

One of the best known gods of Hinduism is Lord Krishna, which is the eighth incarnation of the god Vishnu (Parrinder, 1985). When a god becomes incarnate, Hindus refer to that human form as an avatar. Lord Krishna is by many Hindus considered the "full" descent of the deity Vishnu, the lord of grace, mercy, and peace (Narayanan, 2003). Lord Krishna is often depicted as playing the flute, representing the spread of the melody of love to people. He is the personification of love and compassion for all living beings. Thus, he represents the very essence of what Adlerians refer to as social interest—love and compassion towards one's fellow human beings.

It may seem contradictory that Hindus speak of worshipping the one and only God, yet they simultaneously recognize and accept the worship of a number of other Gods. But Hinduism recognizes one God expressed in different forms. God is formless and timeless, and has no definition. Because Hindus recognize that God is perceived by humans in different forms, the form God takes is not as important as is the act of worshiping a symbol that points to something beyond the individual. Hinduism urges people to form a lifelong attachment to the God they choose to worship. In this way, the path to God becomes accessible (Smith, 1991).

There are countless numbers of other, lesser gods in the Hindu religion. Psychotherapists working with Hindu clients need to examine which gods their clients favor and worship. Hinduism encompasses a rich and colorful tradition, and, given the vast range of traditions within the religion, psychotherapists need to take time to learn about their client's particular values, religious beliefs, and practices. The therapist will need to understand not only what god the patient worships, but, more importantly the patient's perceptions of that god. What kind of god is it? What are the mythological stories associated with the deity? What does the deity expect or demand of the individual? What is the nature of the relationship between the individual and the deity? These and many other spiritual questions must be raised if the therapist wants to fully understand the patient's personal religion. Understanding why patients admire a particular deity can give the Adlerian therapist a glimpse into the patient's style of life.

Myths are particularly important among Hindus. Ethical and moral values, rules regarding behavior and worship, and other religious beliefs are often derived from the life stories of the various gods. Take for example the sacredness of cows amongst Hindus. Cows are associated with Lord Krishna. Myth has it that as a child, Krishna's playmates were cowherds. It is also been said that he had a fondness for dairy products such as milk and butter. Cows also appear in many other religious epics, and Hindus believe that the animal plays a role in guiding the human soul toward God (Sharma, 2006). Hence myths play an important role in the lives of Hindus. Many myths are central to the religion, but mythologies also vary depending on geography, language, and community.

Religious Texts

Although Hinduism does not have a specific holy book similar to the Christian Bible, many Hindus refer to the Bhagavad Gita as the Hindu holy book. The Bhagavad Gita (song of the Blessed One) constitutes a conversation between Krishna and Arjuna (who represents the human soul) on a field of battle. Krishna teaches Arjuna about the nature of the human soul, God, and how to reach liberation. Throughout the story, Krishna tells Arjuna that God can be reached through devotion, selfless action, and knowledge (Narayanan, 2003).

Other important scriptures include the Vedas (knowledge), of which there are four volumes. The most famous of the Vedas is the Rig Veda. Also well known are the Upanishads, consisting of 108 books containing the teachings on the nature of the self (atman) as one with Brahman. The Upanishads reveals the spiritual truths and way to liberation from the endless cycle of birth, death, and rebirth (samsara).

The authorship of these Hindu scriptures is unknown. The Hindu scriptures were all written by anonymous authors, and so it is uncertain exactly who may have written the various texts. The question as to why nobody took credit for the work still remains a mystery. Viswanathan (1992) speculated that leaving the authors unknown was a statement of how these scriptures are eternal truths, and thus questioning authorship would be fruitless.

The Four Stages of Life

Hindus believe that the individual moves through four stages in his or her lifetime: student, householder, retirement, and sannyas (spiritual pursuit) (Sharma, 2006). The first part of life involves learning. Children are often expected to learn and be educated in an area consistent with the family's caste. Unfortunately for many children, those who do not achieve academically are frequently a source of embarrassment to the family, which may lead them to seek psychotherapy for their children. Adolescents are also expected to choose a career path that is considered prestigious. This expectation opens the door for conflict between parents and their children when the child chooses a career that is perceived as having low status or is otherwise contrary to the family values.

The second stage of life often begins with marriage. As a householder, the Hindu individual focuses on work, providing for family, and providing for the community. Thus, the stage of householder stretches beyond the home to include work. Because Adlerians consider the student role an aspect of the work task, the student stage and householder stage both parallel what Adler (1956) referred to as the tasks of work. Furthermore, the focus on family, community, and marriage has obvious implications for the tasks of love and society. So in this stage of life, the individual is focused outward. He or she concentrates on meeting the needs of others and contributing to the community.

Retirement makes up the third stage of life. Here, the individual turns his or her attention inward. As the person's physical ability to contribute declines, Hinduism teaches that one must look inward and attempt to understand who one really is (Sharma, 2006). As Hinduism holds that all final answers are within, the individual searches within himself or herself to find the truth. A short scriptural stanza quoted in Viswanathan (1992, p. 4) illustrates this point:

> Nobody knows what is right or what is wrong;
> Nobody knows what is good or what is bad;
> There is a deity residing within you;
> Find it out and obey its commands.

Building on the search within during retirement, Hindus search for salvation in the fourth and final stage of life. According to the Bhagavad Gita, the final stage of life, sannyas, is defined as "one who neither hates nor loves anything" (Zimmer, 1951, p. 158). It involves the pursuit of salvation, to be with God. A sannyasin is someone who has become unattached from the world and the things in it. He or she has no expectations and has achieved freedom (Sharma, 2006).

Addressing the stages of life in psychotherapy can be useful for both therapist and client. For example, in terms of assessment, being mindful of an individual's stage of life gives the therapist a framework from which to evaluate potential concerns. A client in the householder stage is more likely to be concerned with issues such as providing for one's family and developing a successful career than someone in the last two stages of life, where he or she is turning attention inward. A client presenting for psychotherapy in the sannyas stage may be more likely to seek help for spiritual and religious issues.

As we move through these stages of life, what makes it seem meaningful? What do we want? What do we seek? Striving toward some goal is something we find everywhere in life. Adlerians recognize that there are the long-term goals of the lifestyle and the immediate goals of any given situation. In its own way, Hinduism addresses both. Hindu scriptures teach us that people want four things. The main aims or wants of life are Kama (sexual love), Artha (material gain), Dharma (right conduct), and Moksha (salvation, liberation) (Viswanathan, 1992). These goals are all natural and worthy and should be pursued with both physical and metal effort.

The first pursuit is the search for sensual pleasure and love. Hindus view pleasure as a natural thing that should be pursued, and although pleasure seeking has not been made the highest goal, it is certainly not condemned. As long as the basic rules of morality are obeyed, people are free to seek all the pleasure they want. Smith (1991) expressed the Hindu attitude toward the search for pleasure: "If pleasure is what you want, do not suppress the desire. Seek it intelligently" (p. 14). But as much as people may seek pleasure, Hinduism acknowledges that there will come a time when sensual pleasures cease to satisfy the individual. When this happens, attention turns to material gain.

The second major goal of life is worldly success. Included here are things such as wealth, power, recognition, and fame. As with the search for pleasure, Hinduism encourages the individual to seek worldly success, arguing that such success is essential not only for survival, but also to encourage the individual to partake in civic duties. Personal success is also seen as contributing to the individual's sense of dignity and self-respect (Smith, 1991). People are encouraged to seek worldly success, as long as they think that is what they want and need. Denying or repressing our desires will do us no good. However, the individual's search for material gain will also cease to satisfy. This leads us to the third goal of life, duty and contribution.

The third goal of life is the pursuit of right conduct, or the desire to serve others. This goal is consistent with the Adlerian concept of social interest. Here, the individual desires to give back to the community, to be selfless, and to help others. But as much as the pursuit of duty and selflessness are essential for salvation, Hindus believe it will eventually cease to provide meaning to life. Therefore the final human goal must lie elsewhere.

The most important goal of life, according to Hinduism, is to be one with God (Brahman). Thus, pleasure, success, and right conduct are not the ultimate goals in life; salvation is. We all want joy, knowledge, and life, but we want these things indefinitely. We want release from the finitude that restricts human life. Hinduism teaches us that this can be achieved through God-realization. Hinduism assumes the existence of a true self (atman), which is hidden beneath a false self (asrava). The main goal of life is to discard the false self and thereby attain liberation. Only by realizing that the hidden self (atman) is no less than Brahman can an individual come to experience being one with God. Hindus refer to this experience as satchitananda (sat = being, chit = awareness, ananda = bliss) (Sharma, 2006). It is here that the individual can overcome ignorance and desire and achieve release from the endless cycle of death and rebirth.

Hinduism's discussion of life goals is particularly interesting to Adlerians. The idea that people pursue four main goals throughout their lives suggests that our behaviors are goal oriented. The first three goals may be considered part of the short-term goals of life, whereas the goal of salvation parallels Adler's concept of the final goal of superiority. The difference between salvation and the goal of superiority is that salvation is an objective reality (as is the case with Christian's and Muslim's idea of salvation), which the individual is well aware of. The goal of superiority, however, is a non-conscious fictive goal. What is important to note, however, is that from the perspective of Hinduism, people live their lives searching for the divine (Pargament, 2007). This search for salvation becomes the main motivating factor for Hindus. If salvation is the ultimate goal in life, then how do we find it? Hinduism's answer to this question is what we will turn to next.

The Four Paths to God

Hindu's believe that there are several spiritual paths to God, and they view other religions as legitimate alternative paths. However, Hindu scriptures address four main paths, also known as yogas. The goal of the yogas is to unite the individual with God and to maintain that closeness and living out of it. The first step of any yoga is to cultivate a moral base that includes habits such as truthfulness, noninjury, self-control, selflessness, discipline, and a compelling desire to reach the goal (Smith, 1991).

Jnana Yoga—Finding God through Knowledge

Because people are different, each must seek God in a way that fits his or her personality style. Jnana yoga is designed for those who have a strong reflective and intellectual mode. This path is not necessarily for intelligent people, but for those who live in their heads and who daydream frequently. People who fit this personality style are encouraged to meditate and contemplate. Hinduism proposes several ideas for contemplation that are designed to encourage the individual to shift his or her focus from the finite self to the infinite or divine self (Sharma, 2006; Smith, 1991). This insight may be achieved through listening to scriptures, intensive reflection, and thinking of oneself as Spirit. One example of how to separate oneself from the small self is to think of the self in third person (Smith, 1991). Instead of thinking "I am walking along the road," the person may think "There goes Rahul walking along the road." Jnana yoga is a difficult path to God; one that Hindus consider easier is Bhakti yoga, the path of love.

Bhakti Yoga—Finding God through Love

Bhakti yoga is the most popular of the yogas. The goal of this path is to love God for love's sake alone. Christianity is considered a form of Bhakti yoga. The path to God through love is illustrated in the story of a sixteenth-century mystical poet named Tulsidas:

> During his early married life he was inordinately fond of his wife, to the point that he could not abide her absence even for one day. One day she went to visit her parents. Before the day was half over, Tulsidas turned up at her side, whereupon his wife exclaimed, "How passionately attached to me you are! If only you could shift your attachment to God, you would reach him in no time." So I would," thought Tulsidas. He tried it, and it worked. (Smith, 1991, p. 32)

This path is best suited for those with an emotional bent. Here, symbolism becomes very important. Hinduism recognizes that people often need to have a physical object to love. Therefore, Hindus who follow this type of yoga will form an attachment to a particular god that they love and admire. Whether that god is Lord Krishna, Vishnu, Shiva, or Jesus Christ, is irrelevant. What matters is that the individual devotes himself or herself to an image of God and seeks to love that God ceaselessly and unconditionally. The goal of Bhakti yoga is not to identify with God as in Jnana yoga, but to love God with every part of his or her being (Smith, 1991).

Karma Yoga—Finding God through Work

For individuals who are active, Karma yoga may be an appropriate way to seek God. Because work is an essential part of living, Hinduism teaches that God may be found through work, and people can choose to devote themselves entirely to work in an effort to find God. However, when attempting to find God through work, one must work for God, not for oneself. "Throw yourself into your work with everything you have, only do so wisely" (Smith, 1991, p. 37). So a calm focus and right concentration are important—performing each task as if it is the only thing that matters. Again, we see the importance of focusing one's attention outside oneself. Hinduism emphasizes this point repeatedly and believes that God can be found only by focusing on something beyond the self.

The Karma yogi can be combined with Jnana and Bhakti yoga as well. Some may approach work in a reflective and intellectual manner, whereas others may approach their labor with love. Again, the goal of the yoga is to transcend the finite self, either by identifying the self with God or by shifting one's focus and love toward a personal God.

Raja Yoga—Finding God through Psychological Experimentation

Raja yoga is designed for those who are of a scientific bent. As Westerners tend to think of science being directed toward the physical world, Raja yoga involves experimentation directed at the individual's mind. The Raja yogi experiments with his or her own mind by engaging in various mental exercises and then observing their phenomenological effects. The goal of Raja yoga is to discover one's true nature by meditation and other mental exercises. By uncovering and exploring the deepest layers of one's own mind, the person hopes to find God. No yoga will be a perfect fit for every person. People are different, and so they may need to experiment with any combination of the paths to reach God.

The paths to God can be used effectively in Adlerian psychotherapy. Therapists may encourage clients to follow a particular path based on their self-ideals. Consider Raman, a 56-year-old workaholic, a "driver" (Mosak, 1971), who acted as if the more he did, the more he was. Believing he needed to be number one and outdo his colleagues, he worked tirelessly to compete with them. After his second heart attack, he reluctantly sought psychotherapy after pressure from his family. Being that he was a very religious man, he was encouraged to seek God through his work, karma yoga. In this way he could continue devoting himself to his work, but rather than compete with colleagues, he focused on working for God. Over the course of therapy, he learned to put less pressure on himself, as work was no longer a competition, but a path to God.

Karma and Reincarnation

The belief that karma determines one's place in the next life is a doctrine central to Hinduism. Karma literally means work (as in karma yoga), but the doctrine of karma means the moral law of cause and effect. Every action, thought, and feeling has a consequence. Moral behaviors result in good consequences, whereas immoral or wrong behavior results in negative consequences. This concept of law and effect is extended beyond our present lives. Thus, a person (soul) born into unfavorable circumstances is experiencing the consequences of his or her bad actions in past lives. On the other hand, someone who is born into favorable circumstances is believed to be benefiting from his or her past good deeds.

As the human body dies, the soul takes on another form. This process of endless passage through life, death, and rebirth is known as reincarnation. Smith (1991) points out that, at the subhuman level, the process is automatic, and the soul passes through a series of increasingly complex bodies until it finally gets a human body. With its entry into a human body, the soul attains self-consciousness, and the automatic process ends. With self-consciousness come freedom and responsibility. Consequently, the doctrine of karma suggests that people have personal responsibility and the freedom to choose. The concept is often misused, however, to avoid personal responsibility: for example, "It's my karma; there is nothing I can do about it. There is nothing I can do to change anything." I will discuss this issue further in the section on soft determinism.

The Caste System

The caste system is one of the most well-known and most condemned facets of Hinduism. Viswanathan (1992) referred to it as the "greatest curse" (p. 250) on the religion. The caste system is said to have developed sometime during the second millennium BCE. As Aryan immigrants made their way to India, the clashes between different cultures led to the dividing of people into four different castes: Brahmanas (priestly class), Kshatriyas (royal and fighter class), Vaishyas (business class), and Shudras (labor class).

The Brahmanas are the intellectuals of society. This caste includes religious leaders and those who study and spread ideas, such as philosophers and teachers. Kshatriyas include those who work in government, particularly the military. These individuals are considered to be good at organization and tend to be efficient in their efforts to complete tasks. The Vaishyas, or business class, include farmers, craftsmen, and other business people. The labor class, Shudras, include the unskilled workers, those considered adept only at following orders and supporting the other castes in their affairs.

Over time however, a fifth caste developed—the untouchables. The development of this caste has shed a significant negative light on Hindu society. Contrary to all Hindu ideals, the appearance of the untouchable caste became a source of grave depreciation of Hindu society as well as of its religion. Although the Indian government officially abolished the practice of untouchability in 1949, the caste system in general has led to a series of social problems among Hindus. With the development of castes grew a complex collection of subcastes. Throughout history over twenty-five thousand subcastes have been documented. And about eighteen hundred castes existed at one time within the main Brahmin caste alone. (Viswanathan, 1992). Today, there are about three thousand different castes within the Indian society (Smith, 1991).

The caste system has led to a series of problems with social intercourse (Smith, 1991). Prohibition of intermarriage across castes is one such problem, but the main challenge has to do with social inequality. Hereditary boundaries developed as a result of the system, such that any individual would remain in the caste into which he or she was born. Higher castes have also had more and better opportunities available to them in terms of education, resources, and opportunities for material gain. There may be a high level of equality within castes, but the inequalities among castes are still very much in play to this day.

PHILOSOPHY OF HUMAN NATURE

In our discussion of the four stages of life, the four wants of life, karma, and the caste system, several parallels can be drawn between Individual Psychology and the Hindu philosophy of human nature. Our assumption that people are goal oriented, that they have the freedom to choose, and that they strive for superiority are assumptions maintained by both systems. The phenomenological approach of both philosophies is also interesting to observe. Where Adlerian therapists must pay particular attention, however, is on the issue of equality. Hinduism certainly subscribes to strong traditional roles of men and women, and women are often viewed as inferior to men, despite their perceived useful roles. Some Hindu clients may also carry with them strong feelings about the worth of other people belonging to lower castes.

Phenomenology

Hindu philosophy acknowledges that people see things from their own private perspective. In respect to how we view God, Hindus are very open to individual differences. Viswanathan (1992) discussed this issue and recognized that "When someone calls 'It' Jesus Christ, 'It' comes as Jesus Christ; when someone calls 'It' Lord Krishna, 'It' comes as Lord Krishna" (p. 6).

Hinduism accepts this concept and welcomes the individual differences among people's beliefs. Similarly, Adlerians both recognize and respect the idea that the individual's private reality is subjective and that a person acts in the world according to the way the world is perceived (Shulman, 1977). Given all the different gods available for worship to Hindus and the diversity of beliefs, practices, and traditions associated with each, therapists must take time to learn from the patient about his or her personal god and attempt to understand his or her subjective experience of that relationship.

Soft Determinism

The quote by Lord Krishna that begins this chapter speaks of universal acceptance. But the statement also alludes to the individual's freedom to choose his or her path to God, thus implying that the individual has free will. This creative power to seek God in whatever way we decide suggests that we are in fact active participants and not merely reactors to our environment. Given this fundamental principle, we find that people take an active part in giving personal meaning to life. Hinduism teaches that meaning is found in God, but how we find God is entirely up to us.

Karma, a doctrine central to Hinduism, is often believed to contradict the notion of soft-determinism when it in fact implies freedom to choose. Hinduism informs us that when a soul is reborn and given a human body, the soul is also given self-consciousness. Along with the awareness of self come freedom and responsibility. The misperceptions of karma result from people comparing it to fate, thereby suggesting that our circumstances and our future are determined. Smith (1991) discussed the issue of karma and free will. His statement has an Adlerian tone.

> This idea of karma and the completely moral universe it implies carries two important psychological corollaries. First, it commits the Hindu who understands it to complete personal responsibility. Each individual is wholly responsible for his or her present condition and will have exactly the future he or she is now creating. Most people are not willing to admit this. . . . They want excuses, someone to blame so that they may be exonerated. This, say the Hindus, is immature. (p. 64)

Hinduism speaks of free will, yet our ability to exercise that free will is limited by the circumstances into which we are born, our karma. Similarly, Adlerians accept the individual's freedom to choose, while acknowledging that our environment as well as our genetic inheritance places certain limitations on us. The individual is free to choose within those limitations. For instance, Janaki, a woman in her mid-40s, complained to her counselor that her suffering was a result of mistakes in her past life. Her husband and two children had been killed in a car accident ten years earlier and she still found herself feeling depressed and unable to move on with her life. She had convinced herself that she was doomed to suffer because of her past mistakes. Here, both Individual Psychology and the doctrine of karma would acknowledge that she is powerless to change the loss of her family. But, moving forward, she is free to choose how to respond to her circumstances. From the perspective of Hinduism, she could choose to make an effort to live responsibly while pursuing God, instead of blaming herself for the accident. Acknowledging the devastating loss and moving on with her life would result in better circumstances in her next life. It would also improve her current circumstances, allowing her to live a healthier and happier life.

When a client seeks to avoid responsibility by pointing to karma as fatalistic, the therapist may need to reeducate that client about the doctrine. It should be noted that Hindus are not the only clients who use karma as an excuse to avoid responsibility and to keep from changing their behavior. Many non-Hindu clients often misunderstand the concept of karma and use it to avoid responsibility.

In addition to the implications of personal responsibility inherent in the doctrine, Sharma (2006) discussed two important uses of karma in psychotherapy. First, it can help clients move past difficult life circumstances. Karma implies that there are no accidents. When bad things happen to people, it is the result of wrong deeds in past lives and must be accepted as such. Thus, asking why something happened is a useless activity. Second, clients can come to accept that not everything can or has to be experienced in this lifetime. Sometimes certain experiences are not available to us. Some may not be able to have children, or follow their dreams in terms of education or a career. Others may be limited as a result of illness or disabilities. For these people, as was the case for Janaki, a belief in reincarnation may allow some clients to accept that, although certain things cannot be attained in this lifetime, they will likely have the opportunity to attain them in the next.

Teleology and Striving for Superiority

The main goals of life according to Hinduism—pleasure seeking, material gain, right conduct and duty, and salvation and liberation from samsara—make Hinduism a teleological religion. People are thought to seek certain goals as they move through life. As much as this idea is inconsistent with most psychological theories, it fits with Individual Psychology.

Individual Psychology asserts that people strive from a subjective position of a felt minus to a felt plus. People are motivated to overcome this sense of inferiority and thus strive to achieve a subjective sense of superiority. Striving to be superior to others, however, results in maladjustment and suffering. Healthy striving for superiority—for completion—is characterized by an effort to overcome the challenges facing one's group or community. The individual's goal of superiority will depend on the meaning given to life.

The difference between Adlerians and Hindus is that Adlerians see the ultimate goal as being a subjective and nonconscious one. Consider the narcissistic patient whose subjective final goal includes being greater than others. He may believe that the way to be the greatest is to be admired and respected no matter how he defines admiration and respect. As long as he believes he is admired and respected by those he associates with, he feels content. But the moment someone challenges his subjective sense of greatness, directly or indirectly, he is no longer reaching his goal and must compensate to reestablish his sense of greatness. He may do this by belittling others, creating excuses for himself, or showing how important he is. In terms of religion he chooses a way of worship that allows him to maintain his sense of being the great person he believes he is. He may, for example, choose a less commonly worshiped god, telling himself that others are ignorant for not choosing the same god as he; he may believe he has a special relationship with his god, unlike that of any other person; or he may belittle religion altogether, viewing it as something only weak people concern themselves with. His goal of superiority is subjective and for the most part out of his awareness.

The goal of salvation is an objective reality. Hindus seek to achieve oneness with God and attain a release from the cycle of birth, death, and rebirth by worshipping a god and focusing their attention outward toward that god. Their behaviors are consciously aimed at doing the right things in order to achieve salvation. When they find themselves doing things they believe are wrong, they may feel as if they are not going to attain salvation. For Hindus, they are either moving toward or away from that goal. If a person has made steps toward salvation, he or she can expect to be reborn under favorable circumstances (karma), but those who believe they have somehow made mistakes in this lifetime will likely worry they are going to be reborn under harsher and more challenging circumstances (karma). As with Christians and Muslims, any challenges that life presents that get in the way of reaching salvation may be a source of great stress and lead the person to seek spiritual guidance or psychotherapy.

Social Interest and the Life Tasks

For Adler, salvation is based on social interest (Ansbacher, 1979). Similarly, Hinduism's four paths to God have their moral preliminaries that go hand-in-hand with a sense of social feeling toward humankind. The first step of each path involves the cultivation of habits that are characteristic of social interest. Habits such as honesty, duty, right conduct, and noninjury, along with an absence of self-centeredness and egocentricity, set the stage for each of the yogas. This sense of duty and concern for others is emphasized in the Hindu's relationship with his or her community, family, and occupation. For Hindus, these prosocial characteristics are considered an article of faith.

> I am proud to belong to a religion which has taught the world both toler-ance and universal acceptance. We believe not only in universal toleration, but we accept all religions as true. As different streams having different sources all mingle their waters in the sea, so different paths which men take through different tendencies, various though they appear, crooked or straight, all lead to God. (Swami Vivekananda in Viswanathan, 1992, p. 9)

Hinduism is a relational philosophy. It emphasizes the individual's relationship to his or her family and community. When Hinduism places duty to one's community as one of the goals of life, it acknowledges the individual's connectedness with the community and teaches that meaning and value can be found beyond the self.

Hard work and a sense of duty are both a religious and a cultural expectation among Hindus. Work is considered a vital part of living, and childhood is often seen as a time to prepare for work as much as for life in general. Considering that one can seek and find God by devoting oneself exclusively to work (karma yoga), some Hindus may devote themselves entirely to their careers while neglecting their spiritual responsibilities to their family.

Marriage is of particular importance to Hindus. The concept of a task of sex and marriage is readily applicable to Hinduism. Marriage and child rearing are highly valued, and marriage is considered one of the most important spiritual affairs between a man and a woman. Some Hindus believe that marriage marks the beginning of a person's life. It is a union between two souls that many Hindus believe stretches beyond this lifetime.

Just as Hinduism is difficult to define, its wedding traditions are also hard to describe and classify because of the many variations throughout the Hindu community. But generally speaking, most Hindu marriages are arranged. And Hindus generally do not believe in any kind of court-ship before marriage. Many believe that love is something that devel-ops during marriage, not before. Thus, dating and premarital sex are strongly discouraged. Birth control is generally accepted, and abortion is also accepted among most Hindus.

Through the union of marriage, families are joined together and the woman frequently moves in with her husband's family. Husband and wife have certain roles they are expected to carry out in the marital relationship. Traditionally, women are responsible for caring for the household, raising children, and caring for the family, whereas the husband's role is generally focused on providing for the family financially. The family as a whole, however, is expected to produce children, care for the family, help the poor and needy within one's community, and help each other in their spiritual quest for salvation.

Similar to Islam, Hinduism holds very strong traditional beliefs regarding the differences between man and woman. Women are often considered inferior to men, a belief that directly conflicts with Individual Psychology. Although these traditional beliefs must be respected, increased equality between family members may be encouraged throughout the therapeutic process. Therapists who take great offense at this difference in power structure need to be attentive in their approach to their client(s) as they seek to establish an egalitarian relationship.

Although allowed under some circumstances, divorce is generally not an option. The social stigma associated with divorce and the ousting of women from the Hindu community leads many Hindus (particularly women) to remain in unhappy or even abusive marriages. The most common clinical issues that bring Hindus to psychotherapy center on relationships (Sharma, 2006). In addition, acculturation, cross-generational differences, and conflicts regarding traditional and contemporary values frequently create challenges that Hindus are likely to bring to therapy.

ADLERIAN PSYCHOTHEARPY WITH HINDU CLIENTS

For many Hindus, seeking services from a psychotherapist can be a very difficult decision, as it is considered a major taboo by many in their community. Hindus are generally skeptical of psychotherapy and feel that problems in living should be addressed by the family. However, these concerns regarding mental health treatment vary, depending on one's level of acculturation, cultural background, and education. Second and third generation Hindus are more likely to seek mental health services.

Mental illness is frequently seen as a result of karma. Many Hindus may believe that they are trapped in their karmic fate and therefore can do nothing but endure their suffering. The therapist can move the therapy along by learning about the client's beliefs and understanding of karma and reincarnation and using karma therapeutically to help the client take responsibility. The Adlerian conceptualization of mental illness as discouragement can be helpful in offering Hindus a more positive view of their presenting problem. By reframing their struggles as normal human experiences, clients can move beyond any stigma associated with psychological problems.

Adlerian therapists who work with Hindu clients can do so effectively as long as they remember a few key points. The religious and cultural beliefs and practices vary significantly between Hindus. Thus, therapists need to learn about specific religious beliefs and values from the client. Paying attention to myths that the client admires is also important, as Hindus frequently model their lives after these mythological figures. For instance, it may be useful to address the symbol of Sita when working with Hindu women. Sita is one of the most popular goddesses of Hinduism, considered to be the ideal daughter, the ideal wife, and the ideal mother. Learning about these myths and helping the client find new and positive ideals in mythology, folklore, or media can have tremendous therapeutic benefits (Reddy & Hanna, 1995).

Another important thing to consider when working with Hindus is the importance they place on their families. Many Hindus are likely to put the family's concerns before theirs. Consequently, they will be very reluctant and even fearful of acting in ways that do not take their family's need into consideration. A Hindu woman in her late thirties had sought counseling for her mildly autistic son. Fearful that the boy would never develop appropriate social skills, she would interact with him constantly. She had remained loyal to her family's needs, but any extra time was spent playing with her autistic boy. She was exhausted and stressed, feeling as if she was on the verge of collapse. Given her desperate need for relief, the therapist gave her permission to let her son play by himself for a short period of time each day. He reasoned that learning to play independently was an important part of children's development. So setting aside a half hour each day for independent play was an important part of his treatment. Her worries subsided significantly, and she was able to find time, although very limited, for herself. Last, therapists must consider the conflicts that arise between traditional and contemporary values. Helping clients explore contradictions they experience as a result of these differences is likely to play an important role in the therapeutic process.

Case Example

Deena, a 21-year-old Hindu woman, came for therapy due to stress and acute anxiety. Two weeks prior to her first appointment she had learned that her parents had found the man they wanted her to marry. Deena was the youngest of three children born to immigrant parents from India. She was born and raised in the United States. Deena described herself as Hindu, but acknowledged that many of her Christian friends had had a great influence on her. She considered herself to be "spiritual" as opposed to "religious." By that she meant that God played a very important part in her life. Although she did not attend temple, she found great comfort in her conversations with God.

Deena was the youngest in a family of three children, two girls and one boy. Growing up, Deena always felt she was being ignored by her parents. She always tried to please them, but to no avail. She described herself as an intelligent child and an excellent student. Education was very important to her parents, but she felt she always fell one step short of her siblings' accomplishments.

During her adolescent years, Deena continued to work hard in school, hoping for her parents' acknowledgment. She dated on a few occasions without her parents' knowledge, but for the most part did what the family expected of her. By the time she came for therapy, Deena was a college senior and had her eyes on graduate school. Her father's demand that she marry a man of his choosing had disrupted her plans entirely. She experienced significant stress and anxiety resulting from what she knew was an inevitable confrontation with her parents.

Deena had never challenged her parents' authority. And despite her feelings of being ignored, she had continued to do her best at home and at school to please them. Now, she found herself feeling angry and scared. As therapy progressed, Deena expressed feelings of anger toward her parents for never acknowledging her. "What makes things worse," she said, "is that they expect me to sacrifice everything I have worked so hard for." But despite her anger, Deena knew she was not good at confrontations, and she worried that she might find herself giving in and going along with her parents' wishes. She was not particularly troubled by the idea of an arranged marriage. What she was concerned about was the timing of the event and the potential disruptions to her career.

Over the course of growing up, Deena had found meaning in hard work. She had devoted herself entirely to doing well in school, hoping her parents would notice her. And despite their lack of praise, she came to enjoy her studies and found that friends and colleagues acknowledged her for her accomplishments. She had found a place for herself in the academic environment. If she gave up her career for a married life, she stood to lose what was most precious to her. On the other hand, were she to disobey her parents she would dishonor them and thereby disgrace herself and her entire family.

In session, Deena talked about her relationship with God. She had no specific Hindu God that she worshiped, but knew that God was out there. For her, God represented a higher power that looked after her. As she continued talking about her perceptions of God, Deena explained that God had always acknowledged her accomplishments. She knew that whenever she got good grades or did a good job on an assignment, God was pleased. "What I have been looking for in my parents, but never found," Deena said, "I have found in God."

Deena's worries about confronting her parents gradually subsided as she processed her feelings with her therapist. She eventually decided that her schooling and her career were too important to give up. She had found a sense of purpose and a connection with God in this area of her life. She came to see that sacrificing her career for marriage was equivalent to giving up her relationship with God. That seemed to explain her feelings of panic when she learned about her parents' plans for her to marry.

Through her discussions with her counselor, Deena quickly began to gain a wider perspective on things. She began to see the possibility of marrying and continuing to pursue her career at the same time. She eventually decided to confront her parents and talked with them about her desire to go to graduate school. She was surprised at her parents' response and how they respected her wishes to pursue her career. She eventually agreed to meet the man her parents wanted her to marry.

SUMMARY

Hinduism is an exceptionally diverse religion with hundreds of various divisions depending on language, geography, caste, and community. There is no specific creed or teacher that is viewed as central to Hinduism. Nor is there a single Holy Book similar to the Christian Bible. There are, however, central tenets that unify Hinduism as a religion. The belief in Brahman—the Supreme Being—is at the core of the religion. Brahman is an infinite, formless life force that cannot be described. Another core belief in Hinduism is that of samsara, the endless cycle of birth, death, and rebirth. The highest goal for the individual or the soul is to achieve liberation from this continuous cycle of life and death.

The four main doctrines of Hinduism were discussed in relation to Individual Psychology. In discussing the four stages of life, the four goals of life, the four paths to God, and karma and reincarnation, several comparisons were made between Hindu philosophy and Adlerian psychology. The main differences between the two philosophies have to do with issues of equality between men and women as well as among people of different castes.

Therapists working with Hindu clients should remain mindful of the potential shame associated with seeking services and the stigma often associated with mental illness. In addition to addressing the client's cultural background, social status, and level of acculturation, therapists should pay close attention to the role of mythology in the client's life, the importance of family relationships, and the potential conflicts between traditional and contemporary values.

SUGGESTED READINGS

Reddy, I., & Hanna, F. J. (1995). The life-style of the Hindu woman: Conceptualizing female clients of Indian origin. *Journal of Individual Psychology,* 51(3), 216–230.

Sharma, A. R. (2006). Psychotherapy with Hindus. Chapter in P. S. Richards & A. E. Bergin (Eds.) *Handbook of Psychotherapy and Religious Diversity,* pp. 341–365. Washington, DC: American Psychological Association.

Smith, H. (1991). *The World Religions.* NY: Harper Collins.

Viswanathan, E. (1992). *Am I a Hindu?* San Francisco: Halo Books.

9

Adler and the "Truth" of Human Existence: A Comparison of Buddhism and Individual Psychology

We are what we think. All that we are arises with our thoughts. With our thoughts, we make our world.
— **Siddhartha Gautama**

Buddhism takes its name from Siddhartha Gautama, the Buddha, who was born around 536 BCE in a small province of northern India. The Buddha claimed to have seen the reality of things and to have developed significant insight into the nature of the human condition. He argued that this ability to develop insight and see things as they really are is available to anyone through the practice of meditation (Kyabgon, 2001). His teachings quickly spread across India and into other parts of Asia, significantly affecting cultural and religious life in countries such as China, Korea, Japan, Burma, and the Indonesian islands (Eckel, 2003). Today, Buddhism continues to grow worldwide, and there are an estimated 350 million Buddhists throughout the world. In North America there are approximately 2 million practicing Buddhists (Barrett & Johnson, 1998).

The Buddha, or "Awakened One," was born an Indian prince. But he renounced his life of royalty to win freedom from the eternal cycle of birth, death, and rebirth (samsara) (Eckel, 2003). After a period of prolonged study, meditation, strenuous fasting, and self-denial, the Buddha finally, one night while meditating under a Bodhi Tree (Tree of Awakening), became enlightened about the dharma (Universal Truth)

167

of human existence. In his awakening, the Buddha developed knowledge about his previous births and knowledge about the births of others. Last, he developed knowledge about the "Four Noble Truths": the truth of suffering, the truth of the origin of suffering, the truth of the cessation of suffering, and the truth of the Path. The Four Noble Truths are the essence of all of Buddha's teachings. All later Buddhist interpretations are based on these "truths" (Kyabgon, 2001). Despite differences in how Buddhists train in meditation, morality, and wisdom, they all agree on the importance of understanding the Four Noble Truths. All Buddhist practices are based upon these fundamental principles (Kyabgon, 2001).

As with any other religion, there is a variety of different schools of Buddhism. The two main schools of Buddhism are the Mahayana and Theravada schools. These groups consist of several subdivisions, each maintaining slight differences in beliefs and practices.

The dialogue between Western psychology and the Buddhist understanding of human nature has undergone major developments in recent times. A number of therapists and Buddhists have attempted to integrate Buddhist practices into psychotherapy (i.e., de Wit, 2008; Epstein, 1995; Kawai, 1996; Rosenbaum, 1999; Rubin, 1996; Zhang, 2004). For many people, particularly Westerners, Buddhism is considered a philosophy of living more than a religion. And some consider it to be a psychological system, due to its focus on thoughts and beliefs. Lama Govinda (1990) acknowledged these different outlooks and argued that Buddhism can be thought of as a philosophy, a psychology, and a religion.

> Thus we could say that the Buddha's Dharma is, as experience and as a way to practical realization, a religion; as the intellectual formulation of this experience, a philosophy; and as a result of systematic self-observation and analysis, a psychology. Whoever treads this path acquires a norm of behavior that is not dictated from without but is the result of an inner process of maturation and that we, regarding it from without—can call morality. (p. 30–31)

There are several similarities between Buddhism and psychotherapy, particularly the basic psychotherapeutic listening technique, the focus on the therapeutic relationship (or teacher-student relationship in Buddhism), and the cultivation of psychological insight (Finn & Rubin, 2006). But in addition to the technical aspects of psychotherapy, Individual Psychology and Buddhism share several theoretical concepts as well. Given the vast overlap between Individual Psychology and other world religions, it is not surprising that it is also compatible with Buddhism. The basic assumptions that Individual Psychology maintain are for the most part consistent with Buddha's teachings.

Adler's notion of striving for superiority parallels the Buddhist concept of Karma. Other philosophical assumptions such as soft determinism, striving for superiority, and teleology, are also similar in many ways to the Buddhist teachings. The holistic perspective and the notion of social interest are also comparable. Additionally, both Buddhists and Adlerians emphasize the importance of subjective (phenomenological) experiences.

So for Buddhists, it is not God who has created the world, but our own mind—the mind is the one responsible for all our experiences: joy, happiness, pain, suffering. This is not only in terms of what we experience; the mind also fabricates the kind of world that we live in. The world that we live in is created by our mind (Kyabgon, 2001, p. 13).

A major point of disagreement between Adler and religion is the idea of God. Whereas Christians, Jews, Muslims, and Hindus view God as real, Adlerians view God as an Idea. Thus, the quote by Kyabgon suggests agreement on this issue between Adlerians and Buddhists. Both theories also acknowledge that suffering is created by the individual's private view of the situation (Sakin-Wolf, 2003). Although both theories acknowledge that some suffering is inevitable, such as old age, sickness, and death, there is also self-created suffering.

Most of the literature on Individual Psychology and Buddhism has focused on various aspects of the religion, such as Zen Buddhism (Croake & Rusk, 1980; Huber, 2000), or different assumptions of Adler's system such as holism, soft determinism, social interest, and private logic (Leak, Gardner, & Pounds, 1992; Noda, 2000; Sakin-Wolf, 2003). This chapter reviews the historical background of Buddhism, its basic teachings, and its philosophy of human nature. Its teachings are compared to the principles of Individual Psychology, and the Buddhist practice of meditation is assessed from an Adlerian viewpoint.

HISTORY AND TEACHINGS OF BUDDHISM

Siddhartha Gautama was born around 536 BCE in a small province of northern India. He was born to royal parents in what is now southern Nepal. According to legend, he was raised in his father's palace and married a princess with whom he had a son, Rahula. Around the age of thirty, Siddhartha wanted to explore life beyond his father's palace. He had never ventured outside the palace, and it was here he had his first exposure to suffering. Having ventured out into the world, Siddhartha witnessed three sights: a person in old age, a sick man, and a corpse. On a later excursion he witnessed a wandering ascetic and vowed to follow his example in an effort to find release from human suffering (Eckel, 2003).

In his search for freedom from suffering, Siddhartha gave up his royal status and began the life of a wanderer. He began by practicing strenuous fasting and self-denial, but he soon found his efforts to be ineffective. He decided to follow a more moderate path and avoid extreme self-denial as well as extreme self-indulgence—what Buddhists refer to as the "Middle Way." In a final attempt at freeing himself from the cycle of death and rebirth (Samsara) he seated himself under a fig tree (known as a Bodhi tree—tree of enlightenment) and sometime during the evening he achieved profound insight into the nature of human existence. After this experience, the Buddha eventually became a religious teacher wandering northern India and teaching the Dharma (Universal Truth) for the next forty-five years.

As his teachings spread across India and other parts of Asia, several schools of Buddhism developed. The two main existing schools today are the Mahayana and Theravada traditions. The Theravada (Teaching of the Elders) tradition is the oldest of the Buddhist schools. It is considered to be more conservative than other traditions. Theravada Buddhism is practiced predominantly in Sri Lanka and South-East Asia.

The Mahayana (the Great Method) tradition is the second and largest of the two main schools of Buddhism. The Mahayana Buddhists followed a less strict and less literal interpretation of the monastic discipline (Parrinder, 1985). Mahayana Buddhism is practiced in China, Japan, Korea, and among the Tibetan Buddhists. Ch'an Buddhism (also known as Zen) is a school of the Mahayana tradition. The word Ch'an is derived from the Sanskrit word Dhyana, meaning meditation. Ch'an Buddhism emphasizes meditation and experiential wisdom rather than theoretical knowledge and the study of religious writings. It teaches that all people have the potential to attain enlightenment through meditative practices and discipline. Ch'an (Zen) Buddhism is perhaps the most well-known school of Buddhism in North America today.

Holy Texts

Religious instruction and particularly meditation practice is often taught by an experienced religious teacher. Although readers can find a plethora of literature discussing how to meditate and live a Buddhist life, many Buddhists encourage people to learn directly from a religious teacher.

There are no "holy" texts in Buddhism similar to the Bible, the Torah, or the Koran. There are, however, many sutras, which are the recordings of what the Buddha taught. The Buddhist scriptures vary among the various Buddhist schools, and an in depth look at each of these is beyond the scope of this work. Suffice it to say, however, that the Tripitaka is the canon of scripture used by the Theravada Buddhists. The Kangyur refers to a list of Tibetan Buddhist scriptures. And Dà Zàng Jīng refers to the Chinese Mahayana Buddhist scripture, meaning "Great Treasury of Scriptures." It is a body of Buddhist literature deemed canonical in China, Japan, and Korea. One of the more well-known discourses of the Buddha is the Sigalovada Sutta, which provides detailed guidance on how to meet the life tasks.

The Buddhist scriptures are collections of offences that are to be avoided, social duties of monks and lay people, mindfulness and meditation practices, and even poetry. At the core of Buddha's teachings are the Four Noble Truths. These are the basic philosophical principles upon which all later Buddhist interpretations are based (Kyabgon, 2001). Let us examine each one.

The Four Noble Truths

Buddha's teachings were given within the context of the Indian tradition. At the time, many believed that only those with a certain social standing had the ability to seek higher religious goals. People of "lesser" social value did not have this ability (Kyabgon, 2001). It was also believed that only men had the ability to develop themselves spiritually. The Buddha rejected these cultural standards and taught that anyone who makes an effort to develop insight into the nature of things can become enlightened. And so he encouraged people of all social, cultural, and religious backgrounds to strive toward enlightenment.

At the time of the Buddha there were two major Indian traditions. The first teaching came from the Upanishads. It emphasized the importance of realizing the nature of one's own self as being identical with reality. The second position, called Ajivikas or Lokayatas, was materialist based and rejected the existence of consciousness and moral responsibility (Kyabgon, 2001). Buddha rejected both views, believing reality could not be found either in the world or in the self. He argued that these were fictions created by people, but were not available to human experience (Kyabgon, 2001). It was in response to the followers of the Upanishads and the Ajivikas that Buddha taught what he called the Middle Way. He realized that people tended to either be overindulgent or engage in extreme ascetic practices. So he emphasized the importance of restraint and moderation. This teaching is found in the Four Noble Truths, in which he explains how to practice the Middle Way (Kyabgon, 2001).

The Four Noble Truths depict the symptom, diagnosis, prognosis, and treatment plan for human suffering (Finn & Rubin, 2006). They state that human suffering is inevitable, that it is caused by desire, attachment, and craving, and that human suffering can be eradicated by achieving enlightenment. Enlightenment can be reached by developing moral sensitivity, a concentrated mind, and wisdom.

The first Noble Truth is suffering, or duhkha, a Sanskrit word for meaninglessness, unsatisfactoriness, and suffering. Buddha taught that suffering is universal, and all life events such as birth, growth, and death, cause suffering. There are three kinds of suffering. First, there is suffering caused by old age, illness, and death. Second, there is suffering caused by changes in our lives. Changes in ourselves, our relationship to others, our occupation, and our environment can all cause suffering. And finally, by becoming attached to things that change, we set ourselves up to experience suffering. Despite all this suffering, Buddha also acknowledged that there is happiness. But every time we experience happiness, it is not permanent. Unless we are able to truly understand and accept the fact that happiness is temporary and that dissatisfaction is part of life, we can never really find true happiness.

The second Noble Truth is the origin of suffering. The Buddha taught that suffering is caused by excessive and exaggerated forms of desire, craving, and attachment (Kyabgon, 2001). Thus, Buddhists understand the cause of suffering to originate from within ourselves. According to Buddhism, suffering develops when we insist on having the things we want and when we refuse to accept that life changes. The individual decides to cling to things, people, or events as if they were permanent. These behaviors also direct the individual's attention to what is happening to himself or herself rather than the individual taking responsibility for others in the here and now.

Adlerians agree with Buddhism that suffering originates from within the individual. What the Buddha considered exaggerated forms of desire and craving are what Adlerians refer to as basic mistakes (Dreikurs, 1989). "I must be rich in order to feel like people accept me," "I can never be happy unless I have a man in my life," "Bad things should never happen to me," or "I should always get what I want" are just a few examples of basic mistakes, i.e., cognitive distortions (Beck, 1976) or irrational beliefs (Ellis, 1974). The other point here is that our desires are exaggerated. Similarly, Adlerians consider neurotics to be overly ambitious. They set standards and expectations of themselves and others that simply cannot be reached. Consider for example the obsessive compulsive who believes she must be in control all the time. Because total control is humanly impossible, she eventually becomes discouraged and develops symptoms in an effort to excuse herself and safeguard her self-worth. Buddha said that humans should strive to overcome exaggerated forms of desire. This is not to say that people should attempt to completely eradicate craving and desire, but we should rather look for balance and be flexible in our strivings. Balance and flexibility are key words in counseling and psychotherapy as well. Adler (1956) taught that the goal of psychotherapy was not to create perfect individuals but rather to substitute smaller errors for larger ones.

The third Noble Truth is that suffering can be eradicated. According to Buddhism, it is possible to free oneself from desire and achieve a state of complete awakening—Nirvana. Nirvana ("blow out" or "extinguish") is a state of mind characterized by perfect peace and freedom from craving, desire, anger, and other distressing states. The cessation of individualistic desire is also the end of the experience of suffering (Parinder, 1985) because the experience of happiness is no longer dependent on external circumstances (Kyabgon, 2001). Buddhists believe that nirvana is something that anyone can achieve in this lifetime through the practice of the Eightfold Path, which is the Fourth Noble Truth.

The Fourth Noble Truth is the path to the cessation of suffering, the essence of Buddhist practice. These practices are outlined in eight different steps or actions and are therefore referred to as the Eightfold Path. The goal of the Eightfold Path is to develop moral sensitivity, a concentrated mind, and wisdom—the earliest and most basic description of the path. Through the practice of the path, the individual develops compassion and caring for others. A genuine concern for other people, rather than for one's own needs, is the way to alleviate one's suffering. Similarly, Adler (1956) taught that problems in living are interpersonal or social, and that these problems can be overcome through concern for others (i.e., social interest). Neuroticism is in part a result of exaggerated forms of self-interest, an unwillingness to cooperate with others, and a sense of not being part of one's group or community—a lack of social interest. The Eightfold Path encourages an approach to living that helps the individual focus on others rather than on themselves, and it can therefore be viewed in terms of social interest (Croake & Rusk, 1980). Kyabgon (2001) clarifies this concept:

> Through the practice of moral sensitivity we become better individuals, able to overcome our egocentric tendencies. We become more compassionate and more sensitive to the needs of others. Through the practice of meditation our mind becomes more focused, more resilient, and more aware, which in turn gives rise to wisdom. (p. 7)

The Eightfold Path involves:

Right Understanding

Right Thought

Right Speech (addresses the life tasks)

Right Action (addresses the life tasks)

Right Livelihood (addresses the life tasks)

Right Effort

Right Mindfulness

Right Concentration

Preceding morality, meditation, and wisdom, is faith. Through Right Understanding of the nature of the world and Right Thought or inner mental attitude (Parrinder, 1985), comes an understanding and acceptance (e.g., faith) of the teachings of the Buddha, which, after living the Buddhist life of morality and meditation leads to wisdom (Kyabgon, 2001; Parrinder, 1985).

Kyabgon (2001) went on to say that Right Thought means to understand how our thoughts and emotions are related and that engaging in negative thinking results in negative emotions. This view is directly related to the cognitive perspective of Individual Psychology. Adler

(1956) talked about the individual's apperceptive schema and how a person's view of him or herself, of others, and of life also affects his or her emotions. However, Adlerians do not view individuals as victims of their emotions. Although a person may suffer from negative emotional states, Adlerians understand emotions to be purposeful. In other words, emotions are used to bring about a change that is in favor of the individual.

The next three sections of the Eightfold Path (Right Speech, Right Action, and Right Livelihood) address social behavior and offer guidance for a Buddhist way of life; in this way they relate to the life tasks. Right Speech is important, as people are often unaware of their use of language. Negative forms of speech are believed to have a negative effect on ourselves and on others, so to avoid discouragement it is important that the individual be fully aware of the way in which he or she speaks.

Right Action relates to how we interact with other people and our environment and how those actions affect those around us as well as ourselves. Right Actions often include abstaining from killing, lying, adultery, stealing, and drug or alcohol use. Right Livelihood directly addresses the work task. The Buddha thought that people should work and provide for themselves and their families, but that the nature of our work must not cause harm to ourselves or other people.

These three aspects of the Eightfold Path deal with ethical conduct and social behavior. Leak, Gardner, and Pounds (1992) argued that these sections of the Eightfold Path are the most relevant to Adlerian psychology because of their emphasis on ethical conduct, pointing out that: "These pragmatic Buddhist principles agree with Adlerian theory's position that well-being comes from service in the life tasks of friendship, love, and work" (p. 59).

The next part of the path is Right Effort, which consists of four aspects (Kyabgon, 2001) that the individual should strive for. First, the individual should make an effort to prevent unwholesome thoughts and emotions. Second, people should strive to reduce unwholesome thoughts that have already arisen in the mind. The third aspect involves the development of wholesome thoughts and emotions. Fourth, the individual should strive to maintain and further grow and expand on those wholesome thoughts that have already been developed.

Although all of the elements of the Eightfold Path can be addressed through practicing meditation, the last two elements (Right Mindfulness and Right Concentration) deal specifically with practicing mental discipline. Right Mindfulness has to do with becoming more attentive to thoughts, emotions, speech, and actions in meditation. Being mindful and attentive to actions and experiences allows the individual to gain more insight into human nature. Right Concentration goes hand in hand with the other aspects, as it allows the person to maintain focus on his or her thoughts, emotions, and behaviors without being distracted. Following these aspects of the Eightfold Path, a person can achieve nirvana and thus freedom from the endless cycle of birth, death, and rebirth (samsara).

By following the Eightfold Path, the Buddhist individual eventually enters into a realm of awareness and wisdom. As mentioned above, the first realization or truth is that all life is dukkha. In addition to this there is another important realization: everything is anicca (Sanskrit—anitya), meaning impermanent. Nothing remains the same, and nothing is permanent. This realization leads the Buddhist to another realization: anatta (Sanskrit—anatman), the realization that there is no permanent, real soul (atman) within the individual. The Buddha taught that the individual consists of a temporary combination of five factors—one physical and four nonphysical. The five factors include physical form, sensation, perception, volition, and consciousness. The grouping of these five factors is only momentary, as they are in a constant state of flux, ceasing to exist at the death of the individual.

The Buddha denied the existence of the soul, distinguishing his philosophy from other religious philosophies of the time. Some Indian religious leaders even considered his denial of the human soul to be heretical. They argued that without a soul, there is no holder of personal responsibility. Consequently, there is no grounds for moral striving and ethical and just behavior. Without a soul, who is punished or rewarded for good or evil deeds? Without a soul, they argued, it does not matter how we live our lives (Parrinder, 1985).

What the Buddha taught, however, was for people to cease their egocentric and selfish views. He invited people to follow the path in an effort to transcend their current state of desire and attachment to impermanent things. It is this striving, the striving for nirvana, that becomes the guiding line in Buddhism. As such, it provides the motivation for moral and ethical behavior. It also encourages people to go beyond their selfish and egocentric ways to focus on the needs and demands of the community. The Buddha encouraged people to "lose one's individual existence in the common life of the Sangha" (Parrinder, 1985, p. 275). Similarly, Adlerians encourage people to loose their individual existence (selfishness) in one's community.

Ethical Principles

Buddhists believe that one needs to cultivate and increase an attitude that rejects negative actions and thoughts. Self-interest is at the root of self-created suffering. And so Buddhists strive to restrict self-interest in an effort to achieve enlightenment. The Dalai Lama outlined ten nonvirtuous actions that are to be avoided and another ten virtuous actions that are to replace the nonvirtuous ones (Farber & Gyatso, 2006, p. 69–70).

The ten nonvirtuous actions:

> Three physical acts (killing, stealing, and sexual misconduct)
> Four verbal acts (lying, divisive speech, harsh speech, and gossip)
> Three mental acts (jealousy, ill-will, and ignorance)

The ten virtuous actions:

> Protecting and saving life
> Giving and not taking what is not given
> Treating your partner respectfully—respecting your marriage vows
> Speaking honestly
> Speaking with the goal to bring harmony among beings
> Speaking gently
> Refraining from gossip
> Being happy for others' accomplishments
> Being loving toward all
> Having a view that includes karma and understands the middle
> way between the two extreme views of eternalism and nihilism,
> accompanied by the two kinds of accumulations (of merit and
> wisdom)

Adlerians may construe these principles as a guide to social interest. Although there are other ways of exhibiting and experiencing community feeling, these Buddhist principles certainly lend themselves to usefulness. As much as they can be seen as aspects of social interest, they may also be viewed as goals of psychotherapy. A patient who moves away from the nonvirtuous actions and toward the virtuous ones can be said to have recovered from his or her neurosis.

The Four Noble Truths describe the human condition along with its problems, and provide a formula for how to improve these problems (Kyabgon, 2001). In this respect, they provide a very encouraging model.

The model fully acknowledges the individual's suffering (empathy, understanding, relationship), encourages the development of insight into behavior, emotions, and beliefs to alleviate that suffering (lifestyle assessment), and advocates for changes in thinking and behavior to achieve and maintain a state of tranquility and happiness (reorientation). We will look at each of these aspects as we examine the principles of Individual Psychology, the life tasks, and the process of Adlerian psychotherapy.

PHILOSOPHY OF HUMAN NATURE

Individual Psychology and Buddhist philosophies are both humanistic in that they affirm the dignity and worth of all people and the individual's ability to control his or her fate. In terms of how the two understand human nature, there is significant overlap between the two philosophies. Both view human beings as social, unified, goal-oriented, creative, and responsible. Although both theories are holistic, there are some important differences in how they think about and apply the holistic principles (Noda, 2000).

Soft Determinism

Buddhism is a soft deterministic religion. Although there are various ancient philosophies that many Buddhist clients may subscribe to, they are not in line with the teachings of the Buddha. Noda (2000) described three "mistaken" philosophies that relate directly to the issues of free will and personal responsibility. The first is atheistic determinism, which holds that our past lives directly affect what happens to us in this present life (Karma). The second is theistic determinism, which maintains that God decides what will happen to us in this life. The third position is accidentalism, which denies causality and holds that whatever happens, happens only by chance. All three of these philosophies deflect responsibility away from the individual. The individual is allowed to continue doing what he or she wants without having to consider the effects of his or her behavior on others; meanwhile the individual is assured that his or her deeds are the result of some outside force.

The Buddha rejected these viewpoints and in his very last sermon suggested that each person has the freedom to determine his or her own future (Noda, 2000). "All the constituents of being are transitory; work out your salvation with diligence!" (Mahapari-nibbana-sutta, in Warren,

1979, p. 109). Similarly, Adler (1956) saw people as having the freedom to make their own decisions. He believed that the individual freely makes his or her choices within the boundaries set by one's heredity and environment.

When working with a Buddhist client the therapist will need to determine how he or she attributes responsibility. In other words, who is responsible for the client's suffering? If the client's self-created suffering is attributed to Karma, God, or random events rather than the client's own behaviors, the therapist may need to address these issues so that responsibility can be placed back on the client. From there, the client can be encouraged to make an effort to improve his or her situation.

The issue of karma is often used as an argument for determinism. A person believes he or she is suffering as a result of past negative actions as if some powerful force were making him or her suffer for having violated some law or moral directive. But in Buddhism there is no law commanded by God or nature that we have to obey. The Buddha's principles for proper conduct—abstinence from taking life, stealing, lying, alcohol abuse, etc.—are only directives given to help the individual achieve clarity of mind and eventually Nirvana.

Failure to observe these precepts produces "bad karma" or, in Adlerian terms, neurotic striving (Croake and Rusk, 1980). Croake and Rusk compared bad karma with Adler's concept of neurotic striving stating that we are not punished *for* our sins, but *by* our sins. In other words, bad karma results not because some outside force is punishing us, but because all purposeful actions are part of our striving (karma). Karma is one's intentional (conscious or unconscious) actions. It is the working of cause and effect in which positive actions produce happiness, and negative actions produce suffering. So in striving on what Adler referred to as the "useless side of life," (nonvirtuous actions) the individual produces and maintains the constricted self and the biased perspective (Croake & Rusk, 1980). This in turn moves the person farther away from awareness and clarity and consequently makes suffering more likely.

For example, a depressed patient who seeks to avoid others for fear of being rejected reinforces her isolation and her belief that others do not care for her. Her avoidance begins as an effort to safeguard her self-image as someone who always does the right thing (neurotic striving). After she has isolated herself for several months, her friends begin to distance themselves from her, leaving her feeling rejected and unwanted. The rejection of her friends is then interpreted as bad karma. The patient may conclude that she is being punished with bad karma for not spending time with her friends (e.g., doing the right thing) or having violated some personal ethical guideline.

Thus, according to Buddhism the individual is the architect of his or her own suffering and happiness. Although life presents us with inevitable afflictions such as loss, death, and illness, Buddhism teaches that people have sufficient free will to allow the individual to decide how to respond to those afflictions.

Creativity and Private Logic

Both Buddhism and Adlerian psychology are optimistic philosophies in that they emphasize freedom to choose and freedom to act. It is the individual's freedom to make changes, both behavioral and psychological, that allows for healing. Adlerian psychology stresses the creative role of the individual, believing that people are not simply reacting to their environment, but playing an active role in how they move through life. Adler was influenced by Vaihinger's philosophy of 'as if' and believed that all our thoughts, feelings, and actions are based on our biased apperceptions. We act "as if" our private logic is real or true. And as long as our private logic is in line with the common view of our community and our culture, we will likely adapt well. Suffering arises however, when our private view is conflicting with common sense and we become attached (inflexible) to that particular way of looking at things.

Sakin-Wolf (2003) pointed out that the concept of attachment is central to both psychology and Buddhist philosophy. According to Sakin-Wolf suffering is in part caused by one's attachment or private view of the situation. The individual is stuck or attached to the way things must or should be.

> [Private logic] is a major barrier to psychological well-being. However, both the Buddha and Adler saw the causes of suffering also as a means of release from this suffering; meaning, that if persons could change or shift their mental attitudes, then they could eliminate unnecessary suffering. (p. 73)

Both theories acknowledge that suffering is created by the individual's personal creative interpretation of the situation (Sakin-Wolf, 2003). So from a psychotherapeutic standpoint, healing occurs through the modification of maladaptive beliefs. The role of the therapist is to help clients see things from a different perspective and gradually begin to shift their focus towards more positive and flexible (non-attached) thinking.

Holism

Noda (2000) discussed the issue of holism in Adlerian psychology and Buddhism in great detail. He distinguished between holism and elementism as two separate paradigms in psychology. Individual Psychology is strictly holistic, whereas Freud's psychoanalysis and Jung's theories are elementistic. According to Noda, elementistic theories acknowledge and often emphasize intrapsychic conflicts in which two or more competing elements oppose each other (e.g., the id, ego, superego, mind and body, conscious and unconscious). Adlerian psychology rejects the concept of internal conflicts. Instead, Adlerians view people as being in conflict with their community. What Adlerian psychology fails to do, however, is to understand the world as a whole, in which the individual and the universe are in unity (Noda, 2000). Consequently, Noda refers to Adler's concept of holism as "relative holism."

Adlerians assume that conflict between the person and his or her environment develops when the person fails to meet the life tasks. Buddhism, however, takes the concept of holism one step further and views the individual and the universe as being part of the whole. Thus, the world is a "unified harmonious cosmos of which individuals are elements" (Noda, 2000, p. 291). So according to Buddhist philosophy there is no conflict between the individual and his or her environment, and the experience of such conflicts comprises illusions caused by striving, characterized by unenlightened people. Awakened individuals experience no conflict in the world. Therefore, if we are able to accept that we are not in conflict with our environment, but rather a part of it ("absolute holism"), we eradicate our need to strive and to overcome. This, in turn, allows us to truly accept others for who they are and to accept our own place in the universe (Noda, 2000).

Teleology and Striving for Superiority

Individual Psychology assumes that all behavior is goal directed, and the individual strives to achieve a sense of belonging within his or her social group. This teleological concept is also found in Buddhist philosophy (Noda, 2000). The Buddha taught that suffering is caused by desire and by our thirst for sensuous pleasure. In other words, suffering is caused by our expectations, hopes, and cravings—all of which are future directed or teleological.

Individual Psychology asserts that people strive from a subjective position of a felt minus to a felt plus. People are motivated to overcome this sense of inferiority and thus we strive to achieve a subjective sense of superiority. Striving to be superior to others, however, results in maladjustment and suffering. Healthy striving is characterized by an effort to overcome the challenges facing one's community. According to Dreikurs (1971), healthy striving means to find a place in the community by concerning oneself with the demands of the group and through cooperation. Likewise, the Buddha not only acknowledged that the individual's striving is self-centered, but he also encouraged people to shift the direction of their striving toward a concern for others.

The main difference between Buddhism's and Individual Psychology's understanding of human striving is that, in Buddhism, goal-striving is only for unenlightened people. Those who have achieved enlightenment have abandoned all goals (Noda, 2000). Adlerians would argue, however, that such people are still striving, but that their striving is on the useful side of life. For example, following his awakening, Siddhartha Gautama traveled the roads of Northern India teaching the Dharma, showing a concern for humanity, as he attempted to help others escape the inevitability of human suffering. Another example of how enlightened people continue to strive on the useful side of life can be found in the ethical ideal of the bodhisattva.

In North and East Asia, where the Mahayana tradition makes up the greater part of Buddhism, the ethical ideal of the bodhisattva has become the central principle of moral practice. This ethical principle applies to Buddhist monks and laypeople alike. The bodhisattva ideal encourages compassion and wisdom and is expressed in the "bodhisattva vow": May I attain Buddhahood for the sake of all other beings! (Eckel, 2003). Eckel explains:

> The first principle is an active ideal, centered on relieving the suffering of others. This includes helping others to attain nirvana, even to the extent of postponing one's own entry into nirvana in order to do so. The second ideal is more contemplative. It focuses on seeing through the "veil of illusion" that shrouds ordinary experiences, thereby becoming free from suffering oneself. (p. 184)

Social Interest

Adlerian and Buddhist theories both offer a solution to human suffering: concern for others rather than for oneself. Adlerians consider this concern for others to be characteristic of what Adler (1956) called social interest. For Buddhists, the Eightfold Path encourages the individual to focus on others rather than himself or herself. Thus, both theories deal with the relationship of the individual to the community. Compared to Theravada Buddhism, the Mahayana traditions emphasize the importance of compassion and concern for others more forcefully. Theravada Buddhism is more inclined to emphasize self-discipline and disinterest in the everyday aspects of life (Leak, Gardner, & Pounds, 1992). Nevertheless, both traditions emphasize the importance of service to others.

The altruistic aspect of social interest appears to be directly parallel to the Buddhist concept of "nonattached love." Nonattached love is evidenced when one gives freely to others without concern for repayment. Giving is free from any type of self-enhancement (Croake & Rusk, 1980, p. 224).

Buddhist teachings are in complete agreement with Individual Psychology that psychological health, or freedom from suffering, results from concern for others rather than for oneself, and from service in the life tasks of friendship, love, and work (Leak, Gardner, & Pounds, 1992).

The Life Tasks

In terms of the life tasks, Buddhists have a set of moral and social obligations described in one of the conversations of the Buddha called the Sigalovada Sutta (Parinder, 1985). Similar to the Koran for Muslims, the Sigalovada Sutta provides detailed guidance on how to meet the life tasks. This set of duties outlines

> the duties of children to parents, and parents to children; of pupils to teachers, and of teachers to pupils; of husbands to wives, and wives to husbands; of servants to employers, and employers to servants, and finally of lay people to their religious preceptors, i.e., monks, and of monks to lay people (p. 277).

The Sigalovada Sutta addresses immoral behaviors such as the taking of life, stealing, sexual misconduct, and substance abuse. It also addresses the importance of nurturing and protecting friendships, parents, one's spouse, and one's teachers. It acknowledges the social embeddedness of the individual and serves as a guide for social living. This sutta is one of the more well-known discourses among Buddhists. It is particularly well-known in Southeast Asia and Sri Lanka.

The Eightfold Path also addresses the Buddhist's responsibilities to the life tasks, particularly the part that addresses Right Speech, Right Action, and Right Livelihood. Furthermore, Buddhists emphasize the importance of living in harmony and maintaining friendships without disputes. Compassion and loving kindness are highly valued.

The use of alcohol is generally discouraged in Buddhism, and many Buddhists abstain from alcohol and drug use. One of the reasons for this is that intoxicants can negatively affect our relationship with others, as we often become unaware or unable to maintain right speech, thought, and action when intoxicated. However, some American Buddhists advocate moderation in the use of alcohol (Richards & Bergin, 2006b).

On the surface it may appear as if Buddhist monks had given up their commitment to the work task for the purpose of focusing exclusively on reaching nirvana through meditative practices. However, Buddhist monks and monasteries are closely tied to the community, and there is a reciprocal relationship between monks, nuns, and lay people. Lay people provide monks and nuns with food and clothing, and they may assist in maintaining the monastery. Monks and nuns, on the other hand, provide various services to the community, particularly education.

The responsibility of the laity is to maintain the Buddhist society to make it possible for the inhabitants of the monasteries to pursue enlightenment (Eckel, 2003). This includes working and contributing to society, maintaining social order, and marrying and having families.

For Buddhists, marriage is not a religious duty. It is considered a personal choice and a social contract that promotes social living. The Buddha offered no specific rules about marriage, divorce, or childrearing. In terms of homosexuality, there are a wide range of opinions among Buddhists. Although, early Buddhist teachings suggested that homosexuality was forbidden, contemporary Buddhists in North America are generally very supportive of homosexuals (Finn & Rubin, 2006).

Another issue that may bring Buddhists into therapy is the issue of abortion. The prohibition against taking any life is the most important ethical principle among Buddhists. Consequently, abortion is viewed as unethical. The use of contraception, however, is generally accepted (Richards & Bergin, 2006b).

APPLYING INDIVIDUAL PSYCHOLOGY TO PSYCHOTHERAPY WITH BUDDHIST CLIENTS

There are some important similarities and differences between Adlerian psychotherapy and Buddhist teachings that the Adlerian therapist needs to pay close attention to. In terms of similarities, the therapeutic listening technique is congruent with the practice of meditation. Similar to someone who meditates, the therapists attends to the experience in therapy without judgment (Finn & Rubin, 2006), and the therapist's accepting and loving attitude establishes a safe and trusting relationship. Another area of common ground is that of psychological insight. The third phase of Adlerian psychotherapy is geared toward the development of psychological insight when the therapist provides feedback on his or her assessment of the client.

Buddhists are also interested in psychological insight, particularly into those beliefs that cause suffering. Here, the Adlerian therapist can work cooperatively in helping the client understand his or her basic mistakes and motivations. For example, within the context of a safe and trusting relationship, the clinician may reveal a client's tendency to attach to certain objects or beliefs. He or she may also help the client understand how he or she strives in the direction of self-interest and self-protection, and how that striving causes suffering.

Adlerians emphasize the importance of an egalitarian therapeutic relationship. But Buddhist clients may have very different expectations of the therapist, depending on their Buddhist teachings and practices. For example, some Buddhist schools emphasize a more authoritarian student-teacher relationship, and thus the client may expect a similar approach from the therapist. Therefore, clinicians should try to understand the nature of the relationship between the client and his or her spiritual leader. Counseling approaches that contradict the teachings of the client's spiritual leader may be counterproductive and even offensive. Early education about the therapeutic relationship and the role of the therapist, as well as the client, may be helpful to avoid any friction in the therapeutic relationship.

Mindfulness and Adlerian Psychotherapy

Openness and acceptance of Buddhist teachings and practices are obviously essential to any therapeutic success. But for those Adlerian clinicians who work with Buddhist clients, familiarity with the practice of meditation will help facilitate the therapeutic process. Familiarity with meditation is also another way of demonstrating competence and respect for Buddhist practices.

Sakin-Wolf (2003) discussed how Adlerian therapists can integrate the client's early recollections, dreams, and emotional blockages with meditative practices. She argued that by practicing mindfulness, clients can bring about clarity of thought and an instantaneous awareness of the present that may bring about "holistic change" (p. 77) in addition to psychological understanding.

Mindfulness or bare attention is a meditative practice in which the person concentrates and pays attention to what is happening moment by moment. Goldstein (1983) gives the following definition:

> Bare attention means observing things as they are, without choosing, without comparing, without evaluating, without laying our projections and expectations onto what is happening; cultivating instead a choiceless and non-interfering awareness. (p. 20)

Epstein (1995) stated that the practice of bare attention, or mindfulness, is common to all Buddhist schools of thought.

> Pay precise attention, moment by moment, to exactly what you are experiencing, right now, separating out your reactions from the raw sensory events. This is what is meant by bare attention: just the bare facts, an exact registering, allowing things to speak for themselves as if seen for the first time, distinguishing any reactions from the core event. (p. 110)

Practicing mindfulness in psychotherapy can have many positive therapeutic effects.

> the strategy of bare attention is a self-empowering natural healing tool that helps individuals liberate themselves from destructive and debilitating patterns so that they are able to cooperate with others and hopefully become active and responsible members of society, which is the core of Adlerian psychotherapy. (Sakin-Wolf, 2003, p. 82)

But what exactly is it about practicing mindfulness that is therapeutic, besides the obvious physical benefits of relaxing? Looking at the psychodynamics of meditative practices, we notice that the individual who is focused on the here-and-now is not focused on the past or the future. It is through a past or future orientation that a neurosis is maintained. For example, a depression is maintained by focusing on past failures and misfortunes, while maintaining a pessimistic attitude about the future. In terms of anxiety disorders, the individual is usually focused on the terrible things that he or she fears will happen, thus maintaining a future orientation. Consequently, practicing mindfulness requires the individual to direct his or her focus away from convictions that maintain neurotic feelings. Although meditative practices may have few long-term effects when used in psychotherapy (assuming the patient practices only with the therapist), mindfulness meditation in therapy allows the client to be less burdened by disturbing thoughts and thus give room for psychological work to take place.

Sakin-Wolf (2003) outlined a six-step process for using mindfulness to encourage clients to stay in the present.

1. The therapist begins by helping the client focus on what is happening in the present by asking, "What are you feeling right now?"
2. Next, the therapist helps the client relax by using a breathing exercise or by visualizing a positive experience or memory.
3. The client is encouraged to experience the feelings he or she is having in the present moment. The therapist may suggest that the person accept those feelings rather than fight them.
4. The therapist asks the client, "Who is talking to you now?" when he or she is being self-critical. The client is encouraged to recognize self-punishing parts of himself or herself.
5. The client is then asked to see what is in between his or her thoughts and to be in that space in an effort to let go of negative thoughts.
6. Finally, the therapist encourages the client to experience the present moment more fully by asking questions or statements such as "What is happening now?" or "Just stay with what is happening now."

See Baer (2006), Davich (2004), and Gunaratana (2002) for in-depth descriptions of how to practice meditation and how to use meditative practices in counseling and psychotherapy.

Psychotherapists who work with Buddhist clients can benefit from being familiar with Buddhist literature. Having connections with the Buddhist community may also be helpful, as these communities can offer important supplementary services to the client. As when working with other religious individuals, the therapist should also be familiar with the client's cultural, economic, and educational background. The client's level of acculturation is especially important when working with immigrant Buddhists.

Case Example

John, a 24-year-old Buddhist convert, came for therapy following a breakup with his fiancée five months prior to his initial session. He told his therapist that he was feeling depressed and that he worried about what his family and friends thought about him after he was forced to cancel the wedding. He also worried about being alone and said he had experienced panic attacks on a few occasions.

John was an only child. He grew up in a Catholic family, but stated that his parents never really went to church. His mother, he said, was more of an atheist than a Catholic. His father drank a lot and was verbally abusive toward both John and his mother. As an adolescent, John learned about Buddhism and developed several close friendships through a Buddhist temple in his community. He was an avid reader of spiritual, especially Buddhist, self-help books. He had converted to Buddhism when he was 19 years old, but had lost touch with his religious community over the past three years when he started dating his fiancée.

In terms of treatment, John wanted help with his anxiety and his depression. He also questioned whether the breakup with his fiancée was bad karma resulting from not having been a good enough son. His parents had expected him to pursue a college degree, but after one year at the university he dropped out and got a job at a restaurant. At the time of counseling, he was managing the restaurant, but he felt guilty for not having fulfilled his parents' dream.

Although he had never been in therapy, John was open to sharing his thoughts and feelings in sessions. He was used to working with a meditation instructor where he took on a passive and subservient role. John reported that he felt uncomfortable with the leadership of his teacher, but was afraid to discontinue the relationship for fear of offending him. Instead, he slowly began distancing himself from the temple, while experiencing extreme guilt. He was encouraged to take an active role in therapy and urged to discuss with the therapist any concerns about therapy that he might experience throughout the process.

Due to his immediate concerns about the breakup with his fiancée, the therapist did not conduct a formal lifestyle assessment, but chose to focus on his immediate distress and grief. Here, the practice of meditation played an important role in John's therapy. John had not practiced meditation in several years, but he was very familiar with it and needed no instruction on how to practice. Meditation was used in the early stages of treatment when John was feeling overwhelmed and anxious. His therapist instructed him to spend a few moments practicing meditation the way he had practiced it in the past. This helped him to calm down, reduce his anxiety, and clear his thoughts so that he was better able to take part in his therapy. It also helped encourage him to pursue meditative practice on a daily basis. John eventually decided to find a new meditation instructor and became actively involved in a new Buddhist temple.

Having established a safe and trusting relationship, John's therapist decided to challenge him on his assertion that his suffering was a result of bad karma. John and his therapist began the discussion by talking about what he had learned about Buddhist philosophy and what the Buddha taught about karma and the causes of suffering. His beliefs about being a bad son were also processed. These maladaptive beliefs contributed to the maintenance of John's depression. John had convinced himself that he was being punished and that he was unable to have any positive effect on his situation. As a result, he had become increasingly discouraged and hopeless, telling himself that he would never recover from his suffering. John eventually learned to recognize that he had the power and ability to make effective changes in his life. He also came to accept that the breakup with his fiancée was in no way related to his decision to become a restaurant manager.

SUMMARY

Similar to the field of clinical psychology, Buddhism has several different schools of thought. The beliefs and practices within these schools vary widely. Differences in practice are also attributed to differences in culture. The one thing that all Buddhists do agree on, however, is the importance of the Four Noble Truths. These are the essence of all of Buddha's teachings.

The Four Noble Truths inform us that human suffering is inevitable, that it is caused by desire and attachment, and that human suffering can be eliminated by becoming enlightened. The Four Noble Truths can be conceptualized as the symptom, diagnosis, prognosis, and treatment plan for human suffering (Finn & Rubin, 2006). Any psychotherapist who works with Buddhist clients needs to be familiar with these basic teachings.

There are several similarities and some important differences between Adler's psychology and Buddhist philosophy. Examining the principles of Adlerian psychology, we learn that Adler's notion of soft determinism is found in Buddha's teachings. His notion of striving for superiority, teleology, and social interest also parallels Buddhist philosophy. Last, both Buddhists and Adlerian psychology are phenomenological theories.

For therapists working with Buddhist clients, it is important to pay attention to the therapeutic relationship, as Buddhists are likely to have very different expectations, depending on the style of their Buddhist teachers. Familiarity with meditative practices in therapy is also important, not only for its therapeutic benefits, but also as a way of demonstrating competence and respect for Buddhist practices.

SUGGESTED READINGS

Baer, R. A. (Ed.) (2006). *Mindfulness-Based Treatment Approaches: Clinician's Guide to Evidence Base and Applications*. Burlington, MA: Academic Press.

Davich, V. (2004). *8 Minute Meditation: Quiet Your Mind. Change Your Life*. New York: Berkley Publishing Group.

Gunaratana, B. H. (2002). *Mindfulness in Plain English: Updated and Expanded Edition*. Somerville, MA: Wisdom Publications.

Kyabgon, T. (2001). *The Essence of Buddhism: An Introduction to Its Philosophy and Practice*. Boston: Shambhala Publications.

Smith, H. (1991). *The World Religions*. NY: Harper Collins.

10 Conclusions and Future Directions

The purpose of this text has been to examine the common themes of Individual Psychology and the world religions. After reading this book, you have hopefully gained a general understanding of the various beliefs and practices of the world religions from an Adlerian point of view. Hopefully, you have also developed a greater appreciation for Adler's Individual Psychology and for the fact that many of his theories run parallel to the religious understanding of human nature. Throughout this text we have examined the role of soft determinism, Adler's teleological approach, and the striving for superiority, the role of social interest and equality, and the tasks of life within the context of the many doctrines of the world religions. In so doing, I hope that the flexibility of Adler's Individual Psychology and its applicability to working with people of faith has been exemplified.

The most obvious and significant common area between Individual Psychology and the world religions is social interest. Because Adler placed social connectedness at the very center of his theory, its goals are consistent with any religion that seeks to improve the conditions of humankind. The significance of social relationships and social responsibility are found in each of the religions discussed in this text. In their own way, they all impart the message that wellness is found in other-centeredness, rather than self-centeredness. When religious and spiritual beliefs are used as a force to contribute to the community it is characterized by social interest.

Given the wide range of religious values and devotional practices and the cultural diversity present within each religious group, it may seem a daunting task to fully understand and appreciate the various world religions and to consider all the various factors when doing psychotherapy. However, the therapist has to start somewhere, and one very important way for psychologists and counselors to learn about religion is by examining it through the lens of the theoretical orientation by which they practice.

One of the problems with comparing and contrasting a psychological theory to any religion is that the discussion will inevitably diminish the richness and diversity of views within that religion. A psychological examination of religion is also likely to diminish the role of the supernatural, as these experiences are considered psychological rather than real. What is seen as truth to the faithful individual is replaced with discussions of cognitions and convictions by the psychologist. But the Adlerian, who may view God as an idea rather than a reality, remains open to and respectful of the individual's subjective experience in counseling and psychotherapy.

Every religion has its set of subgroups or denominations. These denominations often maintain a wide range of different beliefs and practices. What is more, of course, is that each individual makes his or her own interpretation and use of religion, and thus practices the religion in unique ways. Yet, examining the main doctrines and teachings of different religions gives us insight into the religious client's world view. It helps us understand and appreciate the social context in which the client lives.

Finally, religion and culture are intimately intertwined, so we have to consider both when attempting to understand our patients. This is particularly important when working with immigrant populations, who often bring with them religious values and devotional practices that may conflict with North American culture. Throughout this text I have sought to separate religion and culture in order to offer clarity, while remaining mindful of the danger of minimizing this important aspect of individuals' lives.

RECOMMENDATIONS AND FUTURE DIRECTIONS

We have reviewed the Adlerian literature that seeks to compare and contrast Individual Psychology with various aspects of Christianity, Judaism, Islam, Hinduism, and Buddhism. However, the literature on

Adlerian psychology and religion needs to be expanded to include other religions. And more work needs to be done in terms of practical applications and research. More theoretical discussions, comparisons, and clinical illustrations are needed within each major religion. Such discussions would serve to educate Adlerians and others about the flexibility and applicability of Individual Psychology to clinical work with religious clients. Case studies may be particularly helpful in illustrating unique religious/ spiritual problems intermixed with cultural and individual concerns.

In terms of Christianity, the various Christian denominations such as the Roman Catholic and Protestant traditions can be explored further. Discussions of other Christian groups such as Jehovah's Witnesses and the Church of Jesus Christ of Latter-Day Saints (Mormons) are nonexistent in the current Adlerian literature. As for Judaism, a closer look at the various denominations—Orthodox, Conservative, Reform, and Reconstructionist—are in order. Case studies examining various religious problems, religious affiliations, and cultural backgrounds would constitute valuable contributions to the literature.

As the Muslim population in North America continues to grow, clinicians need to be familiar with the Islamic faith as well as with the cultural variations within this religion. Islam represents one of the most culturally diverse groups in the United States. Discussions about Adlerian psychotherapy with members of different Muslim groups—Arabs, Eastern Europeans, Asians, African American Muslims, and other groups—are very much needed.

There have been several articles published on Adlerian psychology and Buddhism. However, additional discussions on different Buddhist traditions and various Buddhist practices are in order. One area of particular interest to many psychotherapists is the practice of meditation. Some mention of meditative practices in Adlerian psychology exists (e.g., Sakin-Wolf, 2003). However, this is an area ripe for further exploration.

Hinduism, with its various subtraditions, also provides rich avenues for exploration for Adlerians. Reddy and Hanna (1995) explored the life style of a Hindu woman and discussed various cultural issues and concerns regarding acculturation to North American culture. Similar contributions addressing various presenting problems (mental illness, stress, marital problems, and parenting issues) and populations (men and women, families, and children) are needed.

Finally, other world religions are waiting to be explored by Adlerians. Papers that explore the similarities and differences between Adler's psychology and other world religions, including Sikhism, Jainism, and

Taoism, are lacking. A search of the literature resulted in only one article on Confucianism (e.g., McGee, Huber, & Carter, 1983).

In discussions of religion and Adlerian psychotherapy, there is a need for presentations that illustrate Adlerian principles and techniques in working with the religious person. In expanding the area of religion, spirituality, and Adlerian psychotherapy, Adlerians also need to address the cultural differences that are intertwined with religious and spiritual practices. Where cultural values conflict with religious ones and where personal convictions and behavior conflict with religious values also needs to be addressed.

When religious clients present for therapy, issues of sin, guilt, forgiveness, and repentance are likely to be part of the therapeutic discussions. There are some sporadic articles in the Adlerian literature that address these and other religious concepts. For example, Mosak (1987) defined guilt feelings from an Adlerian perspective and outlined the purposes of guilt feelings; McBrien (2004) discussed forgiveness as an aspect of social interest, arguing that the therapeutic goal of fostering social interest applies to issues of forgiveness. However, there is a need for theoretical exploration of these issues, as well as for case studies that illustrate how Adlerians approach these issues in psychotherapy. I would particularly emphasize the lack of case studies in these areas. Case studies and therapeutic illustrations provide rich opportunities for learning. Other issues, such as homosexuality, abortion, divorce, and suicide are included here.

Expanding Parent Education to Different Religious Groups

Adlerians have a long history of offering parent education and child guidance programs (e.g., Beecher and Beecher, 1955; Christensen and Schramski, 1983; Corsini, 1977; Corsini and Painter, 1975; Crowder, 2002; Dinkmeyer, et al., 1997a, 1997b, 1998; Dreikurs & Goldman, 1994; Dreikurs, Grunwald, and Pepper, 1982; Dreikurs & Soltz, 1964; Loewy, 1930; and Popkin, 1983a, 1983b, 1989a, 1989b, 1993). The Adlerian model of parenting is characterized by a democratic and encouraging approach, marked by mutual respect between parent and child. The model also emphasizes the child's psychological and behavioral goals and the use of encouraging techniques, rather than rewards and punishments when disciplining children. The main components of Adlerian childrearing methods include understanding the four goals of misbehavior, the use of natural and logical consequences, and encouragement.

The concept of natural and logical consequences is a group of techniques that allows children to experience the natural or social outcome of their behavior. Natural consequences constitute the direct result of the child's actions. For example, a child who forgets to bring his lunch to school goes hungry. Logical consequences are used when the natural consequences are too dangerous or are nonexistent. They are imposed by the parents and are directly related to the misbehavior. For example, a child brings home poor grades and is required to spend extra time doing homework until the grades improve.

Another Adlerian technique used in child rearing is the Four Goals of Misbehavior. Based on Adler's teleological approach, Dreikurs (Dreikurs & Soltz, 1964) developed the typology to help parents understand and correct their children's misbehavior. The technique is based on the assumption that when children misbehave, they are pursuing one of four goals. The child however, is usually unaware of his or her motivation. The four goals of misbehavior include the following:

Undue attention: The child wants constant attention in order to feel important and will engage in behaviors parents often find annoying in an effort to get their attention.

Power: The child wants to be in charge. He or she becomes defiant or finds other ways of getting into power struggles with Mom and Dad so to feel like he is powerful and cannot be controlled.

Revenge: If a child feels that his parents have hurt him, he may choose to set out to hurt back. When children pursue revenge, they may say or do things that will hurt their parents' feelings. Comments such as "I wish I was never born," "I hate you," or "You don't love me," are common and intended to get even with the parent.

Display of inadequacy: Children who feel they have no chance to succeed set out to avoid having demands placed on them. They display their inadequacy in an effort to keep from having to do what is expected of them. Children may display their inadequacy in one or more areas. Their parents often find themselves feeling hopeless and will tend to want to give up on the child.

The four goals of misbehavior represent a strategy used to help parents understand the reasoning behind their children's misbehavior in order to find constructive and encouraging ways of responding and disciplining. Overall, the purpose of Adlerian parent education is to help parents find ways of instilling courage and building self-esteem in their children. Parents are taught how to understand and show respect to their children while maintaining cooperation and developing responsibility.

In recent years, Adlerians have contributed significantly to the field of child guidance and parent education. Most notable is Rudolf Dreikurs and Vickie Soltz's groundbreaking book, *Children: The Challenge*, published in 1964. Later, Don Dinkmeyer and Gary McKay published the *Systematic Training for Effective Parenting* (STEP) program, which included books and audiocassette based programs for parents. In 1983 Michael Popkin developed the *Active Parenting* program and founded *Active Parenting Publishers*, which publishes instructional materials for parents, including video-based parent education programs. The *Active Parenting* program has since been expanded to include parent education for Christian and Jewish families (e.g., Gardner, 1993; Kober, 1995; Fisher, Miller, & Popkin, 2000). These particular programs incorporate Christian and Jewish teachings and scriptural material to help parents encourage discussions and activities with their children. The programs draw on scripture to illustrate and teach parents and children. *The Active Parenting Today for Jewish Families* program was developed by the Family Services Department of the Jewish Community Center of St. Louis, in cooperation with the B'nai B'rith Center for Jewish Identity and Active Parenting Publishers. These programs constitute a significant contribution to the area of religion and Adlerian psychology. As the North American landscape grows more diverse, similar integrative parenting programs are needed for Hindu, Buddhist, and Muslim families as well.

To conclude, Adlerian psychology has had only a minor influence in the psychology of religion. As Vande Kemp (2000) pointed out, Adler's influence on the integration movement has been small. However, Adlerian psychology is very much relevant in contemporary clinical practice and has a lot to offer to the current discussions on religion and psychology. It is my hope that this book has inspired you to continue the discussion of the integration of religion and psychology, particularly Adler's Individual Psychology.

References

Adler, A. (1987). The concretization of perfection. *Individual Psychology, 43, 4,* 523–526.

Adler, A. (1978). *Cooperation between the Sexes: Writings on Women, Love, and Marriage, Sexuality and its Disorders* (H. L. Ansbacher, & R. R. Ansbacher, Eds.). New York: Doubleday.

Adler, A. (1970). *The Education of Children* (E. Jensen & F. Jensen, Trans.). South Bend, IN: Gateway Editions. (Original work published 1930)

Adler, A. (1898). *Gesundheitsbuch fur die Schneidergerwerbe* [Healthbook for the tailor's trade]. Berlin: C. Heymanns.

Adler, A. (1947). How I chose my career. *Individual Psychology Bulletin,* 6, 9–11.

Adler, A. (1956). *The Individual Psychology of Alfred Adler.* H. L. Ansbacher, & R. R. Ansbacher (Eds.). New York: Basic Books.

Adler, A. (1983). *The Neurotic Constitution* (B. Glueck & J. E. Lind, Trans.). Salem, NH: Ayer. (Original work published 1912)

Adler, A. (1959). *The Practice and Theory of Individual Psychology.* Paterson, NJ: Littlefield, Adams. (Original work published in English 1925)

Adler, A. (1929a). *The Science of Living.* New York: Greenberg.

Adler, A. (1929b). Position in family influences lifestyle. *International Journal of Individual Psychology,* 3, 211–227.

Adler, A. (1964). *Social Interest: A Challenge to Mankind* (J. Linton & Vaughan, Trans.). New York: Capricorn. (Original work published 1933)

Adler, A. (1927) *Understanding Human Nature.* New York: Garden City Publishing.

Adler, A. (1958) *What Life Should Mean to You.* (A. Porter, Ed.) New York: Prestige. (Original work published 1931)

Adler, A. (1914). Das Zartlichkeitsbedurfnis des Kindes. In A. Adler & C. Furtmuller (Eds.) *Heilen und Bilden.* Munchen: Reinhardt.

Allport, G. (1950). *The Individual and His Religion.* New York: Collier-Macmillan.

American Counseling Association (1995). *Code of Ethics and Standards of Practice.* Alexandria, VA: Author.

American Counseling Association (2005). *Code of ethics.* Alexandria, VA: Author.

American Jewish Committee (2005). *American Jewish Year Book.* New York.

American Psychiatric Association (1994). *The Diagnostic and Statistical Manual of Mental Disorders.* (4th ed.) Washington, DC: American Psychiatric Association.

American Psychiatric Association (2000). *Diagnostic and Statistical Manual of Mental Disorders,* 4th edition, text revised. Washington, DC: American Psychiatric Association.

American Psychological Association (1992). Ethical principles of psychologists and code of conduct. *American Psychologist, 47*, 1597–1611.

Anderson, H. (1971). Individual Psychology and pastoral counseling: Some common concerns. *Journal of Individual Psychology,* 1(27), 25–36.

Ansbacher, H. L. (1951). Causality and indeterminism according to Alfred Adler and some current American personality theories. *Individual Psychology Bulletin,* 9, 96–107.

Ansbacher, H. L. (1979). The increasing recognition of Alfred Adler. In H. L. Ansbacher & R. R. Ansbacher (Eds.), *Superiority and Social Interest: A Collection of Later Writings* (3rd rev. ed.) (pp. 5–22). NY: Norton.

Arciniega, G. M., & Newlon, B. J. (1999). Counseling and psychotherapy: Muticultural considerations. In D. Capuzzi & D. F. Gross (Eds.), *Counseling & Psychotherapy: Theories and Interventions* (2nd ed.) (pp. 435–458) Upper Saddle River, NJ: Merrill/Prentice Hall.

Aristotle (1941). Metaphysica [The Metaphysics] (W. D. Ross, Trans.). In R. McKeon (Ed.), *The Basic Works of Aristotle* (pp. 689–926). New York: Random House. (Original Work published circa 350 BC)

Aswad, B., & Gray, N. (1996). Challenges to the Arab-American family and ACCESS (Arab Community Center for Economic and Social Services). In B. Aswad & B. Bilge (Eds.), *Family and Gender among American Muslims.* Philadelphia: Temple University Press.

Baer, R. A. (Ed.) (2006). *Mindfulness-Based Treatment Approaches: Clinician's Guide to Evidence Base and Applications.* Burlington, MA: Academic Press.

Barrett, D. B., & Johnson, T. M. (1998). Religion: World religious statistics. In *Encyclopedia Britannica book of the year.* Chicago: Encyclopedia Britannica, Inc.

Bartoli, E. (2007). Religious and spiritual issues in psychotherapy practice: Training the trainer. *Psychotherapy: Theory, Research, Practice, Training,* 44(1), 34–85.

Baruth, L. G., & Manning, M. L. (1987). God, religion, and the life tasks. *Individual Psychology,* 43(4), 429–436.

Beck, A. T. (1976). *Cognitive therapy and the emotional disorders.* New York: Meridian.

Bedell, K. B. (1997). *Yearbook of American and Canadian churches.* Nashville, TN: Abingdon Press.

Beecher, W., & Beecher, M. (1955). *Parents on the run.* Marina Del Bay, CA: Devorss.

Bergin, A., & Jensen, J. (1990). Religiosity of psychotherapists: A national survey. *Psychotherapy,* 27, 3–7.

Biddle, W. E. (1955). Integration of religion and psychiatry. New York: Macmillan.

Blumenthal, E. (1964). Religion and Individual Psychology. *Journal of Individual Psychology,* 20. 222.

Brack, G., Hill, M. B., Edwards, D., Grootboom, N., & Lassiter, P. S. (2003). Adler and Ubuntu: Using Adlerian principles in the New South Africa. *Journal of Individual Psychology,* 59(3), 316–326.

Brown, J. F. (1976). Parallels between Adlerian psychology and the Afro-American value system. *Individual Psychologist,* 13(1), 29–33.

Brunner, R. (1996). Spirituelle und transpersonale aspekte der individualpsychologie [Spiritual and transpersonal aspects of Individual Psychology]. *Zeitschrift fur Individualpsychologie,* 21(4), 301–312.

Burke, M. T., Hackney, H., Hudson, P., Miranti, J., Watts, G. A., & Epp. L. (1999). Spirituality, religion, and CACREP curriculum standards. *Journal of Counseling & Development, 77*, 251–257.

Carlson, J., Watts, R. E., & Maniacci, M. (2006). *Adlerian Therapy: Theory and practice.* Washington, DC: American Psychological Association.

Carlson, J. M. & Carlson, J. D. (2000). The application of Adlerian psychotherapy with Asian-American clients. *Journal of Individual Psychology, 56*(2), 214–225.

Carter, D. M. (1986). An integrated approach to pastoral therapy. *Journal of Psychology & Theology, 14*(2), 146–154.

Cavanagh, J. R. (1962). *Fundamental pastoral counseling: Techniques and psychology.* Milwaukee, WI: Bruce.

Cheston, S. E. (2000). Spirituality of encouragement. *Journal of Individual Psychology, 56*(3), 296–305.

Christensen, O. C., & Schramski, T. G. (1983). *Adlerian family counseling: A manual for counselors, educators, and psychotherapists.* Minneapolis, MN: Educational Media.

Chung, R. C-Y., & Bemak, F. (1998). Lifestyle of Vietnamese refugee women. *Journal of Individual Psychology, 54*(3), 373–384.

Clark, A. (2002). *Early recollections: Theory and practice in counseling and psychotherapy.* New York: Brunner Routledge.

Clebsch, W. A., & Jaekle, C. R. (1964). *Pastoral Care in historical perspective: An essay with exhibits.* New Jersey: Prentice-Hall.

Clinebell (1984). *Basic types of pastoral care and counseling.* Nashville: Abingdon.

Collins, G. R. (1998). *The soul search: A spiritual journey to authentic intimacy with God.* Nashville, TN: Nelson.

Corsini, R. J. (1977). Individual education. *Journal of Individual Psychology, 33*, 21–29.

Corsini, R. J., & Painter, G. (1975). *The practical parent.* New York: Harper & Row.

Corveleyn, J. (2000). In defense of benevolent neutrality: Against a "spiritual strategy." *Journal of Individual Psychology, 56*, 343–352.

Croake, J. W., & Rusk, R. (1980). The theories of Adler and Zen. *Journal of Individual Psychology, 36*(2), 219–226.

Crowder, C. (2002). *Eating, sleeping, and getting up: How to stop the daily battles with your child.* New York: Broadway Books.

Davich, V. (2004). *8 Minute meditation: Quiet your mind. Change your life.* New York: Berkley Publishing Group.

de Wit, H. F. (2008). Working with existential and neurotic suffering. Ch. In F. J. Kaklauskas, S. Nimanheminda, L. Hoffman, & M. S. Jack (Eds.) *Brilliant Sanity: Buddhist approaches to psychotherapy* (3–18). CO: University of the Rockies Press.

Delaney, H. D., Miller, W. R., & Bisono, A. M. (2007). Professional Psychology: *Research and Practice,* Vol. 38, No. 5, 538–546

Denny, F. (1985). *An introduction to Islam.* New York: Mcmillian.

Dinkmeyer, D., McKay, G. D., & Dinkmeyer, D. (1997a). *The parent's handbook: Systematic training for effective parenting (STEP).* Minnesota: American Guidance Service.

Dinkmeyer, D., McKay, G. D., Dinkmeyer, J. S., Dinkmeyer, D., & McKay, J. L. (1997b). *Parenting young children: Systematic training for effective parenting (STEP) of children under six.* Minnesota: American Guidance Service.

Dinkmeyer, D., McKay, G. D., McKay, J. L., & Dinkmeyer, D. (1998). *Parenting teenagers: Systematic training for effective parenting (STEP)*. Minnesota: American Guidance Service.

Dreikurs, R. (1956). Adlerian psychotherapy. In F. Fromm-Reichmann & J. L. Moreno (Eds.), *Progress in psychotherapy* (pp. 111–118). New York: Grune & Stratton.

Dreikurs, R. (1960). Are psychological schools of thought outdated? *Journal of Individual Psychology, 16*, 3–10.

Dreikurs, R. (1989). *Fundamentals of Adlerian Psychology*. Chicago: Adler School of Professional Psychology (Original work published in German 1933)

Dreikurs, R. (1973). *Psychodynamics, psychotherapy, and counseling: Collected papers of Rudolf Dreikurs, M. D.* Chicago: Adler School of Professional Psychology. (Original work published 1967)

Dreikurs, R. (1971). *Social equality: The challenge of today*. Chicago: Henry Regnery.

Dreikurs, R., Corsini, R. J., Lowe, R., & Sonstegard, M. (1959). *Adlerian family counseling*. Eugene, OR: University of Oregon Press.

Dreikurs, R., & Goldman, M. (1994). *The ABC's of guiding the child*. Chicago: Adler School of Professional Psychology.

Dreikurs, R., Grunwald, B. B., & Pepper, F. C. (1982). *Maintaining sanity in the classroom* (2nd ed.) New York: Harper & Row.

Dreikurs, R., & Mosak, H. H. (1977). The tasks of life II: The fourth life task. In H. H. Mosak (Ed.), *On Purpose: Collected Papers* (pp. 100–107). Chicago: Adler School of Professional Psychology. (Original work published 1967)

Dreikurs, R., & Soltz, V. (1990). *Children: The challenge*. New York: Plume. (Original work published 1964)

Duin, J. (2009, March 3). *Survey: U.S. Muslim women liberated*. The Washington Times.

Eckel, M. D. (2003). Buddhism. In M. D. Coogan (Ed.), *The Illustrated Guide to World Religions*. NY: Oxford University Press.

Ecrement, E. R., & Zarski, J. J. (1987). The pastor-as-counselor: Adlerian contributions to the process. *Individual Psychology, 43*(4),461–467.

Ellenberger, H. (1970). *The discovery of the unconscious: The history and evolution of dynamic psychiatry*. New York: Basic Books.

Ellerbrock, J. (1985). *Adamskomplex: Alfred Adlers Psychologie als Interpretament christlicher Überlieferung* [The Adam complex: Alfred Adler's psychology as interpreter of Christian tradition] New York: Peter Lang.

Ellis, A. (1976). *The case against religion: A psychotherapists view and the case against religiosity*. TX: American Atheist Press.

Ellis, A. (1974). *Disputing irrational beliefs (DIBS)*. New York: Institute for Rational Living.

Ellis, A. (1984). Rational-emotive therapy (RET) and pastoral counseling: A reply to Richard Wessler. *Personnel & Guidance Journal, 62*(5), 266–267.

Ellis, A. (2000). Spiritual goals and spirited values in psychotherapy. *Journal of Individual Psychology, 56*(3), 277–284.

Epstein, M. (1995). *Thoughts without a thinker: Psychotherapy from a Buddhist perspective*. NY: Basic Books.

Erickson, R. C. (1987). Spirituality and depth psychology. *Journal of Religion & Health, 26*(3), 198–205.

Farber, D. & Gyatso, T. (Dalai Lama XIV) (2006). *Living wisdom with His Holiness the Dalai Lama: Study guide*. Boulder, CO: Sounds True.

Finn, M., & Rubin, J. B. (2006). Psychotherapy with Buddhists. In P. S. Richards & A. E. Bergin (Eds.), *Handbook of psychotherapy and religious diversity* (pp.317–340). Washington, DC: American Psychological Association.

Fisher, O., Miller, P., Popkin, M. H. (2000). *Active parenting today for Jewish families: Supplemental parent's guide (for use with Active Parenting Today program)*. Georgia: Active Parenting Publishers.

Fox, L. R. (1980). Adlerian psychology as related to theology and the church. Unpublished master's thesis, American Baptist Seminary of the West, Berkeley, CA.

Frankl, V. (2006). Man's search for meaning. MA: Beacon Press. (Original work published 1959)

Freud, S. (1927/1957). *The future of an illusion*. W. D. Robson-Scott (Trans.). Garden City, N. Y.: Doubleday. (Original work published 1927)

Frevert, V. S., & Miranda, A. O (1998). A conceptual formulation of the Latin culture and the treatment of Latinos from an Adlerian psychology perspective. *Journal of Individual Psychology, 54*(3), 291–309.

Gallup, G. H., Jr., & Lindsay, D. M. (1999). *Surveying the religious landscape*. Harrisburg, PA: Morehouse.

Gardner, F. (1993). *Active parenting today in the faith community: A biblical and theological guide*. Marietta, Georgia: Active Parenting Publishers.

Gartner, J., Larson, D. B., & Allen, G. D. (1991). Religious commitment and mental health: A review of the empirical literature. *Journal of Psychology and Theology, 19*, 6–25.

Gold, L., & Mansager, E. (2000). Spirituality: Life task of life process? *Journal of Individual Psychology, 56*(3), 266–276.

Gordon-Rosen, M. & Rosen, A. (1984). Adlerian parent study groups and inner-city children. Individual Psychology: *Journal of Adlerian Theory, Research, & Practice, 40*(3), 309–316.

Govinda, A. (1990). *A living Buddhism for the West*. Boston, MA: Shambhala Publications. (Trans. by Maurice Walshe)

Grant, B. (1984). Fitness for community: A response to Lang and Kohut. *Journal of Pastoral Care, 38*(4), 324–337.

Gregerson, D. L., & Nelson, M.D. (1998). Striving for righteousness: Perfection as completion. *The Canadian Journal of Adlerian Psychology, 28*, 21–28.

Grenz, S. J. (1994). *Theology for the community of God*. Nashville, TN: Broadman & Holman.

Grizzle, A. F. (1992). Family therapy with the faithful: Christians as clients. In L. A. Burton (Ed.), *Religion and the Family: When God Helps* (pp. 139–162). New York: Haworth Pastoral Press.

Gunaratana, B. H. (2002). *Mindfulness in Plain English: Updated and Expanded Edition*. Somerville, MA: Wisdom Publications.

Hackney, C. H., & Sanders, G. S. (2003). Religiosity and mental health: A meta-analysis of recent studies. *Journal for the Scientific Study of Religion, 42*, 43–55.

Haddad, Y., & Lummis, A. (1987). *Islamic values in the United States: A comparative study*. New York: Oxford University Press.

Hall, G. S. (1917). *Jesus, the Christ, in the light of Psychology*. New York: Doubleday.

Haneef, S. (1996). *What Everyone Should Know about Islam and Muslims.* Chicago: Library of Islam.

Hart, J. L. (1971). Pastoral counseling and Individual Psychology. *Journal of Individual Psychology,* 1(27), 36–43.

Hedayat-Diba, Z. (2006). Psychotherapy with Muslims. In P. S. Richards & A. E. Bergin (Eds.), *Handbook of Psychotherapy and Religious Diversity* (pp.289–314). Washington, DC: American Psychological Association.

Hale, R. D. (2003). Christianity. In M. D. Coogan (Ed.), *The Illustrated Guide to World Religions.* NY: Oxford University Press.

Hale, R. D. (2004). *Understanding Christianity: Origins, Beliefs, Practices, Holy Texts, Sacred Places.* London: Duncan Baird.

Hart, J. L. (1971). Pastoral counseling and Individual Psychology. *Journal of Individual Psychology,* 1(27), 36–43

Hoffman, E. (1994). *The Drive for Self: Alfred Adler and the Founding of Individual Psychology.* Reading, MA: Addison-Wesley.

Holifield, E. B. (1983). *A History of Pastoral Care in America.* Nashville: Abingdon.

Hood, R. W., Spilka, B., Hunsberger, B., & Gorsuch, R. (1996). *The psychology of Religion: An Empirical Approach* (2nd ed.). New York: Guilford Press.

Huber, R. J. (1986). Adler and the Trinity: Reflections on a residency in pastoral counseling. *Individual Psychology,* 42, 413–420.

Huber, R. J. (2006). In search of social interest. Chapter in S. Slavik & J. Carlson (Eds.) *Readings in the Theory of Individual Psychology* (pp. 113–121). New York: Routledge.

Huber, R. J. (2000). Jung and Ch'an Buddhism: An Adlerian reflection. *Journal of Individual Psychology,* 56(3), 346–348.

Huber, J. R. (1987). Psychotherapy: A graceful activity. *Individual Psychology,* 43(4), 437–443.

Hunt-Meeks, S. (1983). The anthropology of Carl Jung: Implications for pastoral care. *Journal of Religion & Health,* 22(3), 191–211.

Hunter, D., & Sawyer, C. (2006). Blending Native American spirituality with Individual Psychology in work with children. *Journal of Individual Psychology,* 62(3), 234–250.

Jahn, E. (1927). *Wesen und Grenzen der Psychoanalyse* [The character and limits of psychoanalysis]. Schwerin im Meckleburg: F. Bahu.

Jahn, E. (1931). *Machtwille und Minderwertigkeitsgefuhl* [The will to power and the feeling of inferiority]. Berlin: Martin Warneck.

James, W. (1902). *The varieties of religious experience: A study in human nature; being the Gifford Lectures on natural religion delivered at Edinburgh in 1901–1902.* New York: Longmans, Green.

William, J. (1890). *The principles of psychology.* New York: H. Holt and Company.

Johansen, T. M. (2005). Applying Individual Psychology to work with clients of the Islamic faith. *The Journal of Individual Psychology,* 61 (2), 174–184.

Jones, S. L., & Butman, R. E. (1991). *Modern psychotherapies: A comprehensive Christian appraisal.* Downers Grove, IL InterVarsity Press.

Kanz, J. E. (2001). The applicability of Individual Psychology for work with conservative Christian clients. *Journal of Individual Psychology,* 57,(4), 342–353.

Kaplan, S. J. (1984). An Adlerian Understanding of Hillel's Maxim. *Pastoral Psychology,* 33(2), 93–95.

Kaplan, S. J., & Schoeneberg, L. A. (1987). Personality theory: The Rabbinic and Adlerian paradigm. *Individual Psychology, 43*(3), 315–318.

Kawai, H. (1996). *Buddhism and the art of psychotherapy.* Texas A & M University Press.

Kawulich, B., & Curlette, W. L. (1998). Life tasks and the Native American perscpectives. *Journal of Individual Psychology, 54*(3), 359–367.

Kertzer, M. (1996). *What is a Jew?* NY: Simon & Schuster.

Knights, W. A., Koenig, H. G. (2002). *Pastoral counseling: A Gestalt approach.* Binghamton, New York: Haworth Press.

Kober, J. R. (Ed.) (1995). *Active Christian parenting: Practical skills for the preschool to preteen years: Parent's guide.* Minneapolis: Augsburg Fortress.

Koenig, H. G., McCullough, M. E., & Larson, D. B. (2001). *Handbook of religion and health.* New York: Oxford University Press.

Kollar, C. A. (1997). *Solution-Focused pastoral counseling.* Grand Rapids, Michigan: Zondervan Publishing.

Krippner, S., & Welch, P. (1992). Spiritual dimensions of healing. New York: Irvington Publishers.

Kyabgon, T. (2001). *The essence of Buddhism: An introduction to its philosophy and practice.* Boston: Shambhala Publications.

Laird, T. G., & Shelton, A. J. (2006). From an Adlerian perspective: Birth order, dependency, and binge drinking on a historically black university campus. *Journal of Individual Psychology, 62*(1), 18–35.

Larson, D. B., Sherrill, K. A., Lyons, J. S., Craigie, F. C., Jr., Thielman, S. B., Greenwold, M. A., et al. (1992). Associations between dimensions of religious commitment and mental health reported in the American Journal of Psychiatry and Archives of General Psychiatry: 1978–1989. *American Journal of Psychiatry, 149,* 557–559.

Lavin, M. (2009). Intolerance in Psychology: The problem of religious gays. Chapter in N. Cummings, W. O'Donohue, & J. Cummings (Eds.), *Psychology's war on religion.* Phoenix, Arizona: Zeig, Tucker, & Theisen.

Lawrence, C., & Huber, C. H. (1982). Strange bedfellows? Rational-emotive therapy and pastoral counseling. *Personnel & Guidance Journal, 61*–4, 210–212.

Leak, G. K. (2006). An empirical assessment of the relationship between social interest and spirituality. *The Journal of Individual Psychology, 62*(1), 59–69.

Leak, G. K. (1992). Religiousness and social interest: An empirical assessment. *The Journal of Individual Psychology, 48,* 288–301.

Leak, G. K., Gardner, L. E., & Pounds, B. (1992). A comparison of eastern religion, Christianity, and social interest. *Individual Psychology, 48*(1), 53–64.

Levinas, E. (1993). *Dieu, le mort et le temps* (God, the dead and time). Paris: Grasset.

Lippman, T. (2002). *Understanding Islam: An introduction to the Muslim world.* New York: Plume.

Loewy, I. (1930). Small children in guidance clinics. Chapter in A. Adler & Associates, *Guiding the child* (pp. 157–165). New York: Greenberg.

Lukoff, D. (1998). From spiritual emergency to spiritual problem: The transpersonal roots of the new DSM-IV category. *Journal of Humanistic Psychology, 38,* 21–50.

Lukoff, D., Lu, R., & Turner, R. (1992). Toward a more culturally sensitive DSM-IV: Psychoreligious and Psychospiritual Problems. *Journal of Nervous and Mental Disease, 180,* 11, 673–682.

Manaster, G. J. (2004). Individual Psychology and Judaism: A Comparative essay. *The Journal of Individual Psychology*, vol. 60(4), 420- 427.

Manaster, G. J., & Corsini, R. J. (1982). *Individual Psychology: Theory and practice.* Itasca, IL: F. E. Peacock.

Mansager, E. (2000). Holism, Wellness, Spirituality. *The Journal of Individual Psychology*, 56, 3, 237–241.

Mansager, E. (1987). One framing of the issue: Adlerian psychology within pastoral counseling. *Individual Psychology*, 43(4), 451–460.

Mansager, E. (2002). Religious and spiritual problem V-code: An Adlerian assessment. *The Journal of Individual Psychology*, 58(4), 374–387.

Mansager, E. & Rosen, M. (2008). *The Presence of Adlerian Psychology within the Psychology of Religion and Spirituality.* Poster Presentation at the APA conference, Division 36 Psychology of Religion. Loyola University, Columbia, Maryland.

Martinez, D. B. (1998). Transcending cultures: The American process. *The Journal of Individual Psychology*, 54(3), 346–358.

May, R. (1940). *The springs of creative living: A study of human nature and God.* Nashville, TN: Abingdon-Cokesbury Press.

McBrien, R. J. (2004). Expanding social interest through forgiveness. *The Journal of Individual Psychology*, 60(4), 408–419.

McGee, V. J., Huber, R. J., & Carter, C. L. (1983). Similarities between Confucius and Adler. *Individual Psychology*, 39, 237–246.

Menges, R. J., & Dittes, J. E. (1965). *Psychological studies of clergymen: Abstracts of research.* New York: Thomas Nelson.

Merler, G. (1998). Adler and the via mystica. *The Canadian Journal of Adlerian Psychology*, 28, 8–24.

Miller, L., & Lovinger, R. J. (2006). Psychotherapy with Conservative and Reform Jews. Ch. In P. S. Scott & A. E. Bergin (Eds.) Handbook of Psychotherapy and Religious Diversity (pp. 259–286). Washington, DC: American Psychological Association.

Miller, W. R., & Thoresen, C. E. (2003). Spirituality, religion, and health: An emerging research field. American Psychologist, 58, 24–35.

Miller-McLemore, B. J. (1993, April 7). The human web: Reflections on the state of pastoral theology. *Christian Century*, 366–369.

Milliren, A., & Clemmer, R. (2006). Introduction to Adlerian psychology: Basic principles and methodology. In S. Slavik & J. Carlson (Eds), *Readings in the theory of Individual Psychology.* New York: Routledge.

Milne, B. (1982). *Know the truth.* Downers Grove, IL: Intervarsity Press.

Mosak, H. H. (1979). Adlerian psychotherapy. In R. J. Corsini (Ed.) *Current Psychotherapies* (2nd ed.) Itasca, IL: F. E. Peacock.

Mosak, H. H. (1995). Adlerian psychotherapy. In R. J. Corsini & D. Wedding (Eds.), *Current psychotherapies,* (5th ed.) (pp. 51–94). Itasca, IL: F. E. Peacock.

Mosak, H. H. (1987). Guilt, guilt feelings, regret, and repentance. *Individual Psychology: Journal of Adlerian Theory, Research & Practice*, 43(3), 288–295.

Mosak, H. H. (1971). Lifestyle. In A. G. Nicely (Ed.), *Techniques for behavior change* (pp. 77–81). Springfield, IL: Charles C. Thomas.

Mosak, H. H. (1954). The psychological attitude in rehabilitation. *American Archives of Rehabilitation Therapy*, 2, 9–10.

Mosak, H. H. (1987). Religious allusions in psychotherapy. *Individual Psychology,* 43(4), 496–501.

Mosak, H. H. (1993). *What every psychotherapist should know about Judaism.* Chicago, IL: Adler School of Professional Psychology.

Mosak, H. H., & Maniacci, M. (1999). *A primer of Adlerian psychology: The analytic-behavioral-cognitive psychology of Alfred Adler.* PA: Brunner/Mazel.

Mosak, H. H., & Maniacci, M. (1998). *Tactics in counseling and psychotherapy.* Itasca, Illinois: F.E. Peacock.

Mosak, H. H., & Dreikurs, R. (1977). The life tasks III: The fifth life task. In H. H. Mosak (Ed.) *On Purpose: Collected papers.* Chicago: Adler School of Professional Psychology. (Original work published 1967)

Mosak, H. H., & Shulman, B. (1977). Various purposes of symptoms. In H. H. Mosak (Ed.), *On Purpose: Collected papers* (118–128). Chicago: Adler School of Professional Psychology. (Original work published 1967)

Narayanan, V. (2003). Hinduism. In M. D. Coogan (Ed.), *The Illustrated Guide to World Religions* (pp. 125–161). NY: Oxford University Press.

Newlon, B. J., & Arciniega, M. (1983). Respecting cultural uniqueness: An Adlerian approach. *Individual Psychology: Journal of Adlerian Theory, Research, & Practice,* 39(2), 133–143.

Newlon, B. J., Borboa, R., & Arciniega, M. (1986). The effects of Adlerian parent study groups upon Mexican mothers' perception of child behavior. *Individual Psychology: Journal of Adlerian Theory, Research, & Practice,* 42(1), 107–113.

Newlon, B. J., & Mansager, E. (1986). Adlerian life-styles among Catholic priests. *Individual Psychology,* 42, 367–374.

Noda, S. J. (2000). The concept of holism in Individual Psychology and Buddhism. *The Journal of Individual Psychology,* 56(3), 285–295.

Nuttin, J. (1962). *Psychoanalysis and personality: A dynamic theory of normal personality* (G. Lamb, Trans.). New York: New American Library. (Original work published 1950)

Nystul, M. S. (1987). Mental health syndromes among the Navajo. *Individual Psychology: Journal of Adlerian Theory, Research, & Practice,* 43(2), 174–184.

Nystul, M. S. (1982). Ten Adlerian parent-child principles applied to Navajos. *Individual Psychology: Journal of Adlerian Theory, Research, & Practice,* 38(2), 183–189.

O'Connell, W. E. (1987). Natural high psychospirituality: Stalking shadows with "childlike foolishness." *Individual Psychology: Journal of Adlerian Theory, Research, and Practice,* 43(4), 502–509.

O'Connell, W. E. (1997). The radical metaphors of Adlerian psychospirituality. *Individual Psychology: Journal of Adlerian Theory, Research, and Practice,* 53(1), 33–41.

Oden, T. C. (1971). A theologian's view of the process of psychotherapy. *The Journal of Individual Psychology,* 1(27), 69–78.

Olsen, D. C. (1993). *Integrative family therapy: Creative pastoral care and counseling.* Minneapolis, Minnesota: Augsburg Fortress.

Orgler, H. (1963). *Alfred Adler: The man and his work.* New York: Mentor Books. (Original work published 1939)

Pancner, K. R. (1978). The use of parables and fables in Adlerian psychotherapy. *The Individual Psychologist,* 15(4), 19–29.

Pargament, K. I. (1996). Religious methods of coping: Resources for the conservation and transformation of significance. Chapter in E. P. Shafranske (Ed.), *Religion and the Clinical Practice of Psychology* (pp. 215–239). Washington, DC: American Psychological Association.

Pargament, K. I. (2007). *Spiritually integrated psychotherapy: Understanding and addressing the sacred.* New York: Guilford Press.

Pargament, K. (1997). *The psychology of religion and coping: Theory, research, practice.* New York: Guilford Press.

Parrinder, G. (Ed.) (1985). *World religions: From ancient history to the present.* NY: Facts on File.

Parsons, R. D., & Wicks, R. J. (1986). Cognitive pastoral psychotherapy with religious persons experiencing loneliness. *Psychotherapy Patient, 2*(3), 47–59.

Payne, I. R., Bergin, A. E., Bielema, K. A., & Jenkins, P. H. (1991). Review of religion and mental health: Prevention and the enhancement of psychosocial functioning. *Prevention in Human Services, 9,* 11–40.

Perkins-Dock, R. E. (2005). The application of Adlerian family therapy with African American families. *The Journal of Individual Psychology, 61*(3), 233–249.

Peven, D. (2004). Ken Wilber and Alfred Adler: Ascendance and transcendence. *The Journal of Individual Psychology, 60*(4), 389–395.

Pew Forum on Religious and Public Life (2008). *U.S. Religious Landscape Survey.* http:// religions.pew forum.org

Piedmont, R. L. (2009). Editorial. *Psychology of Religion, 1* (1), 1–2.

Polanski, P. J. (2002). Exploring spiritual beliefs in relation to Adlerian theory. *Counseling and Values, 46*(2), 127–136.

Popkin, M. (1983a). *Active Parenting.* Marietta, GA: Active Parenting.

Popkin, M. (1989a). Active Parenting: A video based program. In M. Fine (Ed.), *The Second Handbook on Parent Education: Contemporary Perspectives,* (pp. 77–98). New York: Academic Press.

Popkin, M. (1989b). *Active Parenting of Teens.* Marietta, GA: Active Parenting.

Popkin, M. (1993). *Active Parenting Today.* Marietta, GA: Active Parenting.

Popkin, M. & Woodward, H. (1983b). *Active Parenting Videotapes.* Atlanta, GA: Active Parenting.

Power, C. (1998, March 16). The new Islam. *Newsweek Magazine,* 35–37.

Powers, R. L., & Griffith, J. (1987). *Understanding Lifestyle: The Psycho-Clarity Process.* Chicago: AIAS.

Pratt, J. B. (1908). The psychology of religion. *Harvard Theological Review, 1,* 435–454.

Prevatt, J., & Park, R. (1989). The Spiritual Emergence Network (SEN). In S. Grof & C. Grof (Eds.), *Spiritual Emergency: When Personal Transformation Becomes a Crisis* (pp. 225–232). Los Angeles: J. P. Tarcher.

Progoff, I. (1956). *The Death and Rebirth of Psychology: An Integrative Evaluation of Freud, Adler, Jung, and Rank and the impact of Their Culminating Insights on Modern Man.* New York: Julian Press.

Propst, L. (1988). *Psychotherapy in a Religious Framework: Spirituality in the Emotional Healing Process.* New York: Human Science Press.

Rabinowitz, A. (2006). Psychotherapy with orthodox Jews. Ch. In P. S. Scott & A. E. Bergin (Eds.) *Handbook of Psychotherapy and Religious Diversity* (pp. 237–258). Washington, DC: American Psychological Association.

Rafford, R. L. (1972). *Alfred Adler and Paul Tillich on the Nature of Man's Striving.* Unpublished doctoral thesis, Andover Newton Theological School, Newton Centre, MA.

Reddy, I., & Hanna, F. J. (1995). The life-style of the Hindu woman: Conceptualizing female clients of Indian origin. *The Journal of Individual Psychology,* 51(3), 216–230.

Reuder, M. E. (1999). A history of Division 36 (Psychology of Religion). In D. A. Dewsbury (Ed.), *Unification through Division: Histories of the Divisions of the American Psychological Association* (Vol. 4, pp. 91–108). Washington, DC: American Psychological Association.

Richards, P. S., & Bergin, A. E. (Eds.) (2006a). *Handbook of psychotherapy and Religious Diversity.* Washington, DC: American Psychological Association. (Original work published 1999)

Richards, P. S., & Bergin, A. E. (2006b). Religious diversity and psychotherapy: Conclusions, recommendations, and future directions. In P. S. Richards & A. E. Bergin (Eds.), *Handbook of Psychotherapy and Religious Diversity* (469–489). Washington, DC: American Psychological Association.

Richards, P. S., & Bergin, A. E. (2006c). Toward religious and spiritual competency for mental health professionals. In P. S. Richards & A. E. Bergin (Eds.), *Handbook of Psychotherapy and Religious Diversity* (3–26). Washington, DC: American Psychological Association. (Original work published 1999)

Ridenour, F. (2001). *So what's the difference? A look at 20 worldviews, faiths and religions and How They Compare to Christianity.* California: Gospel Light.

Rietveld G. (2004). Similarities between Jewish philosophical thought and Adler's Individual Psychology (Trans. by Eeuwe Ham). *The Journal of Individual Psychology,* 60(3), 209–218.

Roberts, R. L., Harper, R., Caldwell, R. & Decora, M. (2003). Adlerian lifestyle analysis of Lakota women: Implications for counseling. *The Journal of Individual Psychology,* 59(1), 15–29.

Roberts, R. L., Harper, R., Tuttle-Eagle Bull, D., & Heideman-Provost, L. M. (1998). The Native American medicine wheel and Individual Psychology: Common themes. *The Journal of Individual Psychology,* 54, 134–145. (Original work published 1995)

Rogers, C. R. (1951). *Client-Centered Therapy.* Boston: Houghton-Mifflin.

Schellenberg, J. A. (1978). *Masters of Social Psychology.* New York: Oxford University Press.

Rosenbaum, R. (1999). *Zen and the Heart of Psychotherapy.* Ann Arbor, MI: Taylor & Francis.

Rubin, J. B. (1996). *Psychotherapy and Buddhism: Toward an Integration.* NY: Plenum Press.

Saba, R. (1983). A comparison of the thought of Adler and Teilhard de Chardin. *Individual Psychology,* 39, 27–39.

Sakin-Wolf, S. (2003). Adler: east, west, and beyond. *The Journal of Individual Psychology,* 59(1), 72–83.

Salzman, M. B. (2002). A culturally congruent consultation at a Bureau of Indian Affairs boarding school. *The Journal of Individual Psychology,* 58(2), 132–147.

Savage, A. (1998). Faith, hope, and charity: An Adlerian understanding. *The Canadian Journal of Adlerian Psychology,* 28, 81–94.

Seltzer, S. (2000). *When There Is No Alternative: A Spiritual Guide for Jewish Couples Contemplating Divorce.* New York: URJ Press.

Seybold, K. S., & Hill, P. C. (2001). The role of religion and spirituality in mental and physical health. *Current Directions in Psychological Science,* 10, 21–24.

Shafranske, E. P. (Ed.). (1996). *Religion and the Clinical Practice of Psychology.* Washington, DC: American Psychological Association.

Shafranske, E. P. (2000). Religious involvement and professional practices of psychiatrists and other mental health professionals. *Psychiatric Annals,* 30, 525–532.

Shafranske, E., & Maloney, H. (1990). Clinical psychologists' religious and spiritual orientations and their practice of psychotherapy. *Psychotherapy,* 27, 72–78.

Shafranske, E. P., & Sperry, L. (2005). Addressing the spiritual dimension in psychotherapy: Introduction and overview. Chapter in L. Sperry & E. P. Shafranske (Eds.), *Spiritually Oriented Psychotherapy,* pp. 11–29. Washington, DC: American Psychological Association.

Sharma, A. R. (2006). Psychotherapy with Hindus. Chapter in P. S. Richards & A. E. Bergin (Eds.) *Handbook of Psychotherapy and Religious Diversity,* pp. 341–365. Washington, DC: American Psychological Association.

Shea, J. J. (1997). Adult faith, pastoral counseling, and spiritual direction. *Journal of Pastoral Care,* 51(3), 259–270.

Shulman, B. H. (1985). Cognitive therapy and the Individual Psychology of Alfred Adler. In M. J. Mahoney and A. Freeman (Eds.), *Cognition and Psychotherapy* (pp. 243–258). New York: Plenum.

Shulman, B. H., & Mosak, H. H. (1988). *Manual for Lifestyle Assessment.* Muncie, IN: Accelerated Development.

Shulman, B. (2003). The political science of the Ten Commandments. *The Journal of Individual Psychology,* 59(2), 166–175.

Slavik, S., & Croake, J. (2001). Feelings and spirituality: A holistic perspective. *The Journal of Individual Psychology,* 57(4), 354–362.

Smith, H. (1991). *The World Religions.* NY: Harper Collins.

Smuts, J. C. (1961). *Holism and Evolution.* New York: Viking Press. (Original work published in 1926)

Sneck, W. J. (2007). Jung: Mentor for pastoral counselors. *Reseach in the Social Scientific Study of Religion,* 18, 35–51.

Sperber, D. (2008). *A Time to Be Born and a Time to Die: Jewish Customs from the Cradle to the Grave.* New York: Oxford University Press.

Sperry, L. (1987). Brief therapeutic interventions in pastoral care: An integrative training program. *Individual Psychology,* 43(4), 490–495.

Sperry, L. (2001). *Spirituality in Clinical Practice.* Philadelphia, PA: Brunner-Routledge.

Sperry, L., & Mansager, E. (2007). The relationship between psychology and spirituality: An initial taxonomy for spiritually oriented counseling and psychotherapy. *The Journal of Individual Psychology,* 63(4), 359–370.

Steere, D. (1997). *Spiritual Presence in Psychotherapy: A Guide for Caregivers.* New York: Brunner/Mazel.

Sue, D. W., & Sue, D. (2008). *Counseling the Culturally Diverse: Theory and Practice.* (5th ed.) Hoboken, N.J.: John Wiley & Sons.

Tan, S. Y. (1996). Religion in clinical practice: Implicit and explicit integration. In E. P. Shafranske (Ed.), *Religion and the Clinical Practice of Psychology* (pp.365–387). Washington, DC: American Psychological Association.

Tan, S. Y., & Johnson, W. B. (2005). Spiritually oriented cognitive behavioral therapy. Chapter in L. Sperry & E. P. Shafranske (Eds.) *Spiritually Oriented Psychotherapy* (pp. 77–103). Washington, DC: American Psychological Association.

Turner, R. B. (2004). Mainstream Islam in the African-American experience. *Muslim American Society's Web Site.* http://www.masnet.org/

Vande Kemp, H. (1992). G. Stanley Hall and the Clark School of Religious Psychology. *American Psychologist, 47*(2), 290–298.

Vande Kemp, H. (1996). Historical perspective: Religion and clinical psychology in America. Chapter in E. P. Shafranske (Ed.), *Religion and the Clinical Practice of Psychology* (pp. 71- 112). Washington, DC: American Psychological Association.

Vande Kemp, H. (1984). *Psychology and Theology in Western Thought, 1672–1965: A Historical and Annotated Bibliography.* Millwood, New York: Kraus International.

Vande Kemp, H. (2000). Wholeness, holiness, and the care of souls: The Adler-Jahn debate in historical perspective. *The Journal of Individual Psychology, 56*(3), 242–256.

Veltman, D. R. (1973). *Man-as-a-Moral-Being in Depth Psychology and Christian Thought: An Interdisciplinary Study of Man as a Moral Being in the Psychotherapeutic Theory of Sigmund Freud, Alfred Adler, and Karen Horney and the Christian Theology of John Calvin and Reinhold Niebuhr.* Unpublished master's thesis, Drew University, Madison, NJ.

Viswanathan, E. (1992). *Am I a Hindu?* San Francisco: Halo Books.

Wakley, B. D. (1995). Alfred Adler and the Pauline doctrine of justification by faith: A model for Christian psychotherapy. *Dissertation Abstracts International,* 57(01B), 716.

Warren, H. C. (1979). *Buddhism in Translation.* New York: Atheneum.

Watts, R. E. (Ed.) (2003). *Adlerian, Cognitive, and Constructivist Therapies: An Integrative Dialogue.* New York: Springer Publishing.

Watts, R. E. (1992). Biblical agape as a model of social interest. *Individual Psychology,* 48, 35–40.

Watts, R. E. (2000). Biblically based Christian spirituality and Adlerian psychotherapy. *The Journal of Individual Psychology,* 56(3), 316–328.

Weiss-Rosmarin, T. (1990). Adler's psychology and the Jewish tradition. *Individual Psychology,* 46(1), 108–118.

Weiss-Rosmarin, T. (1997). *Judaism and Christianity: The differences.* New York: Jonathan David Publishers. (Original work published 1943)

Wessler, R. L. (1984). A bridge too far: Incompatibilities of rational-emotive therapy and pastoral counseling. *Personnel & Guidance Journal,* 62(5), 264–266.

Westfeld, J. (2001). Spiritual issues in counseling: Clients' beliefs and preferences. *Journal of Counseling Psychology,* 48, 61–71.

Wiesel, E. (1978). *A Jew Today.* New York: Vintage.

Wulff, D. M. (1991). *Psychology of Religion: Classic and Contemporary Views.* New York: Wiley.

Wulff, D. W. (1998). Rethinking the rise and fall of the psychology of religion. In. A. L. Molendijk and P. Pels (Eds.), *Religion in the Making: The Emergence of the Sciences of Religion* (pp. 181–202). Leiden: Brill.

Yalom, I. D. (1980). *Existential psychotherapy.* New York: Basic Books.

Zapata, J. T., & Jaramillo, P. T. (1981). Research on the Mexican-American family. *The Journal of Individual Psychology,* 37(1), 72–85.

Zhang, Y. (2004). *Zen and Psychotherapy.* UK: Trafford Publishing.

Zahniser, C. R. (1938). *The Soul Doctor.* New York: MacMillan.

Zimmer, H. (1951). *The Philosophies of India.* New York: Panthean.

Index

Friendship, task of
  in Islam, 135
  in Pastoral Counseling, 89
*Fundamental Pastoral Counseling:
  Techniques and Psychology* (Cavanagh), 16

G

Gabriel, Archangel, 123, 126
Gallup Center for Muslim Studies
  (2008), 134
Gardner, L. E., 175
Genesis, book of, 101
George Fox College Graduate School of
  Psychology (Newberg, Oregon), 7
Giving alms, in Islam, 129
Goals. *See also* Final goal
  of belonging, 26–27
  of life, 150–151
  of misbehavior, 195–196
God, belief in, 3, 14
  Christianity, 35
  idea of, 42–44
  Islam, 124
  Judaism, 108–109
Godhead, 146
God-realization, and Hinduism, 145–
  146, 151
Gods of Hinduism, 146–148
Gold, L., 18
Goldstein, Joseph, 186
Gorsuch, R., 16
Govinda, Lama, 168
Grace, various aspects of, 91–92
Graduate School of Psychology, Fuller
  Theological Seminary (Pasadena,
  California), 7
Grant, B., and pastoral counseling, 87
Grizzle, A. F., 13
Grof, Christina, 9
Grof, Stanislav, 9
Guidance, pastoral function, 96
Guilt feelings, 194
Gunaratana, B. H., 187

H

Habits, cultivation of, 159
Haddad, Y., 127
Hadith, 125
Haji, pilgrimage in Islam, 129–130
Hall, Granville Stanley, 2

The American Journal of Psychology, 3
Jesus, the Christ, in the Light of Psy-
  chology, 2
The Journal of Religious Psychology, 3
*Handbook of Psychotherapy and Reli-
  gious Diversity* (Richards and
  Bergin), 7, 11
Haneef, S., 131, 134
Hanna, F. J., 193
Hart, J. L., and pastoral counseling, 87
Healing
  pastoral function, 95–96
  resources of, 15
Hebrew Bible, 101
Hedayat-Diba, Z., 127
Hegira, Islamic calendar, 123
Herod the Great, 65
Hillel the Elder, 106, 111
Hindu clients, and Adlerian psychothera-
  py, 161–164
Hinduism, 51, 143–144
  caste system, 155
  Gods in, 146–148
  history and teachings of, 145–155
  karma and reincarnation, 154
  paths to God, 151–154
  philosophy of human nature, 156–161
  religious texts, 148
  stages of life, 148–151
Holifield, E. B., and pastoral counseling, 84
Holism, concept of
  in Buddhism, 181
  in Christianity, 25–26
  in Individual Psychology, 25–26
  in Judaism, 109
Holy Spirit, 65
Homosexuality
  in Buddhism, 184
  in Judaism, 113–114
Hood, R. W., 16
Hope, 77
Householder stage of life, 149
Huber, J. R., 91
Human equality
  in Islam, 134–135
  in Judaism, 109–112
Human nature, philosophy of
  holism, 72
  life tasks, 76–77
  social interest, 72–75